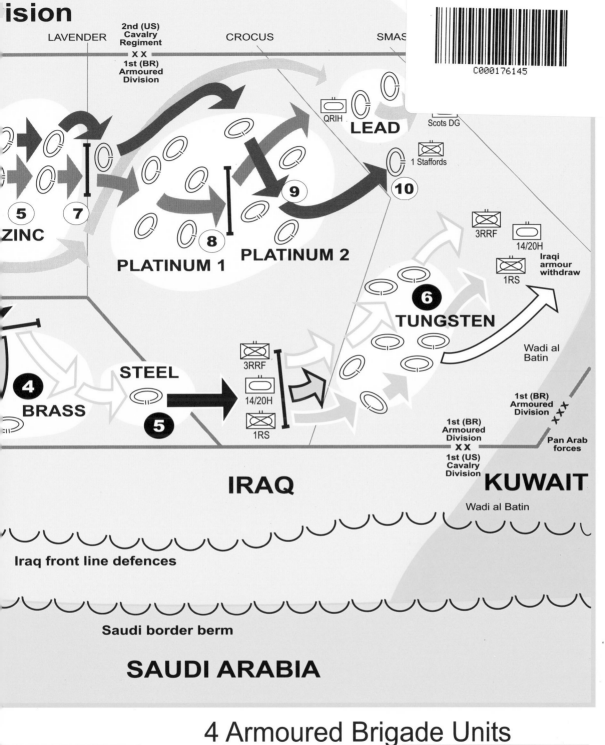

C000176145

ision

LAVENDER 2nd (US) Cavalry Regiment CROCUS SMAS

X X

1st (BR) Armoured Division

QRIH **LEAD**

Scots DG

1 Staffords

⑤ ⑦ ⑨ ⑩

ZINC

⑧

PLATINUM 1 **PLATINUM 2**

3RRF

14/20H

1RS

Iraqi armour withdraw

❻ **TUNGSTEN**

Wadi al Batin

STEEL 3RRF

14/20H 1st (BR) Armoured Division X X X

❹ **BRASS**

1RS Pan Arab forces

❺ 1st (BR) Armoured Division

X X

1st (US) Cavalry Division

IRAQ **KUWAIT**

Wadi al Batin

Iraq front line defences

Saudi border berm

SAUDI ARABIA

4 Armoured Brigade Units

⑥ **0500 hrs, G + 2**

Scotts DG clear waterhole after fighting a fierce battle.

❶ **1930 hrs, G + 1**

4 Brigade leave Forming Up Point.

❷ **2234 hrs, G + 1**

14/20H clear through BRONZE.

❸ **0415 hrs, G + 2**

14/20H attack on COPPER SOUTH, engaging enemy in pursuit battle until first light.

❹ **1045 hrs, G + 2**

14/20H attack on BRASS, clearing brigade complex of infantry and armour.

❺ **1500 hrs, G + 2**

3RRF's main action: clearing enemy artillery on STEEL. Lost 2 Warrior vehicles to A10 aircraft.

❻ **2330 hrs, G + 2**

Heavy artillery bombardment on TUNGSTEN, which is cleared by first light.

From Margaret.
28. 4. 2001
on my Birthday

DESERT FIRE

"The analysts write about war as if it's a ballet. Yes, it's choreographed, but what happens is that, as the orchestra starts playing, some son of a bitch climbs out of the orchestra pit with a bayonet and starts chasing you around the stage. And the choreography goes straight out of the window."

GENERAL NORMAN H. SCHWARZKOPF

DESERT FIRE

The Diary of a Gulf War Gunner

by
Andrew Gillespie

with a Foreword by
Robert Fox

Leo Cooper

First published in 2001 by
LEO COOPER
an imprint of
Pen & Sword Books Ltd
47 Church Street
Barnsley
South Yorkshire
S70 2AS

Copyright © 2001 Andrew Gillespie

A CIP record for this book is available from the British Library

ISBN 0 85052 795 3

*For the wives, mothers and sweethearts of The Rocket
Troop...the real heroes;
and to the memory of my brother-in-arms
Major John Buchanan RA*

Contents

Foreword by Robert Fox ix

Acknowledgements xv

Glossary xvii

Introduction xxiii

OPERATION DESERT SHIELD...1

OPERATION DESERT STORM 53

OPERATION DESERT SABRE..139

THE LONG ROAD HOME...179

Appendix I: Those who fought with The Rocket Troop....237

Appendix II: Silhouettes of tanks and other vehicles...........239

Index...243

Foreword

The trouble with the desert was that it never behaved as expected. In January and February the eastern desert of Saudi Arabia was astonishingly cold, pouring with rain which started grass growing, and on several occasions icicles and frost covered our tents. It was on a dark, though not particularly stormy night in the desert that I ran into the author of this marvellous tale, Major Andrew Gillespie, the Battery Commander of O Battery (The Rocket Troop) of 2nd Field Regiment Royal Artillery.

By that time as correspondent for the *Daily Telegraph*, I had been assigned to the 14th/20th King's Hussars Battlegroup. I recall that on the night in question we were undergoing a half-hearted NBC alert at Battlegroup HQ. I had stumbled from my sleeping quarters semi-naked, having once more lost bits of my NBC kit. On sorting myself out and discounting the alert as a false alarm, I tried to settle down for a brew and a chat with my new acquaintance, shortly to be my host for a month in the desert.

When I say 'chat', I exaggerate. It was one-way traffic. I heard about The Rocket Troop, the King of Sweden, Leipzig, and the significance of the blue and yellow colours. A cease-fire was called only when I finally agreed that the 'Rockets' were indeed the stuff of legends.

I travelled with the battery commander's Warrior, aptly named 'The Optimist,' for most of Operation Desert Storm and its ground component, Desert Sabre. As this book relates, I was not initially welcome...and I think Sergeant Steve Allen had his doubts to the end. Throughout an extremely difficult assignment, The Rockets and the Command Troop of the 14th/20th proved the most agreeable and accommodating of company. They treated me as one of their own, though at the time I was twice the age of all but Sergeant Allen and the Battery Commander. Within the group, discussion was lively on everything from grand strategy to the domestic arrangements with the 'Emperor,' Colonel Mike Vickery's tank. These discussions were led by the Colonel's gunner, an energetic Mancunian known universally as Corporal 'Reds' Redgrave, who reciprocated disrespect by referring to the attached correspondent as 'you fat-gutted bastard.' All in all, relationships were pretty harmonious.

Given the circumstances, I was acutely aware that I had the best of it. The 14th/20th was a close-knit family regiment hailing largely from three centres, Preston, Manchester and Blackpool, whilst The Rocket Troop had its heart firmly centred on Manchester. The Battlegroup was extremely friendly and the patience of the individual soldiers almost saintly. As Corporal Reds remarked, "When your mate has just trodden in your breakfast or on your toothpaste for the umpteenth time, there's no point in having a sense of humour failure." There was the Battery Commander's cramped Warrior, the 'Emperor' now with the addition of the Adjutant, Captain Jonty Palmer, and One One Charlie, the second tank under command of Sergeant Major Gerahty. We weren't exactly a band of brothers but we did keep each other going through the interminable hours and days of training exercises on breaching defences and the passage of lines. After one particularly tedious loop through the desert Corporal Reds vouchsafed from inside his turret, "I am that happy, I could shit!" to which the Adjutant immediately riposted, "said a highly placed Army spokesman."

The Battlegroup took me into their confidence and I was briefed and hosted by the supporting arms and teams and allowed to eavesdrop on the planning as it built up. I also had two meetings with the GOC, General Rupert Smith, whom I had known in previous incarnations. "Hello Chum," he said when we met behind a sand berm after he had briefed the Hussars. "I am not sure if we are supposed to speak to each other. All I can tell you for sure is that when you go through the breach (in the sand wall into Iraq) you're likely to be gassed." I suddenly realized that I had dumped my gas mask a staging area back, so I would have to rely on the NBC defence qualities of the Warrior and the skills of Sergeant Allen.

It was difficult to know what to write about. Clearly I could not write about the plan though it would not take the brains of an archbishop to work out that the NATO trained forces of the American armoured and mechanised infantry divisions, along with their little cousin the 1st British Armoured Division, would do what most NATO armoured forces do - execute a left hook. Operational Security was, however, the order of the day; the various allied deception plans proved successful and the Iraqis never quite knew where the main armoured attack would come from. Despite the need for security, several journalists did try to reveal the plan, fortunately with little success.

It might surprise those around at the time that I found the assignment difficult. It was in many ways infinitely more so than my assignment nine years before when I was with 2 Para in the Falklands. There it was all go, tabbing and yomping across the peat or thumbing a ride with helicopters. There was always something to do as priority one. The reporting and recording often came last. Relationships of trust between the commanders and the journalists working at the front grew quickly. In the desert it was different, not least because of the difference in scale, where nearly 40,000 British forces were committed in the ground operation. In the Falklands many of us had been irked by the presence of 'minders' – government civilian information officers who were supposed to filter our copy and radio dispatches. Once we were ashore, however, the press was handled by soldiers, and it worked very well. After the Falklands there were numerous enquiries about media-military relations and we were assured that next time correspondents were to be accredited for a full-scale operation, things would be different. They were! They were much worse.

Part of the problem was the American belief that the lesson from the Falklands campaign was that the press should be kept out. The real difficulty in the Falklands was the remoteness and the primitive nature of satellite communications – most commercial messages could be sent only by merchant ships equipped with the new Interstat. For the Gulf the Americans ordained that correspondents accredited to the forces should be heavily escorted and that censorship should be strict on security grounds. This led to a policy almost of 'print anything provided it can't remotely be described as news.'

The British followed the American lead and the result was not very happy. This time however, the minders were in uniform. Some made the mistake of trying to tell the journos, the 'hacks', how to do their job. The brighter ones just let the hacks get on with it – and in some respects the reporters with the 4th Armoured Brigade had a better time than their colleagues with 7 Brigade HQ. We were allowed to go to our allotted units and to work with them.

The correspondent with The Rocket Troop and 14th/20th had to find ways around the restrictions, of reporting what it was like to be with the forces, but not to say what they were about to do for real. It was a variation of colour on a theme of boredom. The brigadier took me on trips to visit the Americans and to Div HQ. I visited the Royal Scots, which was like leafing through the archives of my wilder ancestry. I was challenged about whether to describe The Rocket Troop as 'colourful' or 'legendary'.

One of the biggest difficulties was writing for the *Daily Telegraph* which had a formidable following in the military. The editor was an acknowledged military writer, its defence editor a widely read military historian and its proprietor a notable Napoleon buff. From occasional chats through the Div HQ satellite link, it was clear that they were having trouble in catching on to what was about to unfold in the desert. They had little idea where the main point of effort would come in the armoured battle, and why. To that extent Desert Sabre and the strategy of Desert Storm still remains something of a story untold.

The other obstacle at *Telegraph* HQ, more a challenge really, was trying to get a notice into the Court and Social pages. We managed to insert the notice of the pre-battle supper and mess night in the desert for 7 February after much negotiating between the custodian of the pages and the editor. After much "we've never done it this way before Mr

Hastings," the editor's wish became command. The results can be seen later in this book.

Of course much of this talk of minders, censorship and security is now obsolete. With the advent of the mobile phone, WAPS and the like, a reporter can get a signal through from almost anywhere This doesn't mean that military formations should not take reporters along with them, brief them and establish a basis of trust so that what is being done can be understood. This is probably needed as much as ever. In the Kosovo operation, when NATO forces moved in, they found more than 3,750 journalists and TV crews in their path. They had become an obstacle and what might have been a very tricky piece of peacekeeping had become a media circus.

When the desert battle opened, described so vividly in these pages, we were all good and ready. By this time I had realized some lifelong friendships – particularly with Mike Vickery and Andrew Gillespie – were being forged. As the 14th/20th set off to do battle in Iraq for the third time in a century, Mike Vickery said he recalled a letter from a sergeant who had served in the Regiment in 1941, "if there's one road duller than the one from Preston to Blackpool, it's the road from Kuwait to Basra."

Frustratingly, I had a rear-view perspective on the breaching of the berm and the advance into Iraq. I was banged up in the back of the Warrior and could only hear Andrew Gillespie's commentary. Once through we formed up and waited. Against a pea-green sky the artillery began working, firing and manoeuvring. As the 155mm guns opened up and shot darts of flame skywards, forks of lightning came crackling down far out in the desert. The guns, their limbers and support vehicles moved forwards like great herds of buffalo on the prairie and the MLRS rocket system fired spectacular and deadly streaks of light into the sky.

The opening phases were the customary mixture of action and inertia, excitement and boredom. As we formed up before breaching the berm, we found ourselves next to columns of the 1st (US) Infantry Division (Mechanized) 'The Big Red One'. I was able to trade some of our compo rations for some coffee with the agreeable second-in command of one of the American brigades, Lieutenant Colonel Clint Anker, who has also become a lifelong friend. Clint was only too delighted to hand over an outsize jar of Maxwell House. To kill the time we chatted of this and that as the desert wind strove to freeze off our nether regions. One subject was the impending troubles in a place called Yugoslavia.

After the advance into Iraq we were witness to the biggest armoured battle involving British forces since the Second World War – perhaps it may be the last such engagement for British troops ever. Who knows? The weight of artillery firepower that Rupert Smith's Division could call upon was heavier than that at El Alamein. Across the theatre between

300,000 and 400,000 allied troops were involved. Even so, the order of battle of both sides represented less than one seventh of the forces engaged at the opening of Operation Barbarossa, the German invasion of Russia in 1941.

The sights were awesome and unforgettable; the sky purple with illumination and High Explosive rounds as the Iraqi prisoners came through the sand berms, the Hussars manoeuvring at speed, changing formation and line of battle - all done by drill and with the minimum of fuss, the fire-plans being called, batteries of guns and rockets joining and leaving the battle. In the back of the 'Optimist' there was kicking and shouting to stay awake. As always it is easy to sleep in the lull of battle. At one point I kicked Gunner Lyons, "Come on Killer, wake up...we can save a few lives." He did not welcome the intrusion on his slumber, but prisoners were appearing in hundreds.

One of the surprises of this book is to discover just how much we came under enemy fire. Cocooned in the back of the 'Optimist', I was not always aware of our situation. At one point Sergeant Allen opened up with the chain gun against an Iraqi tank crew about to fire at us. The Hughes gun clicked away like a demented typewriter. It was the skill of the Hussars and the O Battery team that perhaps ensured that I am still here today.

Sergeant Allen was the hero of one of the most dramatic episodes when inadvertently the Hussars shot up the Spartans of the Air Defence troop protecting 7 Brigade. As they were fellow Gunners, Sergeant Allen was determined that the 'Optimist' and her crew should render all possible assistance. He prepared to go onto the burning hulls twice, as the account in this book explains. It was an act of real mental and physical bravery. As the crew in the back prepared to help with the rescue, I was given one of the best pieces of advice I have ever received. Bombardier 'Pip' Wilkins handed me the First Aid kit and said, "When we go, follow right behind us – don't think, just do it. You think too much - all the time! When you do things like this you have to stop thinking! STOP BLOODY THINKING!"

Sadly this act of heroism did not find space in the *Telegraph*. Iraqi prisoners were pouring round us by the thousands, terrified and leaderless. Some had not been so lucky. Across the desert for the next few weeks we would find vehicles blasted away by tanks, artillery, helicopters and aircraft and with only fragments of human remains to mark who had been in them.

Before the end of the ground war I was taken away from the 'Optimist' and her crew to be briefed by Brigadier Christopher Hammerbeck about another melancholy episode – the attack on the Fusiliers' Warriors by American A10 aircraft that had mistaken them for Iraqis. The brigadier's briefing was exemplary. He told us everything he knew, gave us the exact total of casualties and told us to print it. There would be no excuses and no cover-up.

This book is the most vivid account of the land war in Operation Desert Sabre. As it so ably explains, the mission for the 3rd Army Group was 'to destroy the Republican Guards' - by implication once the lighter Coalition forces had got into Kuwait City. In other words the plan was to destroy Saddam Hussein's military power base. Once this had gone, he would go. In the Preliminary Orders it was plain that the allies ground operation was to take anything from a week to four weeks...at least.

It didn't happen. After barely 100 hours President George Bush called a cease-fire. Why then? Kuwait had been liberated, but some of the Republican Guard divisions were escaping into Iraq. The simple explanation is that President Bush was so horrified at the images of the 'turkey shoot' on the Mutla Ridge that he ordered an immediate halt to proceedings. Matters were probably altogether more complicated. The plan to replace Saddam Hussein appears to have sprung a leak. Just as the armoured divisions were closing with the Republican Guard, somebody somewhere in the alliance changed their mind. It is said that the Saudis did not want Saddam replaced after all. Another view is that the Coalition did not have a realistic candidate in the military hierarchy of Baghdad to put in his place.

Being with the British Armoured Division, I knew that a plan, designed to be executed over weeks, was cut short in four days. Quite why and how it happened has never been fully explained either in Britain or America. Perhaps now it should. Saddam Hussein is off the hook, in the saddle and making life misery for millions of Kurds and Shiites in his own population. The Forbes list puts him among the ten richest heads of state in the world.

The Gulf War, as Desert Storm came to be known, was followed swiftly by other crises. First came the expulsion of the Kurds and the bombing and shelling of the Marsh Arabs - then came the ragged wars of Yugoslavia, Rwanda and Congo, East Timor and Sierra Leone. Each war has a different pattern and brings a dreadful roll of victims and atrocities. British forces have been involved in trying to bring peace in a fair share of the new, open-ended, turf wars. In most I have witnessed, they have done more than required, proved ever resourceful, imaginative and courageous. The crew of the 'Optimist' and the 14th/20th were typical, which is in itself a compliment. Their company was always diverting and I return the compliment they paid me by their help, trust and courtesy. They show why our forces should have the support and understanding of our public and media. In the case of the latter, they deserve better and more professional coverage than they often get.

Robert Fox
November 2000

xiv

Acknowledgements

I wrote this account for two reasons. Firstly, to keep alive the history of the Battery I hold very dear. When I commanded The Rocket Troop I could go to the records and find out exactly what the Battery was doing on the 2nd of February 1869, where we were, whom we had, what we did. I could not tell you about 1969 because no records had been kept. I was therefore determined that the Battery's exploits in the Gulf War should be recorded. My intention was to produce a few sides of paper but over the years, like Topsy, 'it just growed'. The second reason, and if I am honest probably the real reason, is that it helped exorcise some powerful ghosts.

Although I am the scribe, this is the account of many people's war. It was short and sharp, but we did have casualties. It is already fading in the memory of the nation and will never rank alongside Waterloo or the Somme, but for those of us who went to war, the worries, expectations and fears for our lives were as real as in any conflict and will have left lasting impacts. It is the story of ordinary soldiers at war. I say ordinary because we were a few in so many, but we did extraordinary things and are now permanently bound by a common fellowship. We went to war together.

I would like to thank Brigadier Dick Applegate, Colonel Peter Williams and the Committee of the Royal Artillery Institute who have been the driving force and enablers behind the publication of this book; to the contributors, Graham Ambrose for the loan of his diaries, Vanessa Aitken for her letter, Mike Vickery and Chris Steadman who checked my facts, all who sent their treasured photographs and Robert Fox for his thought-provoking Foreword. My thanks also to those who helped in the production, Mary Rattenbury for her typing, Kay Hopkins and David Lyon my proof readers, Trevor Browning and Paul Folkard of Media Services Royal School of Artillery for their superb graphics and of course Tom Hartman, my wise editor. Particular thanks must go to David Rowlands for allowing his magnificent painting to provide the cover.

Finally I must thank my wife, Annie, and all the wives, mothers and sweethearts who, left behind with their thoughts, endured the media prophets of doom and the long lonely terrors of uncertainty. Their love and support was beyond value. They waited patiently but fearfully at home and had the worst war of all. It is to them that this tale is dedicated.

To avoid unneccessary repetition, I have put in brackets after each caption the initials of those who kindly lent me photographs. They are as follows:

MV	Mike Vickery
PW	Peter Williams
MH	Mathew Hubbard
GM	*Gunner Magazine*
HM	Hulan Morgan
AC	Alan Collett
AW	Alastair Wicks
PS	Peter Sincock
PN	Pete Newell
LEP	*Lancashire Evening Post*
KW	Keith Wilkinson

Those attributed to AG were taken by the author.

Glossary

1 RS	First Battalion, The Royal Scots.
14/20H	14th/20th King's Hussars.
2Lt	Second Lieutenant.
3RRF	Third Battalion, Royal Regiment of Fusiliers.
A1 Echelon	Combat supplies – ammunition, fuel, water.
A2 Echelon	Food, clothing, spares etc.
ACP	Ammunition Control Point.
AFV 432	British tracked personnel carrier/command post.
APC	Armoured Personnel Carrier.
APES	Azimuth Position Elevation System – vehicle-mounted inertial navigation system.
ARRV	Armoured Repair and Recovery Vehicle. Based upon a tank chassis.
B52	American strategic bomber.
BAOR	British Army of the Rhine.
Battalion	An Army formation subordinate to a *Regiment* or Brigade, commanded by a Lieutenant Colonel. It comprises between 650 and 1,000 men and is usually sub-divided into companies.
Battery Guide	SNCO responsible for reconnaissance and assisting in deployment.
Battery	A sub-unit of a Royal Artillery Regiment, it is commanded by a Major and has about 100 men in peace but can expand to over 200 in war.
Battlegroup	A mixed formation of different arms, commanded by a Lieutenant Colonel and his Headquarters, which has been assembled for a specific operational task.
BC	Battery Commander (Major).
BCR	Battle Casualty Replacements.
Bdr	Bombardier. Artillery equivalent of Corporal.
Bedford MK	Standard British Army 4 tonne, 4x4 truck.
Berm	Large sand wall built as part of a defensive system.
BFME	British Forces Middle East.
BFPO	British Forces Post Office.
BK	Battery Captain (Kapitan), the Battery second in command.
BQMS	Battery Quartermaster Sergeant (Staff Sergeant) responsible for logistics.

Brigade	An Army formation subordinate to a division and comprising 3,000 – 4,000 men. Commanded by a Brigadier. In war its sub-units make up battlegroups.
BSM	Battery Sergeant Major (Warrant Officer Class II) responsible for ammunition and discipline.
Cam Net	Large net with patches of plastic scrim attached used to hide the visual and thermal signatures of vehicles and equipment.
CASEVAC	Casualty Evacuation.
CBU	Cluster Bomb Unit (delivered by an aircraft).
Challenger 1	British Main Battle Tank.
CMA	Convoy Marshalling Area.
CO	Commanding Officer. (Lieutenant Colonel)
Combo Pen	Atropine injection system to combat the effects of a chemical attack.
Company	Normally a formation of about 100 men and a sub-division of a battalion. Commanded by a Major, it is sub-divided into three platoons.
Compo	British combat rations.
COS	Chief of Staff. In a brigade he is a Major.
CPO	Command Post Officer (Second Lieutenant/Lieutenant) responsible for commanding the guns in action.
CPX	Command Post Exercise. Used to exercise command and communication systems only.
CRA	Commander Royal Artillery (Brigadier) responsible for command of the Divisional Artillery Group.
Division	An Army formation comprising two or more brigades. Subordinate to a corps and commanded by a Major General, it usually has in excess of 10,000 men.
DROPS	Dismountable Rack Offloading and Pick-up System.
ECP	Equipment Collection Point.
EME	REME officer responsible within the battalion/regiment for equipment maintenance.
Emperor	Traditional name of the Commanding Officer 14th/20th King's Hussars' tank.
FDC	Fire Direction Centre responsible for co-ordinating the fire from more than one battery.
Fire Plan	The formal co-ordination of artillery and other fire systems in support of an operation.
FMA	Forward Mounting Area - in this case the port of Al Jubayl, Saudi Arabia.
FOO	Artillery Forward Observation Officer (Captain) responsible for co-ordinating and directing artillery fire.

FRAGO	Fragmentary Order. Usually a simple sketch with arrows and the minimum of formal instructions.
FTX	Formation Training Exercise. One where troops and their equipment, not just the commanders, are exercised.
FUP	Forming-up Position.
Giant Viper	Rocket-propelled explosive hose used by Royal Engineers to clear lanes in minefields.
GOC	General Officer Commanding (Major General).
GPO	Gun Position Officer (Lieutenant) responsible for deployment and reconnaissance.
GPS	Global Positioning System (Satellite Navigation System).
GRANBY	The code-name given to the British operation to liberate Kuwait.
Gunner	Rank in the Royal Artillery equating to private soldier; generic term for all members of the Royal Artillery.
H Hour	Time of the main event, usually an attack.
HE	High Explosive.
HMMW V	High Mobility Multi-Wheel Vehicle. American 4x4 utility vehicle.
HQ	Headquarters.
II	Image Intensifying.
Int	Intelligence.
KTO	Kuwait Theatre of Operations.
L/Bdr	Lance Bombardier. Artillery equivalent of Lance Corporal.
LCpl	Lance Corporal.
Limber	Vehicle used to transport ammunition.
Lt	Lieutenant.
M109	American-built 155mm self-propelled howitzer.
M548	American built tracked logistic vehicle.
M578	Tracked recovery vehicle equipped with winch and crane.
MCCP	Movement Control and Check Point.
MLRS	Multiple Launch Rocket System.
MRE	'Meals Ready to Eat'. American combat rations.
MSR	Main Supply Route.
M–Star	Small portable surveillance radar.
MTLB	Soviet-built armoured personnel carrier.
NAAFI	Navy, Army and Airforce Families Institute.
NAIAD	Nerve Agent Immobilised Enzyme Alarm and Detector.

NAPS	Nerve Agent Pre-treatment Set (tablets).
NBC	Nuclear, Biological and Chemical.
NCO	Non-Commissioned Officer.
NTM	Notice to Move.
O Group	Orders Group.
OP	Observation Post.
Ops	Operations.
PADS	Position Azimuth Determining System (Inertial Navigation System).
POD	Truck mounted re-fuelling system.
PR	Public Relations.
PX	Post Exchange. The American Forces' equivalent to NAAFI.
QARANC	Queen Alexandra's Royal Army Nursing Corps.
QM	Quartermaster, responsible for battalion-level logistics.
REME	Royal Electrical and Mechanical Engineers. responsible for equipment maintenance.
RMP	Royal Military Police.
RCT	Royal Corps of Transport.
Regiment	The term when used by Artillery, Tanks, Aviation and Engineers can refer to a battalion-size unit commanded by a Lieutenant Colonel. It can also have a wider meaning, embracing many battalions from the same arm or cap badge.
REPLEN	Replenishment.
Respirator	Gas mask. (S10)
RHQ	Regimental Headquarters.
RSM	Regimental Sergeant Major. (Warrant Officer Class 1)
RV	Rendezvous.
Sabka	Salt marsh.
SATNAV	Satellite Navigation System.
SCRA	Brigade secure radio net.
Scud	Soviet-built tactical missile.
Shamal	Sand storm.
SITREP	Situation report.
SOP	Standard Operating Procedure.
SQMS	Squadron Quartermaster Sergeant, responsible for the squadron's logistics.
Squadron	A sub-division of a battalion-size organization, it is commanded by a Major and in the British Army usually refers to sub-units of the Royal Armoured Corps, Royal Engineers, Army Air Corps and logistic units with trucks. The number of men varies widely depending on equipment.

Sultan	Light armoured command vehicle.
Tac P	Tactical Air Control Party.
Tac	Tactical.
TAP	Trans-Arabian Pipe. A long and strategically important oil pipeline.
Task Force	American equivalent of a British battlegroup.
TI	Thermal Imagery.
TOGS	Thermal Observation and Gunnery Sight. (Fitted to Challenger tanks).
TOW	American anti-tank missile. (tube-launched, optically-tracked, wire-guided).
ULC	Unit Load Container. (steel box holding 17 x 155mm rounds)
Warrior	British-made Infantry Fighting/Artillery Observer vehicle.
WO2	Warrant Officer Class 2.
WRAC	Women's Royal Army Corps.

Introduction

On the 2nd of August 1990 the army of Saddam Hussein invaded the small Gulf state of Kuwait. This action set in train the series of events that became known as the Gulf War. Great Britain's initial response was to send elements of the Royal Navy, the Royal Air Force and the 7th Armoured Brigade. The ground force consisted of a brigade headquarters, two armoured regiments, an armoured infantry battalion, an artillery regiment and engineer and logistic support. Its task was to help protect Saudi Arabia and to hold the ground until the politicians sorted out the mess. The operation was given the uninspiring title of Operation GRANBY.

From the start the Government made it clear that there would be no general mobilization of reservists. The only way to bring 7 Brigade up to its full war strength was to strip men and equipment from other units in Germany. By October the brigade had undergone an intensive period of training and had begun to deploy. With no indication of how long the crisis would last, the military staff started to plan to relieve 7 Brigade in six months time. As a consequence, on 11 October 1990 the 4th Armoured Brigade was warned for Operation GRANBY 2.

With more time to plan and prepare, the problem of fully manning and equipping 4 Brigade was approached with the wisdom of experience and the knowledge that there was not much left in Germany from which to choose. There were insufficient tanks to provide a second, tank-heavy, brigade. GRANBY 2 would therefore comprise the Challenger tanks of the 14th/20th King's Hussars and the infantry Warriors of the 1st Battalion, the Royal Scots and the 3rd Battalion, Royal Regiment of Fusiliers. A squadron of tanks from the Life Guards and the Warriors of the Queen's and Number 2 Company, 1st Battalion, Grenadier Guards would provide the necessary reinforcements. It would be commanded by Brigadier Christopher Hammerbeck, and his headquarters staff.

The 4th Armoured Brigade's close support artillery regiment was 2nd Field Regiment, Royal Artillery, equipped with the American-built, M109 self-propelled Howitzer. For GRANBY 2, 2nd Regiment would provide the core of the command and logistics, but its own three batteries would have to combine to provide one at full war strength. The other two batteries for the Regiment would be formed using the strength of 27 and 49 Field Regiments, Royal Artillery. This had the advantage of providing three powerful and cohesive units with their own command structure. Each regiment could provide its best troops and the additional equipment and vehicles known to be necessary, but beyond the resources of a single unit.

In late November it became clear that a division would be required and that 4 Brigade would not relieve 7 Brigade but join it. Operation GRANBY 2 became Operation GRANBY 1.5. Before deploying, the three gun batteries of 2nd Regiment combined under the standard of O Battery (The Rocket Troop) with its proud battle honour, 'Leipzig 1813'. They were joined by 23 Battery from 27 Regiment and 127 (Dragon) Battery from 49 Regiment. I had the privilege to command The Rocket Troop and what follows is my personal record of events.

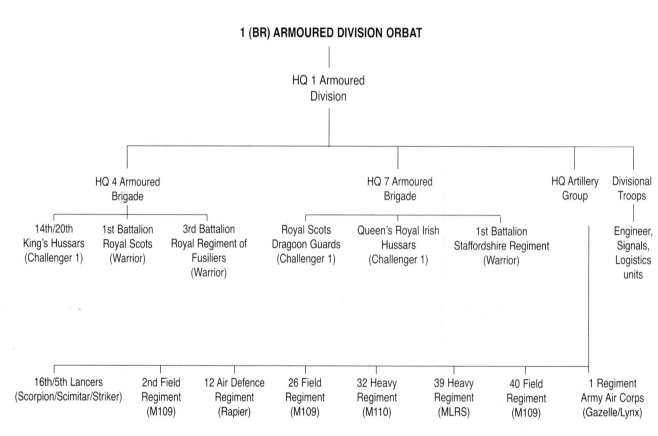

1 (BR) ARMOURED DIVISION ORBAT

HQ 1 Armoured Division

HQ 4 Armoured Brigade

- 14th/20th King's Hussars (Challenger 1)
- 1st Battalion Royal Scots (Warrior)
- 3rd Battalion Royal Regiment of Fusiliers (Warrior)

HQ 7 Armoured Brigade

- Royal Scots Dragoon Guards (Challenger 1)
- Queen's Royal Irish Hussars (Challenger 1)
- 1st Battalion Staffordshire Regiment (Warrior)

HQ Artillery Group

Divisional Troops

- Engineer, Signals, Logistics units

- 16th/5th Lancers (Scorpion/Scimitar/Striker)
- 2nd Field Regiment (M109)
- 12 Air Defence Regiment (Rapier)
- 26 Field Regiment (M109)
- 32 Heavy Regiment (M110)
- 39 Heavy Regiment (MLRS)
- 40 Field Regiment (M109)
- 1 Regiment Army Air Corps (Gazelle/Lynx)

OPERATION DESERT SHIELD

(The defence of Saudi Arabia)

26 DECEMBER 1990

As a career officer in the British Army it is strange to relate that I never ever expected to go to war. For my generation of soldiers, the age of Super-Power overkill meant that military action divided neatly into low-intensity localized operations or Armageddon. An internationalized fast moving war was not considered a credible option. It was therefore not surprising that we who were leaving felt confident that nothing was going to happen and had the firm conviction that the sooner we left, the sooner we would be home. The consensus of opinion was that the Iraqis would certainly back down (after all it would be madness to take on the Americans) but we would probably sit on our backsides in the desert for six months before Operation GRANBY 3 flew out to relieve us. For the wives and sweethearts left behind, this spirit of optimism and certainty was sadly missing. Their men were going to war, perhaps never to return.

I left home at 06.30 on Boxing Day morning after a very traumatic farewell to my wife, Annie, and my three small children. Annie was very brave, but I was extremely glad that I had arranged for one of the other Battery Commanders to give me a lift into camp. The middle of an Army parade ground is not a good place to say goodbye. We journeyed from the married quarters via the prosperous but staid German suburb of Gremendorf, now waking to another day of festivities, and through the gates of Waterloo Barracks, Münster. This array of single-storey huts, built on the old Luftwaffe airstrip in 1945 from the rubble of the bombed city, was the home of 2nd Field Regiment, Royal Artillery. I was dropped off outside the building with a large blue and yellow sign proudly proclaiming 'O Battery (The Rocket Troop) Leipzig 1813'. Even at this early hour a surprisingly large crowd had gathered to see us off.

I spent about thirty minutes going through the final documentation and loading my luggage. The old tin hangar at the end of the Regimental parade square had been emptied of all its war maintenance equipment in order to make room for scales, tables and piles of personal kit. Once checked through, the kit was loaded onto 4-tonne trucks and dispatched, along with all our personal weapons, to Hanover. After a leisurely breakfast in the Mess, I killed time by signing off the last few letters in the office. Already Sergeant Murphy, who was to run the Battery's rear party, had started to transform the block into what would be the base for all our family welfare. I remember thinking, as I looked around my own office now stripped of files, charts, intrays, etc that we had not gone to this trouble for our recent UN tour in Cyprus and wondering how they would cope if we really did go to war.

We left Münster at 09.00 on very smart and comfortable German civilian coaches. We were all in remarkably good spirits and glad to be on the move. The journey itself was pleasant and uneventful until we reached Hanover airport. The final MCCP (Movement Control and Check Point) was in a massive hangar, requisitioned by the military to move thousands of troops. Entry to the airfield was by a gate in the perimeter fence, very close to the hangar. We were a convoy of three coaches, mine being the middle. As the first coach reached the gate it was stopped by a German policeman. He and about ten others were shepherding some sixty demonstrators. The crowd was a mixture of young and old, scruffy and well dressed, aggressive and peaceful. Some carried placards opposing any military intervention in the Gulf. 'No blood for oil' was just one that I remember. Others tried to pass leaflets through the windows, whilst some just shouted in English 'Don't go, don't go.' As each coach reached the gate it was stopped just long enough to allow the crowd to make its point. It was alarming because it was so unexpected, and some of the younger soldiers were clearly quite shaken by the experience. Up to this point we had rather thought of ourselves as international knights in shining armour. Clearly not every one felt that way about us. Reaction inside the bus ranged from bewilderment to anger.

All thoughts of demonstrators, moral ethics and man's inhumanity to man were swept from our minds, however, as we entered the hangar and fell into the clutches of the Joint Services Movements Staff. This is the only military organization which totally refuses to acknowledge that it is part of any military organization. This is home for the rejects, the socially disadvantaged and the psychopaths of the three Services. Only here is the power to move, feed, transport and accommodate a division's worth of troops vested in the hands of a RAF Corporal. Only here will you hear a Royal Navy Petty Officer address an Army Brigadier as 'Luv.'

Inside the hangar hundreds of troops wandered aimlessly amongst the tons of luggage. Some just sat about gloomily on this the second day of Christmas. My group joined the new arrivals line and was herded past one checkpoint after another. Next of kin forms and ID cards all had to be checked and compared with flight manifests and nominal roles. Personal baggage had to be first identified then retrieved before struggling past the final control point where we were weighed yet again and the occasional unfortunate soul searched. The one small NAAFI canteen could not cope with the demands of so many, and so, in characteristic NAAFI fashion, had given up. Some of the troops had been travelling for many hours and were very hungry. Once I had got rid

2

of my kit I sat chatting or wandered about looking for familiar faces in the crowd.

At midday precisely we were called into lines. Clasping my hand baggage I filed past the last mover, walked across the tarmac and onto the aircraft. It was an ex-British Caledonian DC10, now in the new Caledonian Airways livery but still with the familiar tartan-clad air hostesses. The management settled themselves at the front of the aircraft for what was to be a very pleasant flight. A meal was produced almost as soon as we were airborne and there was a real holiday atmosphere. It was like one enormous package tour. One of the younger soldiers was soon dressed up in a tartan skirt and top and helped serve. Most memorable of all was the hostess looking after those of us in the forward cabin. She had the most amazing bust line. Shaped like a heroine out of a comic strip cartoon, she only had to walk down the isle for everyone to fall into disbelieving silence. I am quite sure the experience has done me lasting psychological damage. If that was not enough, they took it upon themselves to show the video 'Pretty Woman'.

Our short stop at RAF Akrotiri in Cyprus was a welcome break, a chance to stretch legs and indulge in a last beer. I remember that each can was blessed with a motto or proverb for the edification of the drinker. Dick Haynes, BC 49 Battery, drew 'He who lives by the sword, shall die by the sword.' A real morale-booster! As I sat with my beer in the departure lounge I took the opportunity to read a letter that I had been handed just before the flight. It had 'Not to be opened before 13.00 hrs' on the envelope and, not immediately recognizing the handwriting, I assumed it was from some well-wisher, too shy to talk to me direct, or words of great wisdom from one of my superior officers. I was wrong on both counts. It was from my three FOOs (Forward Observation Officers) who had entitled themselves, 'The Fugitives.' The letter read:

14 December 1990

Dear Andrew
This letter is not designed to alarm you – but it would probably be best if you were to sit down. Please find enclosed a Captain's rank slide as a symbolic gesture of our departure. After much soul-searching we have decided that, however strong we believe the justification for war to be, we are all yellow bellies. Balloons at parties used to frighten us (they still frighten Bungie) and the thought of all those loud bangs in the desert is unbearable.

We would all like to wish you the very best of luck in the impending battle. We will all be thinking of you and the Battery on January 15th. We appreciate the fact that you will wish to mark our departure with the traditional presentations. Please forward our 'Rocketeers' to the address below. We understand that it will be

3

almost impossible to fit in a dine out prior to your departure. We do, however, look forward to coming back to Münster in happier times so that this may take place.
Yours in hasty retreat,
Derek, Bungie, Graham.

I enjoyed the joke and was touched that they had gone to such trouble to cheer me on my way. I confess, however, that I had a degree of sympathy with their sentiments. Statisticians still argue over who in the Army has the shortest life expectancy in battle, a Forward Observation Officer or a Battery Commander.

The second leg of the flight was uneventful with most of us trying to sleep. As we touched down onto Saudi soil the captain of the aircraft wished us all good luck and added, "For all of you in the front of the aircraft who were wondering.....no they weren't real." I am still trying to come to terms with the disappointment.

27 DECEMBER 1990

We landed at Dhahran military air base at almost exactly midnight. Without any form of ceremony we walked straight from the aircraft and onto a fleet of buses. Literally within minutes we were on our way again. The airfield itself was a mass of activity and clearly gearing up for war. Security was evident everywhere with armed Saudi and American troops on all exits. All was lit by blazing orange floodlights and as we drove from the runway we could see row upon row of aircraft. In front were Saudi Tornadoes and US Air Force F16s, whilst behind were massive Galaxy transporters of the US Military Airlift Command.

The buses themselves really defy description, but I shall try. Firstly they were old, probably early 1970s. It was impossible to tell what make they were for makeshift doubledecker bodies, clearly of local manufacture, had been bolted on to the original chassis. They had been both unsophisticated and uncomfortable when they were new; now these migrant worker buses, with their windows missing, torn seats and strong smell of urine, were requisitioned troop transport. We had arrived. We were not impressed.

The road from Dhahran was straight and lit by innumerable harsh yellow lights. Every now and then a road would join at right-angles escorted by the mandatory yellow glare. In Saudi Arabia the size of the electricity bill was evidently not a factor. For most of the journey many just sat in a jet-lagged dream while others toyed with the packed meal we had been given, grateful for the darkness which denied them a sight of the contents of their sandwiches. For myself, I sat and watched the lights passing by, occasionally catching a glimpse of a single red which marked the location of an oil rig, the only features in this dark, flat, sand world. Traffic on the road consisted of a few military convoys and the odd dilapidated bus, returning empty to collect another consignment of troops.

The oil port of Al Jubayl, our FMA (Forward Mounting Area), first appeared as millions of bright dots on the horizon. It was still dark when we reached the dock area and were off-loaded into Shed 5, a massive waterside warehouse. This was the reception area for the 1st (British) Armoured Division. Once everyone was safely gathered, there was the inevitable briefing, this time by the Officer Commanding Troops Reception. After a welcome we were told the basic do's and dont's of Saudi culture, in particular their sensitivity over women. Where we were was pointed out on a large map and the Intelligence update left us with just a glimmer of hope that we would live to see the next dawn. We were then split up by units and sent on a 'Round Robin' circuit which included collecting a meal and two weeks' water money, booking in with the Post Office, central documentation and pay. All this took place under the one roof; cleverly keeping hundreds of troops occupied and therefore out of trouble.

It was nearly two hours before the luggage convoy arrived. It drove straight into the centre of the building before disgorging its contents into an enormous heap. Everyone was forced, on pain of death, to stand and watch the baggage party unload their kit and separate it into piles of sleeping bags, kit bags and bergans. Each unit was then allowed forward, in turn, to collect whatever they could find. I had tied blue and yellow ribbon to each piece of my luggage but even so it was some time before I struggled out the door to meet my BK (Battery Second in Command - from the French 'Battery Kapitan'), Geoff Ravenhill, and his trusty Landrover.

The oil refineries at Al Jubayl. (AG)

It was 06.00 when, after a short drive, we arrived at Archiroden Lines. Al Jubayl had been built, largely by British contractors, in the 1970s. Oil was its reason for existing and migrant workers made it work. These workers, from Pakistan, Malaysia, Palestine, in fact everywhere but Kuwait and Saudi Arabia, had mostly been expelled or had fled. Their homes were now our homes. Archiroden Lines consisted of about 150 metres of badly tarmaced road. Off this road, at right-angles, were long, single-storey concrete and wood huts, with small windows and large air conditioners. In the centre were two larger huts which served as the restaurant and recreation centre. It reminded me very much of the first Butlins.

First things first, an English breakfast of eggs, bacon, sausages, tomatoes, fried bread, mushrooms and beans. The proverbial heart attack on a plate. Wonderful! It was served by a cheery Brit civilian called Dennis and his small team of Indian cooks. Freshly oiled and watered, I went to bed. I shared a room with my fellow Battery Commanders, universally known as 'BCs', Majors Dave Marshall (BC 127 Battery), Mark Vye (BC 46 Battery), Alan Collett (BC 23 Battery), and Dick Haynes (BC 49 Battery). The room contained three sets of old steel bunk beds and a wardrobe – next door, en suite, was a small and very grimy bathroom. It was cramped, crowded, dirty and uncomfortable – but it was a lot better than where others were living. With so much kit and so many officers, it took some time to get ourselves organized, but at last I fell asleep.

I had to be up for 14.00 to attend an Intelligence briefing in the recreation hut. While I sat through an update on the political situation and a short synopsis of the current deployment plan, Gunner Newell, my driver, located our Landrover and filled it with fuel. Al Jabayl was large but it could not cope with the numbers about to arrive. Consequently, units were deployed out into the desert as soon as possible. Second Field Regiment had started to deploy that morning and my BK had taken as many men and vehicles as were ready to move. I needed to know my own Battlegroup's deployment plan, so at about 15.30 Newell and I set off to look for Black Adder Camp, temporary home of the Battlegroup I would support in war, the 14th/20th King's Hussars.

Al Jubayl was in fact huge. It consisted of the old original preoil-wealth town comprising a few streets of old shabby shops and dilapidated houses. This area was now populated by Asian traders and 'poor' Arabs, mostly from Egypt - the Palestinians, Jordanians and Yemenies having fled. The old town was strictly out of bounds. Close to it were the docks. This was now an area of tight security with armed troops on all the entry points, a place of quays, cranes, ships and warehouses and above all one of frenzied activity. North of the docks was the smart residential area. This was where the Saudis and their newly arrived Kuwaiti guests lived - straight roads, large luxurious houses, green grass and palm trees. Here the Divisional Headquarters staff had found themselves a comfortable, if temporary, home. It was also subject to constant police patrols and where hapless locals were liable to fall foul of the dreaded Religious Police roadblocks. I was interested in the fourth and largest area, the oil refineries, close to which was Black Adder Camp.

Until quite recently it had been illegal in Saudi Arabia for any 'ordinary' person to be in possession of a map. Being caught with a map of an area as strategically important as Al Jubayl could carry the death penalty. It was not surprising therefore that the Coalition Forces found maps in short supply and that I did not have one at all. Gunner Newell, however, assured me that he had been given clear directions and so with a high degree of confidence we set off. Our planned route took us first south to join the motorway that swept north-west across the desert, bypassing the main town and port. We would then head west towards the oil refineries. Apart from oil and sand, the other commodity that Saudi Arabia has in abundance is space, and they use it to the full.

The oil refineries were built around a system of roads which were themselves based on a grid system reminiscent of an American city. The refineries tended to be situated at the crossing points of the grid, leaving square miles of flat, empty sand in between. Running parallel, on both sides of the road, were pipelines, sitting exposed on their foot-high blocks of concrete and joining refinery to refinery. Occasionally one of these pipelines would rear up in a massive arch and cross the road. Also in the grid system were long, concrete-lined, fresh-water canals, up to 25 metres across. To the untrained eye each of the refineries and their adjoining pipelines, roads and canals all had one thing in common, they looked identical. After driving for over an hour it was clear that we were lost. Hope rose again when a US military policeman assured us that the Camp was "Just down the road, Sir." After a further hour's drive it was clear that concepts of distance vary considerably between England and the American Mid-West. It was getting dark! We went home! It had been a salutary and painful lesson. Sixty members of the Battery were due to arrive tonight. Any noble thoughts I may have had of staying up to meet them were overtaken by exhaustion and jetlag. I went to bed.

28 DECEMBER 1990
I was woken at 05.00 by the high-pitched wail of the Muezzin calling the faithful to prayer. I had breakfast at 07.30 with Geoff Ravenhill who had just driven in from the Battery's deployment location to collect the next batch of soldiers. He made no attempt to conceal his amusement when I related the sad tale of yesterday's trip, but he agreed to take me first to the CMA (Convoy Marshalling Area) then Black Adder Camp

and on to visit 40 Field Regiment, Royal Artillery.

The journey to the CMA took us first to the entrance to the port, guarded by British Royal Military Police, as well as their now-familiar US cousins. The Saudi MP looked on but took little interest in either the stream of vehicles or their contents. We went through the checkpoint, having first shown our identity cards, and proceeded through a chicane formed by large seagoing containers. There were hundreds of them, mostly in the drab olive green of the US Army but there were many civilians amongst them in bright orange and red. Occasionally, crudely chalked signs like 'Royal Corps of Transport' and 'URGENT' could be picked out. The containers had been positioned to provide a compromise between accessibility and the need to reduce damage should the port come under air attack. Once through, we took the left fork at a roundabout and headed away from the quays, running north and parallel with the coast. We passed the now vacant customs post and crossing over yet another roundabout, Geoff pointing out the US PX (their equivalent of NAAFI) that had been set up in a car park. It consisted of one cabin selling soap, T-shirts etc., and a burger bar. The queues for both were either long or very long, depending on the time of day. Still within the dock area, we continued along a kilometre of straight road. To the right, behind hastily erected but totally ineffective hessian screens, were the hundreds of amphibious armoured tracked assault vehicles of the US MEF (Marine Expeditionary Force). On the left, smothered by the sound of permanently screaming generators, was Al Jubayl's main defence - a Patriot missile battery. It was manned almost entirely by women.

At the end of the straight was the lorry park. Most were old Mercedes, but all were long, articulated flat-beds with Arab drivers whose homes were quite clearly their cabs. The trucks were all parked in lines, their drivers either maintaining, cooking or sleeping. It was this massive wheeled fleet, rapidly assembling from all over the Middle East, that would provide the bulk of the Coalition's logistic lift. Opposite the lorry park was the refuelling area. This was an open area of flat sand about 100 metres from the sea. On it, in neat lines but well spaced out, were fuel tankers, both British and American. Any one needing fuel, be they military or contract worker, simply entered the circuit and was directed by the military police to the nearest working tanker.

The fuel park was the last of the installations going north in Al Jubayl, for less than 100 metres further on was the military police post guarding the exit to the port. The road continued to head north, just inland from a narrow line of coastal sand dunes, for about 6 kms and then, just past the point where the main canal system ran into the sea, was the CMA. As its name suggested, the Convoy Marshalling Area was an open area upon which hundreds upon hundreds of military vehicles were lined up.

I remember looking in amazement, never imagining that the British Army possessed so many vehicles. I was then told by Geoff Ravenhill that the bulk of 7 Brigade had already deployed and most of 4 Brigade's vehicles were still at sea. "If you think this is impressive, you should have been here last week," he said. I was here this week and I was more than impressed. For the first time I realized the scale of Britain's military commitment. It was all rather chilling.

Black Adder Camp was indeed on one of the open areas of sand between the oil refineries and we had passed quite close the day before. It consisted of a makeshift security fence of coiled barbed wire and six-foot steel pickets. A sangar built of sandbags and corrugated iron controlled the only entry point. Contract workers were laying hard-core ready to receive the hundreds of prefabricated huts that would be needed to house, in the first instance, transit forces and then perhaps prisoners of war. The arrival of the huts was clearly still some way off and so troops were living at the far end of the complex in old, brown, canvas, marquee tents, which had been erected straight onto the soft sand. The tents were in neat rows, each identified by an already fading chalked number for the individual tent and a letter for the row. One glance served to confirm what I already knew - their occupants were a lot worse off than I was.

The 14th/20th were easily found as they occupied three tents in the very first row. Each tent was identified by the Regiment's distinctive

Vehicles assemble at the Convoy Marshalling Area Al Jubayl. (AG)

hawk emblem on a blue and yellow background. This was the home of my alter ego and from now on I would lead a schizophrenic existence. As a Battery Commander with the radio call sign 'Three Three', I would work to Lieutenant Colonel David Radcliffe, the Commanding Officer of 2nd Field Regiment, Royal Artillery; whilst with the King's Hussars I would command an artillery tactical (tac) party, have a 'One Zero' call sign and work to the Battlegroup. Such is the way that the Royal Artillery does its business; I was now required to prepare my battery for war in the firm knowledge that at the crucial moment I would have to desert them. As we moved towards hostilities the guns would become part of the Divisional Artillery Group, whilst I and my three FOOs would go forward to the sharp end to direct the artillery fire for our Battlegroup.

Known by all as 'Colonel', Lieutenant Colonel Mike Vickery was my Battlegroup Commander and peacetime next door neighbour. He greeted me warmly. We spent about twenty minutes discussing future training and the initial deployment plan and then, with the arrival of the Brigade Commander imminent, I felt it prudent to leave.

40 Field Regiment, Royal Artillery, had deployed at the start of the campaign in support of 7 Armoured Brigade. Their M109 Howitzers were now dug in, some 80 kms north of Al Jubayl, as part of a defensive blocking action aimed at countering a sudden Iraqi advance south. The

Black Adder Lines at Al Jubayl. (AG)

Camels on the TAP Line Road. (AG)

Regiment was centred on a series of limestone quarries collectively known as Fire Base Edinburgh. The journey to Edinburgh took us first due west, away from the FMA, on a new tarmac road, past rolling desert sand dunes and open parched sabka (salt lake) to the junction with the main north-south, Kuwait/Saudi highway. At this point there was not only the now familiar Military Police control point, but dropped in neat rows onto the bare sand, was the US Forces 'Tent City'. I was staggered by its size. It made Black Adder seem like a Boy Scout jamboree. It was reputed to hold 20,000 troops and, as it covered acres, I could well believe it.

We did not follow the slow-moving line of trucks heading north on the main route, but passed under it and continued west for another 700 metres, turning right onto an old tarmac single track, which serviced the oil pipe line running along the side. This was the TAP Line Road, TAP standing for Trans Arabian Pipe. The journey by Landrover took well over an hour of steady, monotonous driving. The road, whilst almost deserted, passed through rough desert, consisting of loose rolling sand and low sparse spindly bushes, some less than six inches high. Occasionally camels, seemingly belonging to no one, wandered aimlessly across the road oblivious to any danger. We passed a traditional Bedouin tent surrounded by litter and junk reminiscent of an English gypsy camp. An old petrol tanker provided water for man and goats alike and the only indication that this was a Saudi Bedouin was the gleaming Range Rover and the satellite dishes.

It was now past midday, the sun was uncomfortably hot and the wind strong. Regimental HQ of 40 Field Regiment was colocated with one of its gun batteries at the forward edge of a working quarry. The limestone when crushed formed a dust as fine as talcum powder which penetrated everything when dry and turned to concrete when wet. Today it was dry and the air was one white, choking cloud. HQ and guns alike were dispersed around, and dug into, the quarry. Rock sangars for ammunition had been constructed close to each gun, and those being

11

used as living accommodation had reinforced tin and rock roofs. There was no need for camouflage as everything and everybody was a universal white. The Commanding Officer, Lieutenant Colonel Rory Clayton, made no attempt to disguise his delight at the arrival in theatre of a sister Gunner Regiment and lost no time in bundling us both into his Saudi-supplied Toyota Land Cruiser to show us his empire. After a very educational couple of hours and some very hairy cross-country driving, time and daylight were running out so we arranged to return the next day. It was dark by the time we got back to Al Jubayl. By way of a morale booster we stopped at the PX in the docks and had an ice cream and so we were lucky to catch the evening meal. Ten more of the Battery arrived during the night.

29 DECEMBER 1990

I did not get back from meeting the flight until 06.00 and with the Commanding Officer's conference at 08.30 I was exhausted before the day had properly started. After the usual cholesterol-charged breakfast I did my first lot of washing in the vain hope that I could get the white dust out of my far from green combat suit. With the advantage of hindsight I can now look back at those futile labours and grin. It was a bright sunny day, like an English summer, but there was a strong wind which threw dust everywhere - in particular onto my dripping wet uniform. Midmorning, Newell and I, my GPO (Gun Position Officer) Lieutenant Nick Greaves, and the BSM (Battery Sergeant Major) WO2 Steadman, set off north again for 40 Regiment. As part of the plan to help the newly arriving forces deploy successfully and to avoid repeating earlier mistakes, each battery in 2nd Regiment had been allocated a 'mentor' battery from 40. My own battery, O Battery (The Rocket Troop) had been given 137 (Java) Battery, and their gun position was now our destination.

It took us two hours to get there and after I had spent an hour with the BC, Major Simon Lloyd, we left Nick Greaves to spend the night and headed north-west to where my BK and BQMS (Battery Quartermaster Sergeant) were setting up The Rocket Troop's initial deployment position. The British 1st Armoured Division was deploying in support of the US Marines. 40 Regiment was already deployed to the west of the TAP Line Road in Fire Base Edinburgh. Now 2nd Regiment was deploying some 10 km to the east, into Fire Base Manchester. To get there we had to leave the road and take a sand road which followed a high-voltage power line. The Regiment was deploying both sides of the Pylon Line Road, but so far the only evidence was a few trucks and tents. It was an inhospitable area of soft, shifting sand, flat and windswept, devoid of any vegetation or life. The BK and BQMS had made the best of a bad job, but if a wheeled vehicle strayed far from the road it bogged

into the sand, and if it stayed too close it was covered in the dust whipped up by the relentless traffic. A few hundred yards to our west, a HMMW V (pronounced Hum Vee and looks like a Landrover on steroids) mounted, TOW missile battalion of US Marines was deployed. They had been there for months and in all that time appeared to have done nothing either to improve their operational state or their living conditions.

My only experience with working with the Americans was the occasional interchanges with their Army in Germany which had taken place in the late 1970s and early 80s. Then they had been going through their post-Vietnam trauma and those initial bad first impressions had stuck. To the smug British, the American Army was everything we were not and their Marine Corps on first sight only served to reinforce past prejudices. They looked in bad order and morale seemed to be low. They had begun to trek across to the Battery in the hope of trading. It was, however, an unequal match; lambs to the slaughter. Already the BQMS had acquired a mass of very useful kit in exchange for things as basic as hot water. Having sorted out numerous problems, and armed with a shopping list of 'wants' from the BQMS, we returned to Al Jubayl. I desperately needed some sleep and I had all the symptoms of the mother of all colds. Tonight twenty-five members of the Battery arrived.

The Battery digs in on the Pylon Line Road. (KW)

13

30 DECEMBER 1990

I woke up with streaming eyes and nose. A cold in the desert, could things possibly get worse? I struggled through the Commanding Officer's 08.30 conference. Lieutenant Colonel David Radcliffe was in cheery mood and informed us that a local expatriate had volunteered to instruct our drivers in the art of desert driving. All available drivers, some still jetlagged and bewildered, were herded into trucks to RV (rendezvous) where the Pylon Line Road met the highway. In Hong Kong my experience with Ex-Pats had been all bad and I saw no reason to assume things would be any better here. I therefore volunteered to lead the convoy of PODs (fuel tankers) from the CMA to the Regiment's deployment position and thus monitor the driver training.

Locating the vehicles, checking them out, filling them with fuel, briefing the drivers and then assembling the convoy all took a very long time. Fully loaded, the 8-tonne vehicles were slow and matters were made worse by the sheer volume of traffic on the route north. It was mid afternoon before we reached the junction with the Pylon Line Road. There stood all the drivers. The Ex-Pat had, true to form, not turned up. Stuck in the sand? I sent the drivers back to Al Jubayl. My small convoy of fifteen vehicles set off down the dust road. After about 5 km we came across a 4-tonne Bedford MK lorry which had come off the track and was now buried up to its axles in soft sand. We were almost at our destination so I sent the fuel PODs on and turned my attention to the casualty. It was the REME (Royal Electrical and Mechanical Engineers) repair truck from one of our sister batteries. They had been the last vehicle in their convoy and because of the dust the vehicle in front had not seen that they were in trouble. I made a mental note to sort out the convoy commander.

The vehicle crew had been stranded for over an hour and apart from the bulldozer which was working in the quarry about 100 yards away, we were the only vehicle they had seen. A bulldozer! I was about to go ballistic, then thought better of it. If these two halfwits could not see the blindingly obvious then nothing I could say would make any difference. I walked across to the bulldozer and asked the Arab driver for a tow. He smiled, shook his head and pointed at what I assumed was his foreman standing next to a Land Cruiser a further 100 yards away. I walked back to my Landrover, put the magazine on my 9mm Stirling sub-machine gun and, slinging it over my shoulder, set off for the foreman. I was determined that he should understand that my polite request for assistance was in no way negotiable. There was no need for dramatics. With a cheery smile, the bulldozer was hitched up and out came the truck. I then took the crew aside and explained in very simple terms that the next time they performed like this they would probably die.

I had yet to collect Nick Greaves, my Gun Position Officer, from 40

14

Host Nation support:
a Saudi bulldozer to
the rescue. (AG)

Regiment, so I only had time to confirm that my own convoy had arrived safely before heading west. The journey home was much quicker, but we passed massive, slow-moving, military convoys going north. Sixty vehicles, nose to tail, was not unusual.

31 DECEMBER 1990

My cold was worse and I felt like death. Nick Greaves met the previous night's flight which had a lot of our own soldiers and the advance party from 26 Field Regiment, Royal Artillery. My day was spent on Exercise CRACKER BARREL 1. This was the first of a series of Divisionally-run study days on offensive operations. It was held in the extremely smart Al Huwaillat Social and Recreational Club. Situated in the heart of the rich Saudi residential area, we had been given free use of its facilities as part of the 'war effort'. Lunch was superb! During one of the breaks I took a stroll outside where I noticed a Landrover with its equipment secured on the roof by a yellow net made of inch-wide straps joined by steel rings. This was clearly an extremely useful piece of kit. Enquiries revealed that it was a US air cargo net and that they were stored in the airfreight warehouse in the docks. I immediately dispatched Sergeant Chauhan, my 'Mr Fixit', to acquire some. That night, after a detailed recce, he and a few of the Battery bluffed their way into one of the most heavily guarded few acres on earth and negotiated the 'indefinite loan' of fifteen

15

nets. No mean achievement as it took a 4-tonne truck to move them. I sent them straight out into the desert. They were to prove a battle winner, enabling the guns and recce vehicles to carry more and deploy quicker.

That evening the CO and all the BCs had to attend a map exercise at Divisional HQ. It was held in an open shed which looked as if it had until very recently held hundreds of bicycles. On the ground in front of us all was a cloth model of a section of the Iraqi main defensive line. We sat in descending order of seniority, brigadiers at the front, the majors and captains cramped and straining their necks at the back. The only lighter moment came when the model was explained. Each element of the defences was pointed out. 'Flat sand desert, wire, mines, an oil-filled trench, more mines and finally...a berm.' At this last pronouncement a voice from the back was heard to say, "Zey have a berm." The back ranks dissolved into laughter as a tide of Inspector Clouseau mimics joined the throng. All to the total consternation of the briefers and the front row.

It was getting very cold by the time we finished. Feeling bloody, I went to bed at 10.30pm. My alarm woke me at midnight. As I sat up on my bunk my thoughts went back to this time last year when on an equally cheerless and chilly night, I had deployed The Rocket Troop between the Greeks and the Turks on the outskirts of Nicosia. "Don't worry," I had announced to one and all, "It will be much better next year." Perhaps it would be third time lucky. We toasted ourselves in the only drink available, the Saudi substitute for beer. This was a brown, fizzy, alcohol-free liquid with a taste midway between Marmite and Dettol. The can was erroneously marked 'Delicious Malt Beverage'. We toasted, drank and went back to sleep. Happy New Year!

1 JANUARY 1991

My cold was worse, but to compensate, my three FOOs had arrived. Captains Graham Ambrose, Derek Hudson and Richard 'Bungie' Farndale. I was extremely pleased to see them. After breakfast the four of us set off on tour. We worked our way through the port complex before heading out into the desert and up the TAP Line Road to 40 Regiment and 137 Battery. After a tour of the battery position we headed west to where the BK and the BQMS were working miracles. No longer were single trucks just dotted in the desert, now there were massive sand-coloured nets under which vehicles and crews lived. Under one net was the cookhouse, under another the BQMS store. All around sandbagged sangars were springing up and long, deep fire trenches were being dug. Their greatest feat, however, was a makeshift shower, fashioned using a wooden frame with a water tank on top. All this was in stark contrast to the US Marines some few hundred yards away. They sat in abject discomfort and bewilderment, a hive of inactivity, watching

16

The Battery
cookhouse on the
Pylon Line Road.
(HM)

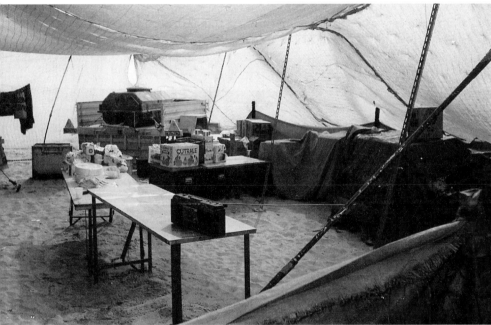

Inside the
cookhouse. (HM)

the British Army move in.

After lunch we decided to drive further out into the desert, due east to the next pipeline. The Regiment's deployment location was on top of what appeared to be a large, gently curving, whale-back feature. From the Battery's position it was evident that the land sloped away to the east, but, because of the heat shimmer, it was impossible to see beyond a few hundred metres. The map showed both an oil pipeline and a sand service road. At first the sand was reasonably firm and we made good speed. However, as we neared the edge of the escarpment we hit a sand sea and only just managed to reverse the Landrover out. It was our first real experience of how diverse and changeable the sand conditions could be over a very short distance. Most alarming of all was the realization that both firm and soft sand looked identical from inside a vehicle.

It was now mid afternoon and the heat and my cold were not happy bedfellows. I had a roaring temperature with alternating bouts of sweating and shivering. We headed back to Al Jubayl and Camp 4 to try and find a doctor. Camp 4 was another 'liberated' migrant worker camp. It was, however, much bigger, more comfortable, and in a smarter part of the town than Archirodon Camp. As a consequence it was full of logistiticians, medics, Royal Military Police and the Women's Royal Army Corps. It was late evening when we arrived, but I was able to persuade a nurse to give me a nasal spray and some tablets.

Apart from the medics, the real advantage of Camp 4 was that it had telephones. We had heard that the queues were interminable but tonight they were down to simple double figures. I fell into line and was rewarded with a brief but very welcome talk with Annie. All was well. It was now too late to catch the evening meal so we decided not to chance our luck with the PX in the port area but to try the PX at the Al Jubayl Air Base. The queues were reported to be smaller. The air base, situated at the south end of the town, had been built for small executive jets. Now, surrounded by barbed wire and the mandatory orange floodlights, it was home to the Air Wing of the Marine Expeditionary Force. As we drove into the base we counted, in the harsh glare, over sixty Harrier aircraft. It was an impressive sight.

2 JANUARY 1991

At 04.00 the ship carrying the bulk of our guns and AFV 432 command and personnel vehicles docked. Considering how long they had been at sea, most started with little difficulty. Unloading was a long and laborious activity. The ship was a Roll On Roll Off, but getting the 26-tonne guns manoeuvred in the hold and then onto the ramps was a nightmare. The ship was not designed for vehicles steered by tracks nor with long protruding barrels. The problem of unloading, however, had to be left to others, as I had to leave at 06.00 to drive up to 40 Field Regiment to watch a demonstration of a gun battery deployment. I bundled the FOOs into my Landrover and Nick Greaves drove a second Landrover with as many of the Gun Line Section Commanders as could be spared from the unloading.

The weather for the journey north was dull and overcast. The wind was strengthening noticeably and we were clearly in for a storm. As it had not rained in Al Jubayl for over five years the prospect of getting wet had never entered our minds. The dreaded white dust was starting to swirl when we arrived and we were only just in time for the 08.00 Intelligence brief. It was given by a Senior NCO from the Intelligence Corps who had been an observer with the Iraqis during the Iran/Iraq war. He was now part of the Divisional Intelligence Cell. I found what he had to say of the greatest interest. Up to now all my briefings had consisted of facts and figures, concluding with the usual bland

'assessment' which told me little more than the BBC's World Service. As a commander I desperately needed to get a feel for the likely task ahead. Most importantly, I needed to be able to speak convincingly to the growing number of young soldiers who asked me, "Are we going to be all right, Sir." What I told them had to both calm their fears and stiffen their resolve. It was already becoming apparent that many of the younger soldiers had an almost childlike faith in my ability to ensure that all would be well.

The NCO spoke extremely well. His talk was aimed primarily at the

Vehicles starting to unload at the port of Al Jubayl. (PS)

Guns moving north to Fire Base 'Manchester'. (AG)

soldiers so was delivered in a punchy and at times very humorous manner. The basis of what he had to say was this:
- In his opinion, of all the Arabs, the Iraqis were probably the best soldiers and certainly the nicest people.
- Their Army is the fourth largest in the world with 1.25 million men under arms, and is well trained and well equipped. They have fought a war with Iran for over 8 years so their soldiers are experienced and combat-hardened.
- As well as nuclear they have a full array of conventional weapons including sophisticated Western communication and optical equipment. They also possess a wide range of chemical weapons and delivery means and have used them not only against Iranians, but also against the opposition to Sadam inside Iraq.
- They are Arabs and therefore have a terror of fighting Western Europeans.
- They are good at the set-piece planned battle but cannot cope with fast-moving manoeuvre warfare. The experience of the Iran/Iraq war was that even when they knew where the Iranians were they took an inordinate amount of time to bring their artillery to bear.
- In spite of the size, the equipment and the experience of the Iraqi army, the Iranians, led by untrained clerics and with vastly inferior forces, fought them to a standstill.

It was the last statement that really put it all into perspective for me and I used it repeatedly on officers and soldiers alike when they needed the threat put into a manageable form. By the time the briefing ended the Shamal (sandstorm) was all but upon us. I left my Gun Line management team to learn what they could about deploying guns in a sandstorm and headed south for the docks. When I arrived the first guns were already being driven off to the CMA. Only one gun (D Sub) and one Observation Post 432 (Romeo 3) was not on the ship. Where they were, no one could say. Ray Fox, the Technical Quartermaster, was in charge of the shipping programme. His office wall in Archiroden was covered in charts showing ships' names, their expected arrival date and likely cargo. Ray pointed out that even the name of the ship could not be relied upon and the vehicles would turn up when they were ready. Ray and I were to spend many hours in that office trying to find my strays.

The issued desert boot, little more than a sand-coloured shoe, was not a success. The procurers were working hard to get a higher, more robust boot which did not allow sand in over the side, but it was a long way from arriving at the front. Consequently the Paymaster, the Regiment's own Mr Fixit, had bought some Saudi Army boots which were sold to all. I bought a pair, confident in the knowledge that under no circumstances would H. M. Government reimburse me. (I never did get issued with desert boots.) As I wanted to meet the next flight I turned in early. I wrote some 'blueys', the free military aerograms, and then the unthinkable happened – for the first time in five years, it rained (We did not know it at the time but this was the start of what would set a 10-year record for rainfall.)

3 JANUARY 1991

After the previous night's flight, the Regiment was complete in theatre, though vehicles and kit continued to arrive. The weather was cool and overcast but dry as I drove out to the CMA where the vehicles were being made ready for the deployment. I retrieved the kit that I had stashed on my own 432 tracked vehicle before it had sailed and took it back to my room to start my final packing. Graham Ambrose was working on our only Warrior. The vehicle had been broken into somewhere on the journey and some of the equipment had been taken. The laser seemed faulty and the Osprey sight was out of alignment. Nothing we could not overcome, given time. The vehicles were to be loaded onto transporters tonight ready to move north tomorrow.

The first large consignment of mail arrived. Two letters from my brother Allan, posted on 27 December, and a large batch of Christmas cards from a school in Walthamstow. I dished the cards out amongst the Battery on condition that they replied. To show willing I took one and also wrote back to the Head Teacher. It made a welcome break from vehicle manifests and loading lists and their letters were much appreciated. Those not at the CMA were doing their own last-minute preparation, and wet washing hung everywhere. I had an Intelligence briefing at 20.00, which told me very little but seemed optimistic that a political solution would be found. I spent the rest of the day and most of the night back at the CMA struggling to load guns and 432s onto a mixed fleet of Royal Corps of Transport tank transporters and Arab contract low-loaders.

4 JANUARY 1991

At 02.30 the final vehicle was secured with chains and the convoy, with its Royal Military Police escort, set off north. A member of the vehicle's crew sat in each cab, the remainder would travel by bus at a more civilized hour. I followed the convoy up later in the morning. So far my tactical party consisted of my ³/₄-tonne Landrover, two Armoured Fighting Vehicle 432s, a Warrior, my own 432 and a Sultan armoured command post which, with its own crew under Sergeant Radcliffe, would provide my foot on the ground at Battle Group MAIN HQ. The AFV 432s were old, slow, poorly armoured, tracked vehicles of 1960s vintage. They were in no way compatible with the new Challenger tanks with which they would have to work. The arrival of the new Observation Post Variant and Battery Commander's Variant of the new, sophisticated and very capable Warrior was expected any moment but so far we only had the one Warrior on which to do our training.

All the BCs were invited to lunch at the Regimental echelon with the CRA (Commander Royal Artillery), Brigadier Ian Durie. It was a pleasant enough lunch eaten on six-foot tables under an enormous cam net. As for information, the CRA could tell us nothing we did not already know, indeed he confessed that the Divisional Intelligence Cell had its ears glued to the World Service like the rest of us. After lunch I made a brief call on the Battery which was now deploying in earnest and doing its best to make the best of a very soft and desolate stretch of sand. I then headed back to Al Jubayl, to Div HQ and another map exercise. Exercise over, I spent the remainder of the evening packing and re-packing my kit. The first issue of the new desert combats had somewhat upset my kit-to-space calculations. There were two real highlights of the day. First, while driving through the port area of Al Jubayl, a brand new American field telephone had fallen off the back of a truck right in front of me. It had instantly joined the British Army. The second was the unfortunate but amusing news that an unwary American Marine had been trying to stare down a camel and had the top of his head badly bitten for his effrontery. Reliable information indicated that sixteen stitches had been required.

5 JANUARY 1991
The morning was overcast, cold, with light rain. I left Al Jubayl via the smart recreation centre and Camp 4. Our Operations Officer, Major John Buchanan, had scrounged a lift but first he had to rehearse, with the CO, a presentation the Regiment was giving as part of the Division's work-up training. To fill the time while I waited for John, I telephoned Annie. She was in bed. Rehearsal over, we joined the hundreds of other vehicles slowly making their way north. We arrived at the Regiment at midday and went straight to A2 Echelon (boots and socks, but the best food) to have lunch with the General Officer Commanding 1st (British) Armoured Division, Major General Rupert Smith. Again we sat round six-foot tables and ate under a massive net. I sat next to the GOC and we chatted for some time. He spoke openly about the problems of the deployment, kit, and training. Most encouragingly, he assured us that if war became inevitable the Coalition forces would not attack until they were completely ready and confident that they had done all in their power to ensure a quick and painless ground victory. Indeed, he explained that the military nightmare was that the Iraqis would attack

BATTERY ORBAT - (217 Officers and Men)

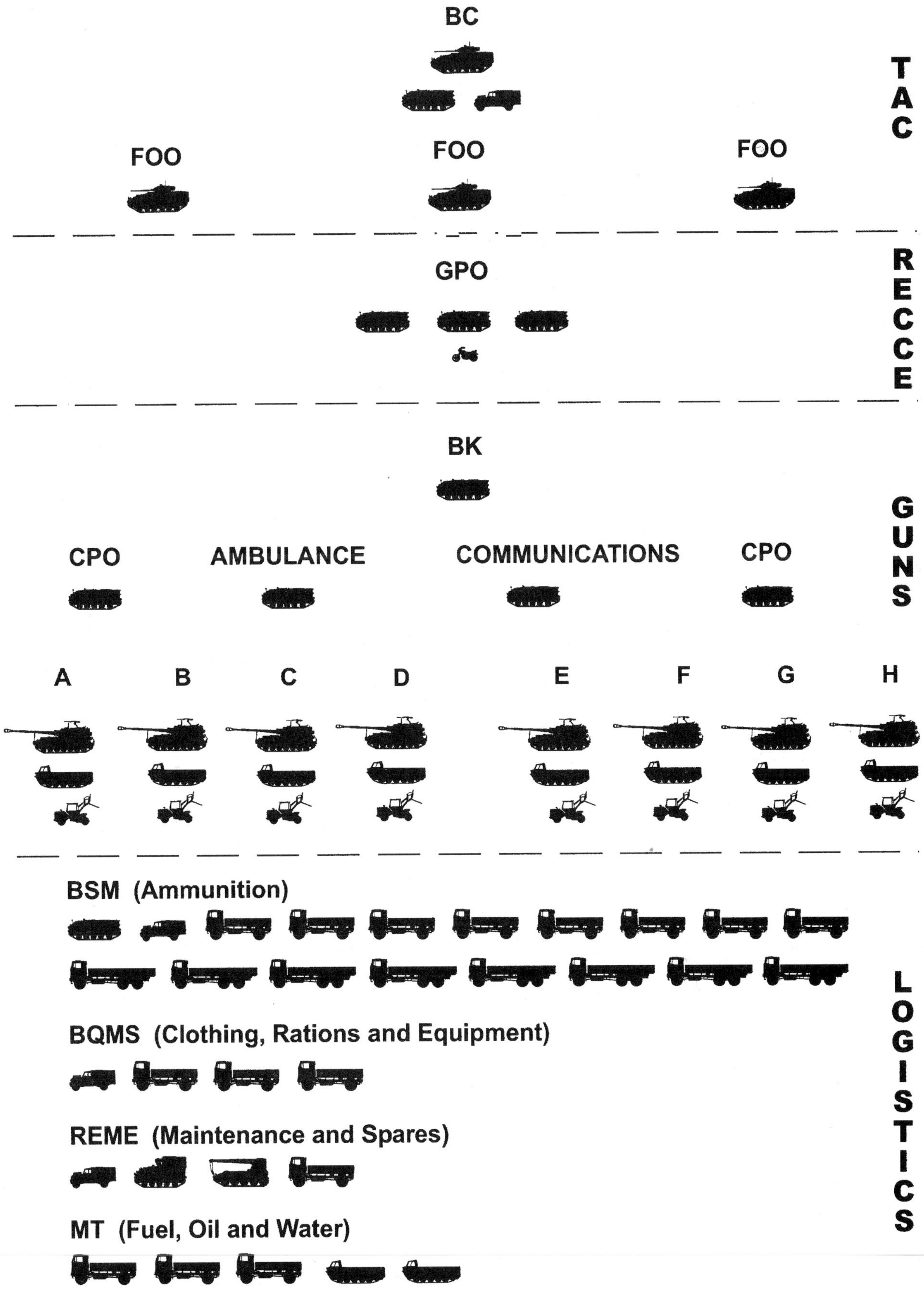

TAC

BC

FOO   FOO   FOO

RECCE

GPO

GUNS

BK

CPO   AMBULANCE   COMMUNICATIONS   CPO

A   B   C   D   E   F   G   H

LOGISTICS

BSM (Ammunition)

BQMS (Clothing, Rations and Equipment)

REME (Maintenance and Spares)

MT (Fuel, Oil and Water)

first and catch the allied forces half-deployed and half at sea. Our current deployment was clearly designed to counter just such a move. I asked him about the injections we had been warned about. Again he was very open, explaining that he had taken the best medical advice and, on the balance of risk, had concluded that we should all be inoculated. He went on to explain that the Bubonic Plague was one of the earliest vaccines and was now tried and tested and that vets, worldwide, were routinely vaccinated against Anthrax. If it was any comfort to us all, he and his staff were going to have them.

The 2nd Field Regiment was now deployed in a linear formation astride the Pylon Line Road. Furthest north was 23 Battery, then 127 Battery, A1 Echelon with our ammunition and fuel, A2 with our food, clothing, etc, and then my own O Battery. On our left was still the Marine TOW missile battalion, but now on our right, and protecting our vulnerable flank, was a US Marine Corps M60 tank battalion. O Battery was deployed with the guns and their limbers in a loose box formation of about 200 by 200 metres on the eastern side of the track. On the west was the Battery's logistic vehicles, the REME mechanics, OP vehicles and my own command post. The formation gave us all-round protection, yet was far enough dispersed to reduce the effects of an air or artillery attack. My concern was that I would lose the missile or tank screen without warning at a critical time. I had therefore ordered the Gun Position Officer to deploy relatively tightly. The problem was the Pylon Line Road, which ran through the middle of the position, was rapidly becoming a Main Supply Route and very dusty. However, I reasoned that in spite of the discomfort, dust was unlikely to kill us, whereas a wide-open flank could.

All work came to a brief halt mid-afternoon while the Battery was lined up and given an Anthrax jab. It was my policy that for 'nasties' the officers always went first in rank order. All eyes watched as I rolled up my sleeve and stepped forward from the head of the queue. The jab was a mixture of Anthrax and Whooping Cough and had to be administered 'deep muscle' which meant that it hurt like hell. I, of course, did not know this, being the first. There was method in my madness. The only light relief for those who had just received their jab was the sight of the Iron Man of the Battery, the Battery Sergeant Major, rocking momentarily on his feet. For those still waiting, the sight held less amusement. Many of the Battery were laid low for up to forty-eight hours afterwards with severe flu-like symptoms.

My own command vehicle had only just deployed so I finished the day by writing to Annie on the wing of my Landrover until it was too dark to see. I spent the night hunched in the back, nursing a very sore arm and listening to the rain beating on the canvas roof.

6 JANUARY 1991

I woke up early, freezing cold and covered in condensation. The back of a Landrover is not the ideal place to spend a night. I was woken by the sound of one of the guns setting off northward along the track. Today was 'Meet the Press' day. The stated aim was to show the newly arrived 4th Armoured Brigade to the Press on the day that we were formally declared complete in Saudi Arabia. It was obvious to even a semi-idiot that the Brigade was nowhere near complete, but one should never ruin a good story with the facts and anyway it could be argued that it was really the Iraqis we were trying to impress. Each type of equipment was to be represented and I had been ordered to supply a gun and crew. I had sent Sergeant Webber who I knew would give his all in the name of PR.

Other than real bullets, nothing is more dangerous than a bad press. Equally no one has greater potential to mess soldiers about than the Army PR staff. I had no intention of letting either happen, so, after the morning fry-up, Newell and I set off to follow the gun. Our route took us due north underneath the Pylon Line, past the forward battery of the Regiment, then down a steep escarpment and across about 800 yards of sabka. Sabka is dry salt lake with a hard brittle crust. We were literally only inches above sea level and where the track crossed the sabka a soft sticky mud was starting to well. Sabka, we were all soon to find, was treacherous in the extreme. Firstly it was often very difficult to spot, particularly if the sand was blowing. Secondly the surface would give way without warning, sucking the vehicle in up to its axles. In soft sand, vehicle follows vehicle, the one in the front compacting the sand to assist the one behind. In sabka, if the ground supported the first vehicle, it certainly would not support the second. This time we got across without too much trouble, but sabka was to prove a considerable problem in the future.

We stayed on the Pylon Line Road for a further 10 kms, alternately crossing ridges and sabka. We then turned right on a tarmac road running east/west. About 15kms further on we arrived at the display area. Nearly every Commanding Officer from the Brigade was there watching the rehearsal. Sergeant Webber and his crew were part of a static display of armoured vehicles and were busily laying out an example of each type of ammunition. The gun itself was an American-built M109 A2/3 Self-Propelled Howitzer, typical of those in service with the Regiment. It was old and unsophisticated but very effective. Its supercharged Detroit Diesel engine, lifted straight from a Greyhound bus, could move the 26 tonnes at great speed over very rough country, while the 155mm gun would fire a 96 lb. shell over 19kms. Most important, it was reliable and simple to operate and maintain.

At about 10.30 buses brought and disgorged some sixty journalists, TV crews, etc. The Press 'Minders' shepherded them up to a rope fence.

Sergeant Webber and crew meet the Press. (AG)

A Royal Engineer Bridge Layer meets the Press. (AG)

After some minutes a tank roared into view from over a nearby ridge and screeched to a halt in a cloud of dust. Brigadier Christopher Hammerbeck, in black overalls and white scarf, climbed down and addressed the assembled multitude. What he had to say was clear and direct and delivered without notes. I thought that he spoke extremely well, but afterwards, listening to the Press talking amongst themselves, it was clear that they did not like the 'Boys Own' arrival routine, so sadly most of what the Commander said went unreported. Afterwards the

Press talked to the troops on the static display, until a deploying Engineer bridge hijacked the show. Initially I had been annoyed that the Engineers had stolen our thunder until I found out that Sergeant Webber had been talking to the *News of the World*. Perhaps I owe the Bridge Layer a vote of thanks.

Once all the journalists had departed, I drove on further east and then north to visit the 14th/20th King's Hussars. They were deployed in squadron leaguers on the edge of a massive area of sabka. The journey was by way of a dummy run as I had to return to the Battlegroup on the 8th to meet the Prime Minister.

By the time I returned to the Battery it was past midday and very hot. I was just in time to see the last of my OP crews getting their Anthrax jabs. The BSM also greeted me with the news that Lance Corporal Ball, our Army Catering Corps cook, had had a negligent discharge with his Stirling submachine gun; fortunately, no one was hurt.

7 JANUARY 1991

My 432 armoured vehicle, with its attached penthouse tent, was now fully deployed along with all the other OP vehicles, so I spent a comfortable night on my camp bed. I was up early to drive back to Al Jubayl to attend the Regiment's presentation on the 'Application of Fire'. It was held in the smart social club and came complete with another equally smart lunch. Immediately it was over I had to dash back north to RHQ to accompany Lance Corporal Ball on CO's Orders. The fact that he could work miracles with a couple of tins of Army rations and an onion was not enough to save him. It was short and sharp. He was fined twenty-one days' pay and marched out.

Today was also the real start of the Regiment's work-up training. The British Artillery Gunnery Staff had, at the request of the American Marines who were apparently unable to do it themselves, built a series of live-firing ranges in open desert adjacent to the coast. It was the largest range complex ever built, covering hundreds of square miles and necessitating the removal of many unwilling Bedouin families who appeared to know nothing of the political or military situation. The passage of information is not exactly encouraged in Saudi Arabia. The Americans christened the ranges 'Devil Dog.' As the British had built them they indignantly added 'Dragoon' to the title, so Devil Dog Dragoon Ranges they became.

Our initial assessment was that we would have two major problems if we had to go to war. The first was navigation which is absolutely vital if artillery fire is to be accurate. The second was the movement of ammunition. The M109 gun can carry just over thirty rounds in its turret, but these are used only in an emergency. The vast amount of

Guns on the Pylon Line ready to move. (KW)

ammunition required for operations has to be carried on wheeled trucks. Our four-wheeled trucks had an 8-tonne capacity, the six-wheelers could carry 14 tonnes. Neither vehicle had the cross-country capability of the tracked guns they supported. The Regiment's first exercise, therefore, was designed to find out just what our war fighting capability really was. As it was to be the guns that were to be exercised, the BCs and FOOs were to be used as controllers. The Regiment's Second-in-Command, Major Steven Young, gave orders to the three Gun Position Officers at midday at RHQ. This gave time for plans to be made and orders to be passed down. The ammunition trucks were loaded to war scales at the ACP (Ammunition Control Point) and then lined up alongside the Pylon Line Road under the watchful eyes of the three BSMs.

Artillery ammunition at the Ammunition Control Point. (AG)

The area of DDD ranges that the Regiment had been allocated was only about 3kms from our current position, but it was the wrong side of

the oil pipeline. To cross required a 10km drive north to the east-west tarmac road, a 5km drive east to where the oil pipeline crossed the road and where the Engineers had made a solid sand bridge over the pipes. It was then a parallel drive south, only this time there would be no road, only soft, shifting, desert sand. The plan was that the Regiment would undertake a controlled move to a Release Point just south of the pipeline bridge. The gun batteries would then move independently to their own pre-arranged positions. RHQ would control the move out, the reconnaissance parties having left some hours earlier. The guns departed mid-afternoon, The Rocket Troop being the most southerly was the last to move.

I had the now daily CO's conference to attend so it was late afternoon before Newell and I set off in the Landrover to chase the guns. We had only been driving about ten minutes when we came across our first casualty. Lieutenant Hewlan Morgan, one of the two CPOs (Command Post Officers), was sitting on top of his stationary 432 Command Post – steam was rising from the engine decks. We stopped to commiserate. Hewlan was philosophical; he had done all that he could. The recovery organization had his position and a good description of the fault. It was now just a matter of sitting and waiting. Better to break down now than in war and being still on the Pylon Line Road meant that there was little chance of him not being found. We left him and his crew to their long vigil.

We made good time to the Regimental Release Point with about one hour of daylight still remaining. There we found Sergeant Tunley, his gun having overheated. He had clearly decided that lone night navigation was not for him and his crew were busy putting up their tent. Progress from this point onwards, however, was desperately slow. I had hoped to join the guns before dark, then at least if we got lost it would be with like-minded friends. This was not to be. The Landrover, even in four-wheel drive and with the diff-locks on, struggled pathetically in the soft sand and with the last ray of sunlight went any chance of following the guns' tracks.

At this point it might be worth saying something about navigation. Gunners do not just need to know roughly where they are, they need to know precisely where they are. The whole artillery system relies upon accurate survey. An error of a few metres when the gun fires can be magnified into an error of hundreds of metres where the shell lands. In Western Europe an accurate fix is attained either by establishing a survey scheme from a known fixation point (there is one of these points in every Grid Square) or by using an inertial navigation machine called PADS. In the desert there were no previously surveyed points and, although our PADS had been modified for use within the Arabian Peninsula, they had yet to be tested. Also, splendid as it was, PADS was designed to fix a position, it was not suited to being a navigational aid. The host vehicle had to stop periodically to enable the machine to update itself, neither the driver nor the commander could see the instrument display while on the move, and it needed accurate maps for gross error checks. That brings me on to maps.

The issue black and white maps were short on detail to say the least, showing only three types of terrain: sand, rock and sabka. Occasionally a road, track or pipeline would be indicated, but contours were marked only to a degree which reflected the basic wisdom that no one who lived in this part of the world was remotely interested in contours. And then there were Grid lines. The maps of the area, like most maps, were drawn originally by the British Army, almost certainly the Royal Engineers, and in happier times. The Army produced detailed local maps, but the charting of the world, the big picture, was the domain of Her Majesty's Royal Navy. When the men from the Admiralty set off east from their fixed point on the ground at Greenwich, it rapidly became apparent that trying to put a world that was round onto something flat and square was not all plain sailing. Indeed the Grid lines became so bent that frequently there was a need to stop and start again with a new series of lines. The problem was where on the earth to put these Grid Interchanges as they became known. Wisely they put one where, in their humble estimation, no one in his right mind would ever wish to go. Consequently the Grid Interchange ran smack through the middle of DDD Range.

I had a map and a compass and it was now dark. In Western Europe it never gets really dark. No matter what the weather conditions, there is always some ambient light from cities, cars, etc. I was hundreds of miles from the nearest house, let alone city, and there was a thick cloud cover. It was dark, totally dark. I later heard someone liken the desert darkness to 'A blind man in a dark cellar looking for a black cat that wasn't there.' Frankly I believe they underestimated the problem.

The Landrover struggled on through the sand and darkness at little

Coastal sand dunes on the Devil-Dog-Dragoon Range. (AG)

more than walking speed for the next hour. The land changed from flat soft sand to undulating soft sand. By now we were conscious of the ominous smell of burning clutch. We made our way slowly forward, at times having to back out of drifting sand or do wide detours to avoid hills we just could not climb. Struggling down and through a deep gully we came across the tail-lights of another Landrover. We made our way past it and when I felt confident we were on firm ground we stopped and I walked back to see what the problem was. It was one of the Battery's own Landrovers and they had broken a drive shaft trying to extricate themselves from a sand dune. There was nothing I could do to help, but meeting them confirmed that we were still on the right route. I returned to my Landrover, then stumbled and groped my way past to try and see what lay ahead. It was a steep hill. We had driven into a bowl and the only way out was up. We set off in the inky blackness, the back wheels spinning. After about twenty yards we were forced to slither back down the hill and try again. This we repeated, taking a different route each time and each time sliding back to the centre of the bowl. The smell of burning clutch was now overpowering. There was still some drive left but not enough to get us up the slope. We were stuck.

8 JANUARY 1991

As we had no real idea of our location there was little point in radioing for assistance. The Battery Fitter Section could stumble around the desert all night and never find us. I resigned myself to the inevitable wait for dawn and tried to go to sleep. I had been dozing for less than an hour when I heard the sound of engines and out of the darkness appeared my three FOOs led by Graham Ambrose in our one and only Warrior. Using the APES (Azimuth Position Elevation System) to navigate by, the Warrior had been leading the other vehicles when they had picked up the heat of the Landrover's engine on the thermal sight and had changed course to investigate. Now with a clear fix we could call recovery to the second Landrover, but I needed to be back with the Battery that night. My own Landrover was therefore attached to the back of one of the 432s by our only tow rope and we set off on what was to be one of the most terrifying journeys of my life.

The tow chain was barely 6 feet long and had to be attached to the spring mount on the front of the Landrover and onto the towing point on the rear of the 432 which, because of the central door, was on the left side next to the track. This meant that I was being pulled at an angle and forced to travel immediately behind the left track which threw soft sand all over the bonnet and windscreen. To prevent sand being ingested into the engine, it had to be switched off. No engine meant no power to the brake servos; no servos meant virtually no brakes. The Warrior was the only vehicle that could see or navigate in the dark, so the 432s were forced to stay right up behind it, each following the tiny glow of the convoy light on the vehicle ahead. Graham Ambrose in the Warrior went as the crow flies and at speed. We crossed sand seas, scaled almost vertical sand walls and slithered down sand embankments. For once not being able to see was a mercy. Newell and I stared through the windscreen desperately trying to see the convoy light of the 432 through the swirling cloud of sand, while all the time we were thrown from side to side, often at angles that, had we not had the momentum of the tow and the resistance of the tow chain, would have rolled the vehicle. At times even trying to steer was a pointless exercise as our combined strength could not prevent the front wheels taking their own chosen route through the sand. Twice I almost jumped from the vehicle, saved only by its last-minute return onto four wheels and a terror of leaping into the total unknown of the darkness.

I cannot begin to guess how long the journey lasted, but I remember the relief of suddenly stopping, the sensation of stillness and silence and then Graham Ambrose's voice at the window. "According to the machine we are here, but there's no sign of any one else." There were a few. They came slowly out of the blackness to investigate the new arrivals. Both the GPO and the BK had made it, if with some difficulty. There was a Command Post and two guns, but the rest of the Battery was still somewhere out there in the sand and the darkness. Occasionally the sound of an engine could be heard, first approaching then receding as the crew searched vainly for their RV.

Assuming that the enemy could hear all transmissions I was not prepared to use the radio to guide vehicles in. It would have been of limited use anyway as few of the crews knew with any certainty where they were, so knowing my location would be of little help. War was yet to be declared and there was no chance of enemy aircraft flying, so, in the certain knowledge that we were still some distance from the border, I ordered one of the powerful Command Post searchlights to be shone vertically into the air. It produced a solid pillar of light reaching up hundreds of feet. Within minutes vehicles started to arrive. Not just those from O Battery, but from other batteries of the Regiment, and even other regiments. Some crews had been wandering for hours and had given up in despair. They now flocked to the light like moths. I went to sleep just after 02.00, lying on the floor of my Landrover, leaving instructions to be woken at first light.

Dawn rose clear and stupefyingly cold. All around, vehicles were parked, their exhausted crews still asleep. I sat on the tailboard of the Landrover rubbing warmth into my frozen legs, watching the sentry walking around shaking people awake. We were a pretty unimpressive sight. Vehicles and crews were strewn everywhere; many were from other units grateful just to be with someone. Some from my own Battery had yet to be accounted for. It was while I was discussing the next move with the BK and GPO that we were startled by a yell from a young Gunner just behind us. He had been scraping the sand away from his vehicle's tracks when he had uncovered a tiny brown coiled snake no bigger than a Biro. The animal was sluggish from the cold and we were later to discover that it had a non-fatal but very painful bite. The excitement ensured that everyone was soon up and frantically searching sleeping bags. I only had time to give a quick briefing and grab a mouthful of breakfast before departing for the 14th/20th and the 09.00 visit of the Prime Minister. My Landrover was all but dead so I requisitioned Graham Ambrose and his new Warrior.

A local hazard. (AG)

The Prime Minister, John Major, was on his first visit to the troops in the Gulf. The 14th/20th Battlegroup had been selected for the visit and I, as their BC, had been ordered to attend. That meant a very long journey northwards along narrow corridors between live firing ranges. There were no roads and I travelled from point to point on the map using the APES navigation system. I could now see that my original plan to use my Landrover was completely impractical. I was travelling very close to the coast now and occasionally, across to my right, I could see the flat, oily sparkle of the sea. The coastal strip was mainly low undulating dunes of soft shifting sand with what looked like small dry twigs stuck haphazardly on the tops, as if placed there by children. By way of contrast, there were areas of the dreaded sabka and of high rock ridges reminiscent of the terrain in a Spaghetti Western. I was some time reaching the now familiar east-west road and only just made my RV with the Battlegroup Commander on time.

Mike Vickery was as annoyed at having his Regiment's training disrupted as I was at being dragged away from my Battery. The 'Emperor', his Challenger tank, was parked in the middle of an expanse of open desert, his wingman to his left rear and the four armoured squadrons in neat rows some distance behind. I took up my usual place to his right rear and settled down in the increasingly hot sun to wait. The plan was that the PM and accompanying army of Press would fly over the 14th/20th King's Hussars spectacularly drawn up in the desert. They would land at the 3rd Fusiliers and then, after the PM had spoken, the Brigade Commander would drive him, in his tank, back down to speak to us. As a consequence of this wonderful plan the crews had to stay with their vehicles until he had flown over, then scramble out and walk, some a considerable way, to a makeshift stand, ready to be addressed. Mike Vickery was far from impressed with the plan that 4 Brigade's HQ had foisted on him and didn't care who knew it. We sat in the sun. Occasionally someone would walk past or call across and we would engage in some shouted conversation between vehicles. Always the topic was the same, the heat, the desert, and HQ 4 Brigade. The PM really did not figure in the equation. He had come to power while we were on our frantic work-up training prior to embarking, and with little time for newspapers or TV, most of us barely knew his name, let alone his face. We sat in, on or beside our vehicles while the sun grew hotter.

After what seemed hours and probably was, six Puma helicopters landed in their own home made sandstorm about 500 metres away and started disgorging their cargo of journalists. Clearly the great plan had stalled on the starting point. I heard the message go out from Captain Jonty Palmer, the Adjutant, cooking inside the Emperor, "There's been a cock up! It looks as if he's here already! All crews to get to the stand as fast as possible." I clambered out of the turret, thankful that I had less than 100 metres to walk in the now crippling heat and saw on the distant shimmering horizon, disgruntled tank crews starting their long journey. Mike Vickery and I were the first to arrive and met the RSM in front of the stand. "These are just the news men, Colonel," reported the RSM, "We are still on the original plan. Shall I send the men back to their vehicles?" "Don't you dare," was the sharp reply. "He can take us as he finds us or not at all." I was starting to get a comfortable feeling about my Battlegroup Commander.

We stood in the heat and watched the PR staff herding Press and TV crews up onto the raised sand vantage-point. They pressed up against the white mine tape and were slowly joined by the tank crews. We waited and it got hotter still. I stood at the back with my own crew hoping for

Brigadier Christopher Hammerbeck arrives with the Prime Minister. (AG)

a fast getaway as soon as it was all over. At last (11.30 to be exact) a Challenger tank with the call sign 14D hove into view and stopped about 25 metres from the stand. Out clambered the Prime Minister and the Brigade Commander. Slowly they walked to the centre of the mine-taped square. The PM stood, looked and asked, "Can you all move a bit closer." Orders were barked, troops moved, the Press and TV swore, and after a manoeuvre understood only by RSMs, I found myself in the front row inches from the great man. The cameras clicked and for the first time in the conflict, BC O Battery was displayed to the world.

John Major spoke for about 15 minutes. He spoke of why the UK had embarked on this adventure, the support for us and the pride felt by those at home. He gave the assurance that a ground war would be the very last resort, but, should we go, we would attack only when we were sure of victory. He spoke not to the World's Press but to us, the troops now seated on the ground. He spoke without notes or hesitation and with real sincerity. I was immensely impressed. As soon as he had finished speaking he walked forward and started to speak to individuals. I was in direct line and he shook my hand and asked me how the training was going and was there anything vital that I needed. We talked for about two minutes. Again the cameras

John Major goes walkabout. (AG)

clicked, but he had made at least one convert that day – me!

Graham and I spent the next thirty minutes or so killing time by seeking out old friends in the crowd and playing spot the news celebrity. Kate Adie was there signing soldiers hats, also my old boss from Hong Kong, Brigadier Peter Sincock, now the Defence Attaché. We had a long talk and he invited me down to stay at Riyadh as soon as I got a chance. He seemed pretty optimistic that the Iraqis would pull out once face had been saved, which was encouraging news. At last it was time for the PM to depart and he flew off accompanied by the world's Press to destinations unknown. I bade farewell to Mike Vickery and wandered back to the Warrior to plot my route back to the Battery.

It was a long way back. Firing on the ranges forced us to make a wide detour, effectively the long way around a square. I was trying to link up with my own CP and the FOOs who had by now deployed to a high rock ridge. The ridge, imaginatively christened OP 1, looked out to sea and in particular out over a small, low and flat sand island. This was to be the target for tomorrow's activity. With the help of US Marine Corps' Harriers we were going to attempt close air support using our own OPs and their Laser Target Markers, coordinated by a British Army Air Corps helicopter. However, my route to OP1 took me first west and then south, indeed along much of the route I had been dragged over the previous night. It was while on the southern leg that I came across two of the Battery's 14-tonners, one bedded up to its axles in soft drifting sand. The Bedford truck with its six wheels was a pathetic sight. Even without its load of 6 x ULCs (Unit Load Containers), each holding 17 rounds of 155mm ammunition, it was little better than a civilian truck; even with 6-wheel drive, its cross-country performance was far from satisfactory. Given a heavy load and soft sand the vehicle was helpless. Bombardier Allison was struggling, with the help of a 432, to drag the truck onto firmer ground but the aged armoured vehicle was not up to the task. The air was acrid with the smell of burning clutches, while fine sand, thrown up by the truck's spinning wheels, fell like mist. It took some time to uncouple the 432 and link up the Warrior. Even with its massive reserve of power it was a struggle for the Warrior to overcome the resistance of the sand. At last, inch by inch, the truck came free, but I did not feel confident enough to leave them to struggle back on their own and so we escorted them the few remaining kilometres to the gun position.

Time was pressing. I did not want to be driving up steep slopes or travelling close to the sea in the dark, so I was only able to spend long enough with the Battery to get a quick update from the BK and GPO. It had taken most of the morning to account for all the guns and it was only now, with the arrival of the 14-tonners, that the Battery was complete. As we had expected, navigation was extremely difficult, but moving the wheeled ammunition vehicles was worse than our most pessimistic predictions. Orders had already been received for the Battery to deploy in support of tomorrow's firing. The BK and the BSM had made elaborate plans to have those trucks that could not be dragged by a gun pulled by the 432s. I gave orders that this was not to happen. Should we have to go to war the tracked vehicles would have to move independently of the wheels and so, if our ammunition could not keep up, now was the time to find out. I was acutely aware that many of the scaling and equipment deficiencies we were now suffering were the result of years of fudging and the acceptance of practices that we knew would be inadequate in war. Now, with war possibly imminent, there could be no muddling through. I had to know what our real capabilities were. I ordered the ammunition vehicles, under command of the BSM, to move as a separate unescorted convoy.

I left the guns as the recce party was also moving off and we travelled together for the first few kilometres, the Landrover drivers grateful for the compacted sand of our tracks. Soon I could see the massive ridgeline of OP1 and, as we drew closer, I could see the tiny dots of the observation vehicles already parked along the summit. As we struggled up the final gradient a very relieved Graham Ambrose steered us to the end of a line of vehicles. The OP 432s and now the Warrior were lined up ready to start work the following day. Behind them, in a loose huddle, were the BC's vehicles. I wandered over to my own crew who, having watched my approach for over an hour, had been able to time dinner to the minute. I sat on the roof of the 432 and tried to see where the guns would be deploying. I was either looking in the wrong direction or the twilight defeated my eyes for I could see nothing. With depressing news from the BBC ringing in my ears, I ate and went to bed.

9 JANUARY 1991

Dawn rose clear and bright and, most importantly, dry. The US Secretary of State was now going to meet the Iraqi Foreign Minister, so expectations were once again high. The CO arrived early to conduct the Joint Air/Aviation day. The aim of the day was to integrate air power with the troops on the ground using a FAC (Forward Air Controller) in a helicopter to tie it all together. The aircraft would be US Marine Corps Harriers.

The day did not start well! We had serious difficulty talking to the helicopter which flew around in circles but made no attempt to land and either sort the radios out or get a briefing. Then, to compound the problem, the Harriers turned up early. We watched the first aircraft do a few lazy circuits of the ridge and then, suddenly, bank hard and start its shallow attack dive. There was a harsh rasping sound as the Vulcan cannon under its wing fired and the ground in the centre of the island erupted. Clearly the pilot was talking to someone; we could only assume that it was the helicopter pilot. A RAF officer arrived, our BALO (Brigade Air Liaison Officer), and confessed he was no wiser about what was happening. At last he managed to talk directly to the Harrier pilots, but by now we had abandoned any thoughts of using the helicopter. As far as most of us were concerned the helicopter was a peacetime training contingency, in the Forward Air Control role for internal political reasons only. None of us seriously thought that an unarmed Gazelle could fly far enough forward during a battle to be able to control aircraft. We were later to be proved right. If we went to war air power, particularly American air power, would be vital. The only people who could control aircraft in 4 Brigade were the artillery tac groups, namely us. We were therefore more than keen to make the most of what might be our only chance to practise and were delighted when the helicopter finally gave up and flew away.

Forward Air Controlling under British doctrine is a very precise art as befits the power of the weapon systems being employed. Radio voice procedure is kept short and formal and a very tight control is kept on the aircraft throughout the attack. The BALO explained that we would be using a heavily modified version of the American system. American because they had by far the most aircraft, modified because of the danger of massed small-arm and anti-aircraft fire. He told us of his experience to date and that the ground station had little real control and procedures and drills were very relaxed. His account sounded like a spoof version of *Top Gun*. Each pilot had his own handle. I seem to recall that one was 'King Eagle,' but no doubt, 'Maverick' and 'Goose' were up there also. The lead aircraft would call on the radio, identify himself, give details of his weaponry and ask if the ground observer had a Laser Target Marker. *'Hello Brit 43 this is King Eagle, inbound Harriers loaded Iron and Mavericks, can you sparkle, over.'* If the FOO had a laser the pilot would then give him a series of coded numbers to set on his laser designator so that the missiles could distinguish their particular beam from the many others on the battlefield. This done, the pilot was given details of the target, the direction of approach and the time the strike was required. The latter was given either as a straightforward 'time on target' or, if the aircraft was to attack immediately, then *'Buster, Buster'* was the cry. The next thing the observer would hear was *'Hack 6, over.'* This meant that the aircraft had started its attack run and was six minutes from weapon release. *'Hack one, Sparkle'* meant that the pilot was one minute from weapon release and he wanted the ground observer to fire his laser target marker. That in theory was all there was to it. If the target was destroyed then the pilot was given a very British *'Thank you very much for all your help, etc.'* if not then *'Frenzy, Frenzy'* would bring the aircraft round for a second run.

However, today was not a good day; with no target as such, i.e. no nice solid armoured vehicle for the laser beam to reflect off, the missiles could not lock on. We tried giving verbal directions so that the Harriers could use their cannons, but the target area was one low, flat, totally featureless sand island at no point more than a few feet above sea level. "Please hit the island for us" was not our idea of forward air controlling. We gave up and the aircraft flew away.

It was now past midday and hot. Visibility was not much further than the now shimmering island. David Radcliffe called each of the FOOs forward in turn and let them fire all three Batteries of the Regiment. As a climax to the day's activity we had been authorized to fire one of the new M483 bomblet rounds. None of us had seen this round fired before but with its cluster of 88 small submunitions it was our principal means of destroying Iraqi armour. The radio net sprang into life,

"Fire, over."

"Fire, out."

There was a sharp report from some way behind us as the single gun fired. Next the eerie whistle as the round cleared our ridge, passing almost directly over our heads. A thud and a small cloud of dark smoke high above the target marked the point where the first charge had split open the shell to eject the small sub-munitions. An agonizing pause then the island erupted in flames and dust. To say that we were impressed would have been an understatement. If we had to go to war, then this bomblet round made us feel much more confident about it.

The excitement over, I made my way back to my command 432 to be greeted by the news that talks were taking place in Geneva and optimism really was the order of the day. I told the crew to get the evening meal on and sat on the roof of the vehicle, watching the FOO crews packing their equipment away and pondered over the problems of directing aircraft. As a tac group we only had one laser target marker and no prospects of getting any more. I had therefore allocated it to Richard Farndale, whom I would place with the armoured infantry company. As we were likely always to lead with the tanks then he would be in a good position to come forward, out of contact, and direct the air attack should the tanks get into trouble. I had hoped that today's activity would at least give Richard confidence that the systems and procedures worked. If anything it had done the opposite.

I waved goodbye to Dave Marshall, the Canadian BC of 127 Battery. He had been parked next to me and was now leading his three FOOs down the steep side of the ridge. I had just enquired how long dinner would be when I was showered in dust by a solid-shot tank round embedding itself in the ground ten feet away at the point BC 127 had only minutes before vacated. This was a war environment and peacetime range safety rules no longer applied. With so many troops needing to fire and with so little time and space to do it, greater risk had to be accepted. I had just experienced the practical effects of that fact. We abandoned the meal and in the evening light made our way hurriedly down off the ridge and headed for the comparative safety of the Battery.

The Battery was deployed on an area of low, soft dunes about two hundred metres from the beach. The beach itself was

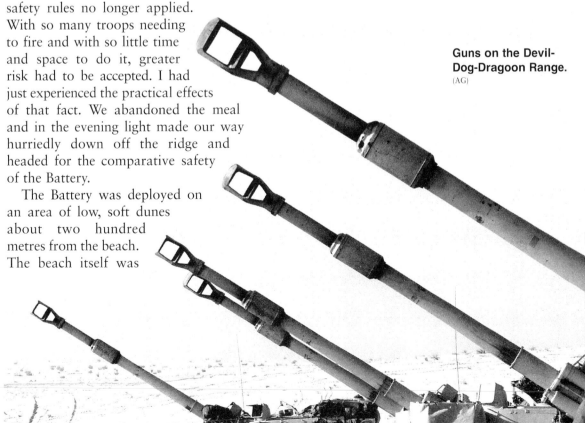

Guns on the Devil-Dog-Dragoon Range.
(AG)

hard, damp sand stretching to the shimmering horizon where one caught the occasional glimpse of water. Inland, the sand dunes were interspersed with acres of the dreaded sabka. The Battery was still deployed in the position from which it had been firing all day, in the now standard box of four pairs, each Gun Section under the command of its own Warrant Officer Gun Line Section Commander. The OP vehicles were directed to a flanking position by WO2 Windle, the Battery Guide, but still within the security ring provided by the guns. As we let the engines run down, it was just light enough for me to make out the two Command Posts, located astride an invisible line which bisected the position. I climbed off the 432 and started off for my evening conference with my management team. The BK, GPO and BSM all gave me a résumé of their story so far. It could be summarized as:

- Everyone in good heart and coping well with the sand, heat, scorpions and uncertainty.
- Guns firing well, no problems with deployments or movement.
- Navigation across country for anyone not following a high tech navigation device was almost impossible.
- Once we had fired the turret ammunition that was it. The wheeled ammunition limbers could not keep up, indeed there were vast areas of the desert where they just could not go.

Two plus points and two minus points! The BBC World Service was optimistic about the Geneva talks; however, I could not rely on just optimism and tomorrow I would have to address the problem of ammunition. After a coffee I set off in the dark to visit the southern two sections of guns. The first gun was about three hundred metres away and I used the light from its crew's cooking stove as a navigation beacon. Those of the crew who were not asleep were seated under the Cam Net, mugs in hand, passing the time. The Gun Line Section Commander, Sergeant Major Eddie Lee, was holding forth from a canvas chair, telling Geordie war stories. The one thing they were all eager to hear about was the bomblet round, in particular what it looked like on the ground. My account did not disappoint them. I spent about thirty minutes chatting about everything and nothing. The BBC seemed to have raised spirits and there was a general feeling that all would be well. Surprisingly, it was the younger soldiers who felt the most positive. The older sweats, with a cynicism born of experience, were of the view that the politicians had not brought us all this way just to send us home again. I made my way round all the guns in the southern sector repeating the same formula, coffee, bomblet round, World Service News, pep talk.

It was strange to find how others viewed the immediate future. Like me, the married men with children feared death or, should I say, we feared the consequences of death. If we were killed, who would look after our wives and children? Would they think we had abandoned them? For the single soldiers death posed no such fear; it was the prospect of horrific injury that filled their nightmares. Being crippled, burnt or horribly disfigured would mean no more girlfriends, no chance for children. – condemned to a lonely sad life. The words of the song "Ruby, don't take your love to town" clearly played on many a young mind and all added to the stress of uncertainty.

By the time I left the last gun it was both late and very dark. All were in bed and there were no lights, not even stars. I set off in what I thought was the direction of my vehicle. I walked and walked, stumbling in the pitch darkness over invisible but solid sand hillocks. I walked for what I judged was sufficient time to bring me to my vehicle plus a good bit more. Nothing! I stopped. I had done the one thing I had gone to extraordinary lengths to prevent my soldiers doing. I was lost. Losing someone in the dark is every commander's nightmare. After our first night in the desert the GPO, BK, BSM and I had all come to the same conclusion and we had each simultaneously cancelled the prowler guards and ordered the sentries to be mounted from the top hatches of the guns. Now, stupidly, I was lost, in the dark, in the desert.

I fought the temptation to panic and started to walk round in a wide clockwise circle, dragging one foot behind me through the sand. It was a good ten minutes before my foot found what I had pinned all my hopes on, one of the telephone lines that link the vehicles to the central command post. I picked it up and slowly followed it. At last my outstretched arm felt the solid metal of one of the FOO 432s. The feeling of relief was almost overpowering. Holding onto the Cam Net, I groped my way until I finally saw the dim red glow of the light my crew had left on for me in my vehicle. I slumped down onto my sleeping bag now stretched out along the crew seat, a great deal older and wiser. As I lay in the dark the tanks were firing, the shock waves making the vehicle tremble. The distant tank exercise included a breach crossing. I was just dozing off when I was all but thrown to the floor. The Royal Engineers had breached their minefield with their own shock wave, a Giant Viper.

10 JANUARY 1991
We were all up early to tune into the BBC World Service, only to hear that the peace talks in Geneva had collapsed. Today was a planned maintenance period to put right all the damage from the exercise. At the morning meeting it was clear that, apart from routine tasks like track tensioning, there was not a lot to do, although the incidence of drive shaft failure on the M109 generators was now causing me concern. Over all, the equipment seemed to be coping well, due principally to the dedication shown by the crews. In spite of the bad political news most

of us seemed to be in good spirits. Navigation and the movement of our logistic vehicles continued to be our greatest difficulty. The navigation problem was out of our hands and would only be solved by satellite navigation systems which we were assured were being procured. The problem, we were told, was that the Americans had cornered the world market in an attempt to meet their own needs. For certain, the Coalition was not going to war without them, so the longer they took to arrive, the better. We had, however, as an interim measure, been issued with sun compasses. These masterpieces of low technology consisted of two cardboard disks with what looked like a lollypop stick protruding up through the middle. Time was set on one disk, direction on the other and when suitably aligned the shadow cast gave the basic navigation information. OK for Lawrence of Arabia but not for us. They were totally useless in the dark and in the overcast rainy weather which seemed to be the norm in this 'desert'. To quote one very senior officer, "Soldiers won't learn to use these overnight!" We were not impressed.

I saw no possibility of help over logistics. We had to move massive stocks of ammunition at a rate and distance that would enable the guns to support the forward troops in contact. The gun itself carried turret stocks for use in an emergency, but certainly not sufficient for war operations. Indeed to cope with larger gun crews and the vast amount of extra equipment that now had to be carried, we had been forced to reduce significantly the turret ammunition holdings. Our ammunition limbers (Bedford 8 and 14-tonne trucks) had been designed for operations in Western Europe. Although they had 4 and 6-wheel drive, they were primarily long-distance load carriers with only limited cross-country capability. Nowhere in Western Europe were you very far from a road or track and so, if necessary, the gun could go and load from the truck. This was not possible in the desert.

We had already given a great deal of thought to the problem. We had tried towing the limbers behind the guns, special ammunition trailers, even designed a crude sledge – all without success. The M109 was a proven and very reliable system, but the technology was old (1950's) and the vehicles tired. Over the years more equipment, radios, a heavier barrel, etc, had been added, without a compensating increase in power. As a result there was little, if any, spare capacity and the additional strain of moving tracks through soft, clinging sand was putting a massive strain on the generators. Somehow we had to cope with what we had.

The BSM, who would take responsibility for the ammunition resupply in war, was more optimistic. He had noticed a small but distinct improvement in the way the drivers were coping and was convinced that much of the trouble had been the 'follow my leader' mentality bred of Germany soldiering. This meant that when one got stuck, they all got stuck. If each driver could be persuaded to pick his own independent route, recognize he was in difficulty early and take the correct action, then the problem might be overcome. In addition he intended to reduce the tyre pressures far below the currently recommended minimum. We talked around the problem for some time and I eventually agreed to let him have all the trucks and drivers to play with for the day. The BK and I watched them depart, not in the familiar convoy but as individuals, each making his own way but always in sight of the others.

The BSM dispatched, I settled down to my own tasks. I spent about an hour in the CP going over signals, logs and maps and the thousands of admin matters that are part of a Battery's life wherever it is. I then did my daily round of the guns, CPs and REME before returning to my own vehicle. By now the sun was high in the sky and the temperature was starting to climb. We had not carried out the expected number of engine changes, so water stocks were unusually high. Everybody was making the most of the time, water and the heat to wash bodies and clothes. I did likewise and had my first desert shower; a black plastic bag with a small rose attachment which was suspended from a pole. Wonderful!

I spent the afternoon working with my own crew before limping my way, in my now very sick Landrover, to the FDC (Fire Direction Centre), for the 16.00 Orders Group. I was relieved to hear that the other batteries were faring worse than we were with endless tales of major breakdowns and bogged lorries. All three BCs confirmed to David Radcliffe the futility of trying to operate over any distance without some means of accurate navigation. It took about an hour to brief us on the next day's deployments so it was nearly 17.30 when I returned to the Battery. The BSM and his trucks had not returned. I made my way over to the in-action Command Post. The CPO, Matthew Hubbard, informed me that the BSM had got himself stuck in sabka less than 2km away and he had dispatched the Battery's powerful M578 tracked recovery vehicle to rescue him. I set off, following the recovery vehicle's track marks. I arrived in time to see the last of three vehicles being dragged from the thick, clinging mud. I expected my BSM to be somewhat sheepish over the incident. Far from it. He considered the sabka to be nothing but bad luck, the problem of movement across the desert had been cracked. The secret lay in dispersing the vehicles and dramatically reducing the tyre pressure. Yes, there were areas that a truck could never manage, but this problem could be circumvented given time, patience and a lot of skill. Already the drivers were taking routes that would have been impossible two days before. Things were looking up and morale soared when, on returning to the Battery, I was greeted by a request from Regimental HQ to borrow my M578. Both 23 and 127 Batteries had convoys stuck in the sabka.

Less encouraging, today Iraq had stated that it would attack Israel if war broke out, and Russia had threatened to intervene. On a more positive note, Turkey would send troops if the 15th deadline was not met.

11 JANUARY 1991

We were due to fire again, but as the guns were already in their deployment positions, all the GPO had to do was a Check Bearing accuracy test and they would be ready. It was the OP parties who had to get up early and move, this time to another high rock ridge about 3km inland. This we imaginatively christened OP 2. The guns were primarily firing in support of helicopter crews, so it was to be a slow day for us. We were all required at the OP for the visit of the Corps Commander from Germany, General Sir Peter Inge. There was little likelihood that I would have much to do, so I left both of my crews and their tracked vehicles with the guns. We set off at dawn, the Warrior, the two 432s and my Landrover, still limping along with its sick clutch.

On arrival we set ourselves up with the rest of the Regiment, FOOs in the front, BCs behind. It was a long day. There was some mid-morning drama when we were placed on air alert YELLOW for a short time but we never discovered why. (Air attack states were RED: Imminent, YELLOW: Possible, WHITE: Nil) The helicopters were slow firing the guns, the FOOs had only a few shoots and the Corps Commander's visit came and went, leaving us none the wiser as to future events. To keep myself amused I spent some of the time with the crew of a Listening Post from a Cymbeline Radar, which drove up and calmly announced that they were to be attached to the 14th/20th Battle Group. They were very welcome, but if we were ever to be in need of a mortar locating radar then someone had got things badly wrong.

Shooting over, we were given orders to return, via a Regimental replenishment point, to our original positions astride the Pylon Line Road. The REPLEN had been positioned to suit the location of the guns and meant a massive dogleg for the OPs. It would be dark well before we could reach it, always assuming we could find it. The whole thing seemed simply an aberration of the Second in Command who probably had no idea where we were anyway. With fuel tanks reasonably full, the BCs' union decided to ignore the order and head straight for home. It was almost dark when I reached my now well-setup 432. It was like coming home. The BQMS greeted me with the news that we were to send four soldiers to the Combined Services Entertainment show in Al Jubayl tonight. Clearly hostilities were at least 24 hours away. The World Service gave us the news that the Secretary General, Pérez de Cuéllar, had instigated peace talks and the speculation was that Saddam Hussein would be prepared to withdraw for the UN, thus saving face in the Arab world and still defying the Americans.

12 JANUARY 1991

My cold had all but gone and I appeared to have no discernible ill effects from my Anthrax jab. I was looking forward to a short lie in but it was not to be. I was woken at 05.30 by the cries of 'Get an ambulance.' One of the JCB forklift trucks, fully loaded, had accidentally backed into the BK's tent. The BK's driver, Gunner Hough, had been asleep on his cot bed and now had a serious head injury. Fortunately a steel box and then the frame of the bed had absorbed a good deal of the impact. By the time I arrived our own medical crew and ambulance were coping well and he was with the Regimental Medical Officer very quickly. A helicopter had been called for within minutes of the accident but it was three hours before an RAF Puma arrived from Al Jubayl, some twenty minutes flying time away. The injury looked appalling but as we placed him in the helicopter the doctor assured me that he would probably be a week in hospital and have a bit of a scar for a while. (In fact he never returned to the Battery but was evacuated immediately back to the UK. I met him after the war. He had eyesight problems, headaches and the most horrific scar). He was our first serious injury.

I returned to a Battery that was visibly shaken. Gunner Ayres, the eighteen-year-old JCB driver and a close friend of Gunner Hough, was in shock and there was now a dawning realization throughout the Battery that, inevitably, accidents like this were going to hit us. The three FOOs and I, however, had to be with the 14th/20th for a briefing, so, leaving Geoff Ravenhill to settle things down as best he could, I set off north-west in the GPO's Landrover.

I spent most of the rest of the day at Battlegroup HQ talking through how we planned to operate should we go to war. The 14th/20th had finished their own training and were now back in their original deployment position, between the two enormous sabka lakes. Accidents, however, were not the sole preserve of The Rocket Troop. While I was at the HQ I was told that, in the early hours of the previous morning, an officer with the 16th/5th Lancers had been killed. He had been in a Scimitar which had driven over an embankment and into a quarry whilst on a night move. It made our own accident, bad as it was, seem far less terrible.

In spite of the tragedy the 14th/20th were in good spirits. I saw their paymaster, David Taylor, who had driven up from Al Jubayl and we spent some time swapping family gossip from Münster. It was nearly dark when I arrived back at the guns and it was raining heavily. The news was good. The UN Secretary General had gone to Baghdad and sixteen new artillery Warriors were due to dock tonight. In a cheerful mood the FOOs and I cracked a few tins of 'delicious, alcohol free malt beverage', listened to Radio Baghdad's report of the spontaneous anti-war riots that were breaking out all over Britain and the USA, and had a game of Malefiz (a German board game). Richard Farndale won.

13 JANUARY 1991

I was called in the early hours to be told that the new Warriors had docked and were already heading north on low-loaders. We were to send crews to the Brigade RV to collect them at dawn; however, I had to take part in a CPX (Command Post Exercise), Exercise JERBOA DRIVE, which was due to last for the next two days. It was still raining heavily, tents and vehicles were leaking badly and it was very cold. After a late breakfast, I set off in the Sultan with Sergeant Radcliffe and my Battlegroup MAIN HQ crew, to join the exercise. I navigated from the turret while the rain soaked me, in spite of my wet proofs, and poured into the vehicle through thousands of unseen holes. I had been travelling north along the Pylon Line Road for about fifteen minutes when I met the first of the new Warriors returning. A brief chat to the crew confirmed that three had indeed arrived, but one had lost its track while being unloaded and the second vehicle had stayed with it to help. The best news was that this one was a Warrior BCV (Battery Commanders Variant) so was for me. I would no longer have to go to war in my trusty, but very slow and tired, 432.

We were a long time finding Brigade HQ and the exercise. The rain was heavy, the desert flat and featureless and visibility greatly reduced. We drove across this depressing and increasingly sticky landscape for over two hours. As a single vehicle I had no one to help check my navigation and was about to turn around, fearing I had gone too far, when I spotted some radio masts in the distance. In a shallow bowl was a huddle of about ten forlorn and bedraggled vehicles, their crews struggling to erect the canvas penthouses that would link them all together. We were not happy. The exercise, primarily designed to practise the Brigade staff, was slow and laborious for those who were representing the tactical players. The inside of the vehicle was awash and some of the crew had motion sickness from the drive out.

The Sultan was an extra vehicle issued for the campaign. It would allow me to keep my crew under armour, at Battlegroup MAIN HQ and provide a stable foot on the ground should I have to go forward and fight in my tac vehicle. I had asked for a Sultan as this was the vehicle the rest of the HQ was equipped with. It was not a vehicle with which I was familiar, but our recent experience had shown it to be cramped, far from weather-proof, uncomfortable to travel in; with its aluminium armour, it afforded about the same degree of protection as a baked bean can. Sergeant Radcliffe, who commanded my MAIN HQ crew, was particularly disparaging. It would have to go! Besides, the 14th/20th RHQ's all-Sultan fleet had been so augmented, with every shape and size of vehicle, that any attempt at standardization was now a nonsense.

I whiled away the time as best I could with Sergeant Radcliffe coping easily with anything the exercise passed our way. I had a long talk with

Mike Vickery who confided that yesterday he had met Sir Peter de la Billière. The message was not good and the General's prognosis was that war was 90% certain and that the current flurry of diplomatic activity would produce nothing. Just a few hours after our conversation came the news that the 1st (British) Armoured Division was being moved from the Marines and was to join VII (US) Corps away to the West. With 146,000 soldiers (US & UK) and nearly 50,000 vehicles, this would make VII Corps not only the most powerful corps of the Coalition but the most powerful corps ever assembled. I spent a very depressed and unsettled night squashed in the commander's seat of the Sultan, headphones on my head and rain dripping down my back. The Dog Watch!

14 JANUARY 1991

After an atrocious night of heavy rain and gales the dawn was a long time coming. The CPX dragged on. During the morning I elicited David Radcliffe's agreement that with the arrival of the Warriors I could swap the Sultan for my now redundant 432. Godfrey Tilney, the 14th/20th second-in-command, was only too delighted to take the Sultan off my hands. Every cloud has a silver lining.

The rain finally stopped at 10.00. We left the exercise after lunch and headed back to the Battery. Although there was the occasional glimpse of sun between the scudding clouds, the desert was now a very different place. In fact, as over one and a half inches of rain had fallen, we were technically no longer in a desert. The small stunted twigs now sprouted green shoots and small blades of grass were everywhere pushing their way through the sand. The flat parched sabka now had a dark menacing appearance and in many areas was already flooded. We made slow progress, having to make wide detours to avoid the most obvious hazards. Someone had clearly not been so cautious and we passed close to an abandoned JCB buried over its axles in black clinging mud. Only a few kilometres from home we saw a 4-tonne truck stuck fast, its unhappy crew perched forlornly on the roof. On reaching the Battery, I dispatched the M578 to rescue them.

Stuck in the dreaded Sabka. (AG)

It was still daylight when we finally rejoined Sergeant Allen and the tac crew. They were wet but in good heart as we had just received a large delivery of mail. As I wandered around the newly arrived Warriors, Derek Hudson related his tale. As instructed, he had arrived at the Brigade RV armed with a driver and commander for each vehicle. They had travelled some 25 miles north up the Pylon Line Road, in the dark and the rain and, miraculously, had managed to negotiate the sabka without incident. The Warriors were on the back of 'Host Nation' transporters. These were Arab-owned and driven articulated flat-bed trucks designed for civilian tasks. The Warriors had only just fitted with a good proportion of their steel tracks overhanging the sides. Derek described unloading as 'Like walking a high wire wearing ice skates.' While reversing Romeo Three Three Bravo, the driver tracked too close to the edge and the vehicle was left with barely an inch of its right hand track supporting its weight and with the trailer lurching alarmingly to one side. Two passing REME armoured recovery vehicles were then co-opted/commandeered and their recovery winches set up to try and drag the Warrior back into the centre of the trailer.

After over an hour of concentrated effort, disaster struck. A cable snapped, whiplashed across the Warrior and 26 tonnes of armoured vehicle crossed the flatbed and fell off the other side, leaving one track on the truck and the other on the ground. At this precarious angle the driver somehow managed to reverse it off. The only apparent damage was to one of the front drive sprockets. Much relieved, Derek had assembled his small convoy and, with my Warrior leading, set off for the Battery. They made less than 500 yards before Romeo Three Three Bravo threw a track. With minimal tools, little knowledge of the new track linkage, soft sand, driving rain and only the crew's muscle, it took over three hours to get the track back on.

Before I turned in I held a meeting of the senior management of the Battery and told them that they were to tone down the "They are bound to back down" rhetoric and start preparing the boys for war. I did not want an instant about turn as I was sure that we were a long way from any ground offensive; however, there now needed to be a definite change of emphasis. In particular, the younger soldiers needed to be made aware gently of the realities of our situation. My message was supported by the news that the Baghdad talks had collapsed.

The post had brought a letter and a parcel of goodies from Annie. I lay in bed, still wet and cold, munching, reading and listening to the sound of a full-blown sandstorm raging outside.

15 JANUARY 1991
Dawn rose sunny and warm with a clear sky. The GKN-built Warriors seemed to be in good condition in spite of having been rushed from the

factory. Weighing some 26 tonnes, with a 550-horsepower supercharged diesel engine, they could do in excess of 85 kph, extremely fast for any armoured vehicle. The OP variant was a sophisticated beast. It was equipped with built-in thermal and image-intensifying sights, a laser rangefinder, an inertial navigation system and a battery management system. My own BC variant was more downmarket, missing the navigation system, rangefinder and thermal sight. The vehicle was also missing much of the computer hardware its designer had intended (it was still under development) so cables criss-crossed the turret joining those components that were there and bypassing those that were not. Heath Robinson would have been impressed. All variants had one thing in common – the amount of equipment crammed into the turret left no room for the main armament and the fearsome-looking 30mm Rarden Canon was simply a dummy. The only firepower came from a 7.62mm Hughes Chain Gun. It sounded a lot more impressive than it really was and had yet to arrive. However, we were all absolutely delighted with the vehicles and clambered over them like excited children with new toys.

We spent the morning drying out and transferring kit from vehicle to vehicle - Sultan to 432, 432 to Warrior. Once both my 432 and the Sultan were ready I dispatched them north to join the Battlegroup. As an FOO's 432 became available it was transferred over to the guns to provide the BK, BSM, and Recce party with much-needed mobility and protection. There was still no sign of a clutch for my Landrover.

About mid-morning the BQMS came and reported that we had been issued with some Dosimeters, and every man was to carry three Combo pens and NAPS tablets. This was not welcome news. On pure cost alone I knew such an issue would be avoided if at all possible, and to now be getting them, at war scaling, was worrying. We had about twenty Dosimeters, a small device looking exactly like an Army wristwatch except it had a plain black face. When placed in a special reading device it displayed the accumulated radiation to which the wearer had been exposed. Clearly one needed to know the worst case, so I ordered them to be distributed amongst turret crews of the OPs, the Recce party and those gun crews who would be working outside unprotected. I also kept one for myself. One day I might wish to check our real level of exposure against the official pronouncement.

The Combo pens, which we now carried in our respirator satchels, were in what looked like green cigar tubes. They were in fact an immediate antidote for Nerve Agent poisoning. As soon as the symptoms showed, the pen had to be placed firmly against the fleshy part of the thigh and the trigger squeezed. A high-pressure spring fired a half-inch needle through the clothing and gave a deep-muscle injection of atropine. The pain was said to be excruciating. The NAPS (Nerve

Agent Pretreatment) tablets looked like foil-packed contraceptive pills, even marked with the days, and were exactly as their name suggests, a pretreatment to help the body withstand the shock of the Combo pen. The issue of these three articles did nothing for morale.

It was a busy day for everyone but helped by the 70°F+ temperature. Apart from just trying to get sorted after the rain, the BK, BSM and BQMS had to attend Exercise CRACKER LOG, a logistic presentation run by 26 Regiment, Royal Artillery. It was during this exercise that they were informed of the imminent arrival of M548s. Each Battery would get twelve of these old, but still very effective, tracked logistics vehicles which had been hurriedly begged, borrowed or stolen from American war stocks. One would go to each of the eight guns, the balance to the BQMS. This would significantly improve our ability to keep ammunition, fuel and water up with the guns. On their return they told me the good news with great satisfaction, then, after a pause, gave me the bad news. Our first line scaling of ammunition was to be four SPGs (Staff Planning Guide) per gun. One SPG was 150 rounds or nine ULCs (Unit Load Containers), each of seventeen rounds. We therefore had to deal with a total of 288 ULCs. As a Battery Commander the ULC was the standard unit for all my calculations. These steel containers were the smallest unit it was practical to deal with, single rounds only being broken down to load turrets or immediately prior to firing. Each shell weighed in excess of 96 lbs, so keeping them in their ULCs was the only way to move bulk ammunition, each gun having its own JCB fork lift.

It was a long time before the magnitude of the problem fully dawned. We could put sixteen ULCs in the gun turrets and forty-eight ULCs on the M548s. That left a balance of 224 ULCs to be moved by the Battery. A quick calculation showed that this would require 56 x 8-tonne trucks or 38 x 14-tonne trucks or 28 x DROPS vehicles or 25 x Chinook helicopters. The BQMS was already advancing ideas, including the construction of sledges, when I stopped him in full flight and told everyone we would give the matter no further thought. Any ammunition we could not lift became a logistics problem and therefore Div HQ could lose sleep over it. We would not.

Kit and spares of all kinds continued to be delivered and there was the endless round of briefings and Orders Groups. At one such briefing we were informed of the Coalition's solution to security. From now on we would abandon the simple well-proven British system of challenging with two letters, e.g. HH, and replying with two more, e.g. JD, the letters changing daily. Now in recognition of their relative status in the Coalition, we would adopt the American and Arab systems, both of which would be used concurrently. The Americans used two words, one to be used in the opening challenge, the second to be somehow incorporated in the reply. An example:

> *'Hey buddy not much of a GIGGLE standing here all day.'*
> *'Sure aint, not on the MONEY they pay us.'*

Giggle and Money being the code words of the day. Far from being impressed with the system, we were worried that our soldiers, not to date known for their linguistic dexterity, would be able to cope. Shamrock and Scrapbook, Quicker and Freedom, Tariff and Bottle being just some examples of words we were expected to link in supposedly casual conversation. We need not have worried, and confused GIs had everything from Shakespeare to the unprintable spouted at them in Jock, Geordie, Cockney and Gurkhali.

The Arab system caused greater problems. It worked like our own letter system but was based on numbers. Using fingers by day, torch flashes by night, a number was given and a set number expected in reply. There were several drawbacks to this system which were never satisfactorily resolved. Firstly there could be numbers greater than ten. Secondly, like in England, certain hand gestures hold alternative meanings and in the Arab world the scope for offence is infinite. Finally, no British soldier is stupid enough to flash his torch in the dark at someone he is unsure of. We were not impressed.

Today I was supposed to rejoin the 14th/20th but it was after dark when the PADS Landrover finally dropped me off. Sergeant Allen had parked the Warrior close to the Emperor and Sergeant Radcliffe had set up the 432 as part of the RHQ complex. The complex itself consisted of three vehicles in a T formation, the Plans vehicle (Sultan), my Gunner vehicle (432) and the Operations vehicle (Sultan). All three were parked, facing outwards, at the outer points of the T, with mine, with its large canvas penthouse deployed, making the long leg. A box structure of poles and plastic sheet linked the rear of my penthouse to the open backs of the two Sultans. This was Battlegroup MAIN HQ. It was clear that the only place where orders and briefings could take place under cover was my penthouse, so to the horror of Sergeant Radcliffe, I volunteered its services to the Operations Officer. Sergeant Radcliffe later conceded that the Colonel would have taken it anyway, so better to get some appreciation from the gesture. Orders that night took over two and a half hours, mainly covering equipment and spares problems. I was delighted to learn that the Battlegroup hoped to have a stand-down on the 17th and with luck the services of a bath unit.

The BBC's nightly offering was depressing. The French had proposed a solution only to have it rejected by the US, UK and USSR. The Israelis had threatened to retaliate if attacked and the Palestine Liberation Organization's second-in-command and head of security had been shot in Tunis. The Israelis were being blamed and we in the desert felt totally impotent.

16 JANUARY 1991

At 08.00 local time the UN deadline for Iraq to withdraw from Kuwait expired. Everyone sat glued to the World Service broadcasts. There was an air of disbelief everywhere. We were always so confident that Saddam would back down, even at the final hour.

From now on we would train largely in the organization in which we expected to go to war. The forth tank squadron, a squadron from the Life Guards under command of Major James Hewitt, was detached to join the Royal Scots Battlegroup and we took under command the Queen's Company of the Grenadier Guards, commanded by Major Grant Baker. The FOOs arrived to join the Battlegroup mid-morning and, after a quick briefing, I sent them off to join the squadrons and the company, Graham Ambrose to A Squadron, Derek Hudson to B Squadron and Richard Farndale to the Queen's Company. None were more than a kilometre away. The Sultan was handed over and the washing done. In the afternoon we sat in the sun, the hottest day yet, and received a briefing from the Arabic-speaking prisoner-handling team on how to deal with prisoners of war. The message was that they expected a lot, especially in the initial stages if we had to break through the Iraqi first-line defences which we knew to be held by poor-quality conscripts. The evening Orders Group was at 19.00 and we followed it with a leisurely meal, then sat in the back of the 432 listening to the BBC speculating on the options. That nothing was likely to happen in the immediate future seemed the prevailing opinion; indeed that Saddam would now withdraw, having ignored the deadline, seemed highly probable. If not, so the pundits argued, the Coalition air power would make a ground offensive unnecessary. The radio announced that the American game plan would be Cruise Missiles on the chemical plants and destroy the airfields, then B52 carpet-bombing on a scale never before seen. I went to bed with very mixed feelings.

52

OPERATION DESERT STORM

(The campaign to liberate Kuwait and establish regional peace and security)

17 JANUARY 1991

The night was warm and humid. My American cot bed was on the side of the penthouse and I slept uneasily on top of my sleeping bag. At 04.30, just as the first rays of dawn were appearing, I was shaken awake and told, "Sir, NBC Black, Air Alert Red." I didn't ask why or question anything. I went straight into a reflex-driven drill. Combat kit, boots, NBC suit, then respirator satchel around the waist, ready. All around me people were scrambling into their protective kit. Other than the duty operators passing the alarm, no one spoke. Every thought was focused on the task of getting dressed. A lot of records were broken that morning.

Once I was happy that all my crew were awake and fully prepared I made my way next door to the Operations vehicle, the command centre of the Battlegroup. I was told by an excited watch-keeper that 'Desert Storm, execute' had been given. The air war had started at 03.00 local time with over one thousand air sorties by coalition aircraft. Prior to the aircraft, at 02.30, US ships had launched one hundred Tomahawk Cruise Missiles. Already the Iraqi war-fighting capability was greatly reduced and the increased alert state was simply a precaution that had been ordered throughout the ground force area.

Still in our suits we sat down to breakfast, happier than we had been for a long time. It was now about 07.30 and already we were receiving reports of spectacular allied success. As I munched my way through eggs and bacon burger I remember telling my crew, "Team, this is the first day of our journey home".

No one who heard it will ever forget it, the shock, the panic. As we relaxed over our empty plates, sipping our tea, we heard "Gas, Gas, Gas." Alarms sounded, vehicle horns blared and everywhere people were running and shouting. I ripped open my carrier. Remember the drill! Close your eyes, hold your breath, respirator over the head; when on, blow out and open eyes. Breath normally, fit the hood around the mask, check with someone else - the buddy buddy system.

I opened my eyes to see all of the crew, their respirators now on, in the final stages of sorting their hoods. There was an expression of horror on every face. Mine will have been no different as our worst nightmare erupted around us. Having checked each other, Sergeant Radcliffe and I went around the crew. Outside, those who could had taken refuge inside their vehicles and there was now an audible whine from high-pressure fans. I went to the Operations vehicle which still had its back door open. The duty signaller, now with his microphone attached to his respirator, was sending the Nuclear-Biological-Chemical report to warn all other units. The duty watch-keeper, visibly shaken, was frantically writing in the log. I went outside again. There were a few dazed soldiers standing around fully suited, a look of disbelief on their faces; otherwise all that could be seen were vehicles with their hatches clamped shut and open featureless desert. The sun was shining and there was not a cloud in the sky. I went back into the Ops tent. "Who gave the alarm?" "Don't know, Sir, it came from outside somewhere." Mike Vickery arrived and asked the same pointed question. No one seemed to have an answer.

In all operations of war the British Army accepts, indeed trains for, casualties, regarding the calculated risk as one of the responsibilities of command. Only in NBC have we attempted to produce equipment and drills that will give 100% protection. The bullet and the bomb, even for those who have never been shot at, are things familiar. They fill our film and television screens and, even if we fear their effects, we understand and know them for what they are. Blood, blister and choking agent, nerve gas and bubonic plague have no such familiarity and therefore hold a terror of their very own. For such as these, no risk is acceptable and no risk taken. If there is the slightest suspicion, the alarm is given. We never found out what or who sounded the alarm. However, now that the Battlegroup was masked up we faced the problem of getting it unmasked.

Part of the declared unmasking drill is a procedure called 'the sniff test.' Simply put, a volunteer lifts his respirator and takes a good sniff of the potentially contaminated air. The non-volunteers then watch from the comfort of their own respirators to see if their hapless friend descends into violent muscle spasms or dies. I wonder which clown thought up that little gem. Be assured, armed soldiers do not volunteer to do sniff tests.

For a unit to receive a chemical attack, the enemy has first to find it and then deliver the agent. We were a relatively small force, isolated in the middle of nowhere. We were over 100 km from the Iraqi border and, as no Iraqi plane had flown for months, it was unlikely in the extreme that the enemy had found us. Furthermore, there had been no explosions and no tell-tale vapour trails in the sky. None of the sophisticated alarms had gone off, nor had the detector paper on our sleeves changed colour. We had a quick chat and took our respirators off. We now had to persuade everyone else to do the same.

Soldiers are by nature creatures of caution and their experience in the Army teaches them to play safe and not to fool with things they don't understand. A soldier who believes he has been attacked by gas, having got his respirator on, is inclined to keep it on. The sight of an officer, regardless of seniority, with his respirator off does not impress, indeed it tends only to confirm his worst suspicions. At times of high stress, and many that morning had experienced no higher, people react in different ways. Some had already started to withdraw into themselves, sitting hunched up oblivious to their surroundings. Some, inside the clean, filtered environment of their vehicles, showed a marked reluctance to leave them. That is not to say that the British soldiers' spirit was completely crushed. Mike Vickery later told me that as he made his way around the Headquarters complex he was greeted by the occasional muffled 'Thanks for the day off, Colonel' just audible through the S10 respirators. It took, however, a very long time for the Battlegroup management to get everyone unmasked and settled back down to some semblance of normality. We learnt a salutary lesson that morning.

By about 10.00 the Battlegroup was starting to enjoy its much-deserved day off. Those not on essential duties were now washing clothes, playing football, writing letters. The mandatory NBC sentries were posted, sweating in the increasing heat. Dressed in their 'Noddy' suits, they stood despondently next to their NAIAD detector machines. To our west, MLRS (Multiple Launch Rocket System) batteries were firing on DDD Range, adding to our increasing sense of security. For the top management there was no day off. The American Marines had constructed a replica of the Iraqi defensive line, complete with wire, ditches and high sand walls. It was built in open desert about an hour's drive away and was to be used for training. The Battlegroup had been allocated the site for 19 January and the Colonel wanted to recce it so that best use could be made of the valuable training time. At about 10.30 we set off across country in the Colonel's box-body Landrover. Godfrey Tilney, the second-in-command, drove, Mike Vickery navigated, while the radio operator and I sat, hunched and isolated, facing each other in what little room remained available in the back. The outward journey was cramped, uncomfortable, but uneventful. As a precaution we had kept our NBC suits on, so it was also very hot. When we got out of the Landrover we were confronted by an obstacle belt about 200 metres long consisting of a dummy minefield, a ditch about 1 metre deep and 2 wide, and a sand wall or 'berm' about 5 metres high. The three of us gathered about 20 metres from the back of the Landrover while the operator sat at the rear of the vehicle manning the radio sets, the back door open. The first few minutes were taken up by the entertaining spectacle of a Royal Engineer armoured vehicle practising demolishing the high sand wall. It would run up, stop on the knife-edge pinnacle and then track sideways, collapsing and flattening the sand. After this manoeuvre had been repeated two or three times, a wide, trafficable hole lay in the berm. We were seriously impressed.

We cannot have been there for more than ten minutes when the radio operator screamed "Gas, Gas, Gas.!" Once again I instinctively went through my drills, my heart pounding. With my eyes closed I started to run towards the Landrover. Just as I reached the door, mask on, I blew out and opened my eyes. Oh God! In the hollow ground close to us, white mist was rising. I scrambled into the back of the vehicle, the signaller slamming the door behind me. In the front the Colonel and 2IC were both inside and had started their decontamination. As the signaller began to bash the pad of Fullers Earth around my hands the Colonel yelled, "Who gave the alarm?" "It came over the Brigade net, Sir," was the reply. "The 14th/20th have reported a gas attack. One of their NAIADs has alarmed."

We hurriedly moved off in an attempt to drive out of the contaminated area. We were downwind from the Battlegroup, so we would have to drive in a wide circle if we were to get back safely. "Can you smell anything in the back, Andrew?" I looked up to see the masked face of Mike Vickery. He was trying to peer through the six-inch gap between the roof and the high mound of radios and kit which divided us. "Yes," I said, "new mown hay," the classic signature of Nerve Agent. I sat in the back, desperately trying to brace myself as the Landrover rocked and bucked, flat out, over the sand dunes. My mind raced as I tried to remember the symptoms of Nerve Agent poisoning: distinctive smell, dilated pupils, muscle cramp, uncontrollable twitching, loss of bodily functions, death. We had been told that to defeat our respirators the Iraqis sometimes mixed in a vomiting agent. I stared at the signaller some eighteen inches away and he in turn stared at me. In less than thirty seconds we confirmed to each other that our pupils had dilated.

I felt them and recognized them immediately. I had them on wet, cold, dark nights on foot patrol in Belfast. I had them now. I called them icy fingers. Long, thin, cold fingers that seemed to reach out from the depth of my bowels and squeeze my stomach until I wanted to vomit. I recognized these familiar symptoms all too well. Fear!

An age passed. We still drove as fast as possible over the soft but uneven sand. In the back of the Landrover it was hot from the blazing sun and the bank of three radios. Inside our suits it was almost unbearable. Sweat ran down the inside of my mask, stinging my eyes, yet there was no way I could brush it away. Nausea swept over me in waves. I gripped whatever part of the Landrover would provide me with some purchase and desperately fought down the panic attack which threatened to overwhelm me.

Still more time passed. It started as a dull ache and quickly grew to such intense pain that I wanted to cry out. Severe cramp. I tried to move but there just wasn't the room. My leg went into a fit of uncontrollable muscle spasms. A glance at the signaller confirmed that the spasms were not confined to me. Not only was he desperately trying to massage his thigh muscles but he had taken out his COMBO pen. I also took out my pen and placed it on my lap. We both knew from our training that the impact of the inch-long needle and the high pressure of the fluid was such that few could withstand the pain long enough to give themselves the full dose. We also both knew the penalties of injecting too soon or too late. We sat in silence. We were going to die and we were going to die horribly. I went back through my childhood, my mother and my father, re-living my most treasured moments. I thought of Annie and the children and all the things I wanted to say but now never would. I thought of my daughter Katie, my son John and I thought of little Louise, how she would grow up without even a memory of me, and how they would perhaps never know how and where their father had died.

"We're here!" The voice came from the front. I looked out of the back window to see troops sunbathing and playing football. The feeling of relief all but overwhelmed me and I again had to grip the side of the vehicle to keep some control over my emotions. We drove over to RHQ, the back door was opened and we tumbled out, still in our respirators. We must have looked a comical sight. A glance at our faces as we unmasked clearly stifled any further mirth. Outwardly I put a brave face on the experience; inwardly, I suspect the others' reactions mirrored my own and they also took a good few minutes fully to regain their composure. Perhaps the two in the front of the Landrover, able to see and control their movements, had realized our true situation much earlier and never thought to tell those cocooned in the back. I don't know, but again I had learnt a painful but salutary lesson, a lesson nothing in my training had even hinted at. The imagination, when reinforced, is a terrible thing to control. Yes, the NAIAD had activated and, rightly, the Battlegroup had sent out the alarm. By the time the all clear was given we were out of radio range. There had been no gas attack. The young Guardsman on sentry, in spite of the hours of training, had failed to tell the difference between 'BLEEP, BLEEP there is a gas attack' and 'BLEEP, BLEEP my batteries are running down.' The mist was natural for that part of the desert at that time in the morning. The smell was not hay but the clutch burning out; it failed very soon after. The sickness was normal motion sickness. If you stare closely at anyone their pupils will dilate, and if you sit cramped and tense in the back of a Landrover for a long time, your legs will go first into cramp and then into spasm. Fortunately we were not armed or the temptation to shoot ourselves while we still had control of our limbs may have proved too great. I can relate this tale now with a wry smile at our naivety. However, those few hours were for me the darkest moments of the whole campaign and are still the substance of terrifying nightmares.

One of the few advantages of any kind of command is that you are seldom left long with your thoughts. I had an Orders Group with David

Radcliffe back at Brigade HQ at 17.30 and so missed the Battlegroup Officers' photograph. However, the trip enabled me to call in at the NAAFI and stock up on drink and chocolate bars. I spent the evening writing to Annie in an even shakier hand than usual and trying to exorcise the ghost of the day's events by talking them over with my crew.

18 JANUARY 1991

At 06.00 we received the order to start taking NAPS tablets, the pre-treatment for Nerve Agent. This was not a good sign. NAPS were in short supply and very expensive. Clearly someone on high and therefore presumably in the know considered the chemical threat to be more than just cursory. Sergeant Radcliffe took it upon himself to be our NAPS conscience and would do spot checks on our tablets to ensure we were all taking them.

Today was the start of the Battlegroup's two-day exercise. In slow time we went through a series of attacks on range area Alpha 8. Sergeant Radcliffe on the radio in the 432 played the artillery Fire Direction Centre and, all in all, things went well, that is until the 432 broke down and had to be recovered back to the Echelon. At every opportunity we listened intently to the BBC World Service news. There was great concern over Scud attacks on Israel and a real chance that the Coalition would, as a consequence, break up. Although we were not using live ammunition, during that particular excercise the training was as real as was practical, with many of the peacetime safety restrictions lifted. Across the range our sister Battlegroup, the Royal Scots, was training 'live'. Practising drills and procedures exactly as you expect to do it in war is a vital part of the training for war. Sadly, as the Royal Scots were coming to the end of one of their Battle Runs, a 'Second Captain', who had been supervising what safety their CO had considered necessary, was hit in the stomach by a ricocheting round and seriously hurt. Regardless, the training went on.

Start of the Battle Group work-up training. (AG)

The 14th/20th Battlegroup did a long sweeping night march, moving rapidly in squadron and company columns. There was a clear sky and a moon and I travelled with my face glued to my Image Intensifying sight. The desert was low, rolling sand dunes with the moonlight reflecting off the coarse sand crystals. In the weird world of my sight it was like travelling through green sparkling snowdrifts. It was surreal. I remember being captivated by the vision that was flashing past on my small television screen and wondering if I would ever see real snowdrifts again. We stopped a few hours before dawn and the two tanks and the Warrior, which made up Battlegroup Tac HQ, went into a tight leaguer, guns pointing outwards. The Colonel clambered into the back of my vehicle and with the Adjutant, Jonty Palmer, we worked out the plan for the next part of the exercise. Conference over, I heaved myself onto the top of the Warrior and slept on the back hatches, oblivious of the hinges, bolts and brackets which stuck into me.

19 JANUARY 1991

I awoke cold and very stiff with my foot being shaken by Gunner Lyons who had been on radio stag through the Dog Watch. It was still dark though the grey of dawn could be seen in the east. As a matter of routine one of the crew tuned into the BBC World Service for the morning news update. We were just in time to hear that during the night Iraq had fired eight Scud missiles. Seven had hit Tel Aviv, the other had been fired at Saudi Arabia and been successfully intercepted by a Patriot missile.

I lay for a short time digesting the news, shivering and looking skywards. Above us the navigation lights of a tanker aircraft sketched a lazy figure of eight pattern in the sky. Every few minutes other lights would approach from the south and join in the dance. The Tornadoes, Jaguars and F15s, having taken their last drink of fuel, then headed north, their lights going out as they approached Iraqi airspace. I, together with everyone who watched those lights disappear, wished them 'God speed' and prayed that their efforts would avoid a ground war.

It was going to be a dry and sunny day. While I greedily bolted down my fat boy's breakfast of rapidly cooling bacon burger, Mike Vickery gave orders to the Battlegroup management gathered around the front of the Emperor. There would be no live ammunition but we would practise our procedures both on the ground and on the airwaves. Using the dummy Iraqi defensive line, the Battlegroup would move to a crossing site, effect a crossing and then exploit forward to destroy an enemy position. At 06.00 our Recce, along with the Engineer Recce, would move. At 06.25, B Squadron and No 2 Company, 06.40 Tac HQ, Step Up and half the Air Defence troop. 06.45 A and D Squadrons and the Queen's Company. 07.00 MAIN HQ with the remaining air defence. 07.10 the Regimental Aid Post and 07.15 the Engineer heavy plant and bridges. The Battlegroup was to cross the startline at 07.30. As always I took the opportunity to brief my FOOs on the Fire Plan and sort out any problems.

We started well. The Recce quickly found the American-built obstacle belt and the Royal Engineers identified Grid UL 052335 as a suitable crossing point. Two of the squadrons moved into over-watch positions and the third squadron, with two infantry companies, moved to their staging areas ready to assault forward as soon as the breach was opened. The artillery Fire Plan started on time with a mixture of suppressive HE (High Explosive) and blinding smoke. The engineers moved forward under the cover of fire and successfully breached the minefield, cut the wire, bridged the ditch and bulldozed a lane through the sand berm. While the last few tons of sand were being removed the first Challengers were entering the lane. Within minutes the artillery fire had moved forward enabling the tanks to form and then expand the bridgehead. So far so good. Behind the bridgehead squadron came the three vehicles of Tac HQ. I remember reliving my ordeal as we passed the spot where our Landrover had been parked on the day of the recce. I followed the two tanks down the lane, over the bridge then up and through the gap in the berm. I heard the order for the infantry to start crossing and then disaster struck. The first infantry Warrior drove onto the bridge and toppled over the side.

Fortunately for all concerned it was only a training exercise. There was no live ammunition being fired, no real mines and the trench over which the bridge had been laid was a token one-metre deep. Even so the crew were badly shaken and very lucky that the Warrior landed on its tracks and did not roll over. Normally such an accident would have meant an abrupt halt to all further activity. Not now. If we had to breach the Iraqi defences we would have to drive over these bridges, perhaps under fire. We carried on. That day a total of three Warriors failed to negotiate the bridge, fortunately without serious injury. Those who failed were sent back to do it again. Once the Battlegroup was safely assembled in the bridgehead the breakout started. With the tanks leading, we moved rapidly through an area of deep soft sand interspersed with areas of very low twiglike vegetation. One of the aims of the exercise was to develop and then practice our casualty procedures. In peacetime, each company or squadron has one 432 tracked ambulance, manned by musicians from the band, whose secondary employment was as medical orderlies. The Battlegroup had been given two additional ambulances. In order to make the most of these precious assets and because of the problems of navigation and their lack of speed, the Colonel had grouped them together under the command of a young Royal Tank Regiment subaltern.

For the first part of the exercise the ambulances had moved at the rear of the Battlegroup, practising communication and deployment drills under the direction of their 'Ambulance Master'. Now they felt suitably confident to join the main exercise. About a kilometre from the bridgehead we shook out into our attack formation, the two leading sabre squadrons in line abreast. In the centre and just behind came the tac group and then behind us the remaining companies and squadron, still moving in column. The attack frontage was about 4kms. The Battlegroup started its assault and the second-in-command, over the air, awarded vehicle casualties. Those call-signs designated as casualties stopped and waited for help. The nearest 'healthy' vehicle reported the casualty's position and then carried on with the attack.

All did not go well. Firstly, with their lack of speed, the 432 ambulances rapidly fell behind, even over short distances, and consequently took some time to get to the vicinity of the battle. Secondly, with no navigation aids other than a sun compass and a map, the location given by the closest vehicle to the casualty was at best a SWAG (Scientific Wild-Arsed Guess). The ambulances themselves had no navigation aids either and so were lucky to find the spot even if the fix was accurate. Finally, the troops were working on their own Company/Squadron radio nets, while the ambulances had to work on the Battlegroup command net. Consequently, they were not talking to each other. The Colonel was not impressed and, unusually, vented his frustration on the Ambulance Master. Rightly, he realized that the medical support not only had to work but had to be seen to work by all. Otherwise morale would take something of a nose dive.

We tried to put things right. The ambulances, as a Standard Operating Procedure, would close up behind the assaulting troops just before the attack. The Ambulance Master was given one of the few precious SATNAVs and a drill for communicating was worked out. We tried again and, after a 5km dash, vehicle casualties were again awarded. This time both the Colonel (in a tank) and I (in a Warrior) made ourselves casualties to test the system. On hearing our call sign nominated we stopped and within a few seconds I heard the third vehicle of Tac HQ report that the CO and BC had been hit and give a fairly accurate location. We waited for what seemed an eternity. Eventually, some 20 minutes later, I was lifted out of the turret, strapped to a stretcher, and then with the Colonel, started a very bumpy ride back to the Battlegroup Aid Post. During the journey we talked over the problem and concluded that the medical crews had neither the tactical experience nor the equipment to effect casualty evacuation up with the fighting troops – enthusiasm alone was not enough. Casualty evacuation would have to be done, in the first instance, by the reserve or uncommitted troops. They, with their speed, protection and greater tactical awareness, would ferry the injured back to an RV where the ambulances would be waiting.

We returned to the Battlegroup leaguer area tired but much more confident in our drills, procedures and, most important, our equipment. We arrived back long after dark, having been through a night rolling REPLEN. I was expecting to find the 432 and Sergeant Radcliffe and crew in their old spot or with the maintenance crews. There was no sign of them. Once we were all settled, the Battlegroup management were called to an Orders Group. The Colonel announced that he had been given Orders for the move to join VII (US) Corps. The Battlegroup would move north-west by road and air to Forward Concentration Area KEYES (46E 26.30N). The artillery and engineer groups would move later, after the completion of their work-up training. My FOOs and I would therefore move with our guns. For the 14th/20th the move would start with the Harbour Parties at 16.00 on 25 January and be complete by 18.00 on 27 January.

I went to bed that night with my brain racing. From a gentle almost leisurely pace we were suddenly moving very fast. The move of the Division westward would be a massive logistic task. I took some comfort from the fact that, if we were to fight, VII Corps was the place to be and, because the Artillery Group was not yet fully operational, the ground war was probably still some time away.

20 JANUARY 1991

After two warm, dry days, the morning was damp and cold with thick penetrating ground mist. This was scheduled as a Battlegroup maintenance day, but the three FOOs and I had to go to Div HQ for a study day with the Commander Royal Artillery. There was no sign of Sergeant Radcliffe and his 432, but the maintenance officer assured me it was being looked after. I took the Warrior down to the Battery and then went on in the PADS truck. There was still no sign of a clutch for my Landrover.

The study morning consisted of an update from the Chief of Staff on the artillery deployment to date and I was amazed to hear that 26 Regiment's guns were still at sea. This was followed by a résumé of the artillery move to KEYES. The main subjects for discussion were ammunition resupply and the Iraqi main defences. The morning confirmed what I already knew, the Battery was not expected to move all its ammunition. For formal fire plans, planned well in advance, we would fire initially from our trucks and then the M548s. Once empty, the trucks would go back to an ammunition RV and be crossloaded from second-line transport. For quick fire plans after rapid deployment, the M548 stocks would be used and they in turn would REPLEN from the Battery's own trucks making best speed behind. As usual, ammunition held in the turrets would be used only in an emergency.

The study period over, I returned via the Battery, picked up my

**An M109 of 'O'
Battery (The Rocket
Troop) with a newly
issued M548.** (AG)

Warrior and went on to A2 Echelon to have a TRIMFIX GPS (Global Positioning System) satellite navigation system installed. It took a couple of hours for the installation of the set, which looked like a standard car radio. An aerial, on a short foot-long pole, had to be mounted on the turret roof between the two hatches. I used the time constructively, scrounging a meal and tracking down my Landrover. My worst fears had already started to become reality, for not only was there no sign of a clutch but it was now being cannibalized to keep other Landrovers on the road. I gave orders for it to be back-loaded down the supply chain. With luck I would never see it again and, with even more luck, I would get a new one back in Germany.

Once back with the Battlegroup it proved too windy and overcast to be worth trying to wash any clothes so I indulged myself with a hair wash. Wonderful!

At 20.00 we had the Orders Group for the following day's exercise. Afterwards the Colonel briefed the senior management on the Coalition's projected plan. A summary is set out here:

• The air war, which began on D-day, 17 January, would be in 4 phases. Phase 1, the strategic and counter-air phase, would concentrate on nuclear and chemical plants and command and control targets. Phase 2 would target primarily the Republican Guard Force divisions. Phase 3 would be the tactical phase in which the front-line positions would be attacked with the support of artillery. The artillery raids would involve guns deploying forward and engaging targets selected from air and satellite

intelligence. Phase 4 would be the air support to the ground battle.
• The ground war would start on G day and consist of a preliminary and then 4 phases. The preliminary phase was the movement of 1 (BR) Armoured Division west into concentration area KEYES in VII (US) Corps sector. Phase 1 was the subsequent movement into a forward assembly area. Phase 2 was the artillery raids. Phase 3 was the breaching operation during which the Divisional Artillery would dig in and fire intense rates for 12 hours. Phase 4 was the advance into Kuwait.

This was the outline schedule that the coalition was working to, but the Colonel went to great pains to emphasize that we had only just started. Phases could run concurrently or not at all, depending on how things developed. Above all we should not speculate on G day as it was by no means certain that a ground war would be necessary and the air war could go on for weeks. Equally, should the Iraqi forces crumble, the Coalition forces would move in as soon as possible.

Any chance for detailed discussion was interrupted (21.50) by the news that a number of Scuds had just been launched towards Saudi Arabia. We again scrambled into our NBC suits, but now the note of panic was missing, replaced by resignation. I slept in my suit, determined that I was not going to get involved in the 'suits on, suits off' routine that experience had taught me would go on now for most of the night. It was a fitful sleep aided by the first meal of fresh meat and vegetables for days, or was it weeks?

21 JANUARY 1991

Today was earmarked for the Battlegroup to do live battle runs on Range Bravo. One of the aims of the exercise was to indoctrinate the Battlegroup to the sound of live firing within very narrow safety angles. While everyone was sorting themselves out and moving to the exercise area, Mike Vickery, the Operations Officer and I went to Brigade HQ for the 10.00 Orders Group that would kick us off. On return at 13.00, Orders were hurriedly issued and disseminated. Even so it was not until 14.30 that the Recce finally crossed their Line of Departure. I had little to do other than to monitor the radio traffic and the movement of my FOOs. The guns were firing in support of the FOOs forward with the squadrons. Very little artillery ammunition had been allocated for this exercise, indeed the tanks themselves had very little ammunition. For many of the tank crews it was the first time that they had experienced artillery fire falling close in front of them. For the FOOs, lacking the normal support of a comprehensive safety system, it was also a nervous time. The exercise moved very slowly, due primarily to the poor visibility, and we had started to get bogged down with procedures and

64

Tanks of the 14th/20th King's Hussars firing on the Devil-Dog-Dragoon Range. (AG)

range restrictions when night overtook us.

The Challenger tanks have a sighting system called TOGS (Thermal Observation and Gunnery Sight). A miracle of modern technology, it relies not on light but on heat and can produce a crystal-clear thermal image in absolute darkness. It did literally turn night into day. In spite of the tanks' superb TOGS the range safety staff insisted that the firing range left and right arc limits be marked with burning tyres. We therefore spent over two hours waiting to do the second phase of the exercise while vehicles drove out into the desert, erected the tyre piles, struggled to light them and then return. It was quite late before firing finally finished and, even with the arc markers blazing clearly, one rogue tank round landed very close to some of our own troops. After passing through a night REPLEN at 04.30 we returned 'home'. In all, I felt the day had been something of a disaster, but the Colonel seemed happy enough with the training value of the exercise, if not with its speed of execution.

Before I went to bed I read the daily Intelligence summary. Two Scuds had been fired at Dhahran air base and debris had fallen on the runway. The Iraqis were reported to be dispersing the captured coalition pilots to strategic locations and their aircraft losses were six Mirages, eight Fulcrum, one Flogger and three Foxbats.

22 JANUARY 1991

The weather was dull and overcast. Today was another maintenance day. There was clearly real concern within the hierarchy over the maintainability of our kit as not only were we given every opportunity to do our own maintenance but there was tight control on the amount of movement and therefore training we could undertake. Other than maintenance and training, life now revolved around the fixed times of meals, NAPS tablets, World Service news and radio frequency changes. There was still no news of Sergeant Radcliffe and the 432. However, I was repeatedly assured that they were in the maintenance chain and would be returned through the system as soon as the vehicle was repaired. Today we had one bright spot: the Desert Cinema was due to appear that evening.

The morning Intelligence brief brought the news that Iraq had rejected the Soviet peace initiative, Scud attacks continued, most of the permanent missile sites remained intact and the air war did not appear to be having the catastrophic effect on the Republican Guard divisions that had been predicted. The only cheering note was that the Iraqis were reported to be running short of anti-aircraft ammunition.

I had amassed a large bundle of laundry and hoped to take advantage of the now very efficient laundry system being operated from Al Jubayl. I took it down to the SQMS, all neatly labelled and bundled, only to be told that as a result of the last Scud attack, all the laundry workers had fled. No more laundry. It took me a couple of hours to wash, rinse and hang up. True to form, the crew had improvised a washing machine by using an old tin ammunition box. All it really did was re-distribute the dirt but it saved on labour and, above all, precious water. Having sorted my clothes, I set about myself in what remained of the warm water. Stripped naked I was standing in my bowl, vowing never again to take running water for granted, when disaster struck. I dropped my one and only tablet of soap in the sand. Fate has a habit of kicking you when you are down!

Vehicle and personal maintenance complete, it was now mid-afternoon and I wandered over to RHQ. A large consignment of mail had just arrived, including the first letter I had received from Annie in over a week (posted 15 Jan). There was a letter from my younger brother Allan. He ended his letter with,

> Now that it has started for real I just better add what I hope you would take for granted anyway. If you should not return from the Gulf you know that everyone will look after Annie. I will be on the first flight out to Germany and fix things. I promise you that the children will be OK and that their Uncle Allan will see to their education and make sure they grow up in a way that would make you proud of them. I will see that John learns all the things that matter - all the things that we were so lucky to experience. I will take John to the country and teach him about the flowers, trees etc. - all the things that we learnt in Scotland. I will see that the girls go out with nice boys - In short I promise you that everything will be just fine. You just get on and win the war - we will look after the rest.
> Thinking of you all the time,
> Your Brother.

Good on you little brother! I wondered just how many similar letters were being received that day. Also with the mail was a signal just in from my own Regiment telling me I had to be at OP 1 to start the Commander Royal Artillery's exercise by 07.00 the next day. It was over 30km away so we would have to leave this evening. I could not face a 4am start, then a blunder through the darkness.

It was 17.00 when I put my still-wet washing into a plastic bag, gathered up my FOO crews and set off to join the CRA's exercise. The cinema was just starting and so was the rain. Our route took us south, across the east-west tarmac road and down towards the ridge we called OP 1. It was just getting dark when we reached the base of the ridge. The bulk of the Artillery Division's tac groups were already camped some 100 ft above us and I had to decide whether to attempt a hazardous ascent in the dark in order to join the relative safety of the Regimental group on the high ground or to stay at the bottom, isolated and relatively exposed, and wait until dawn. In the end I decided that the steep climb in the dark was a certain risk, while staying at the bottom was only a presumed risk. Staying at the bottom won. However, I deployed the three Warriors (Richard Farndale with Three Three Bravo still had problems with his front sprocket and would join us the next day) in a tight triangle, the vehicles almost touching, with their turrets facing outwards. We could all sleep in the middle, protected by the vehicles bulk (the chain guns had still not arrived so we had no firepower), yet making a very small and difficult target for enemy aircraft or artillery. After a good meal and numerous cans of 'delicious malt beverage', we went to bed.

23 JANUARY 1991
We rose at 05.00 to the noise of another tac group arriving. I was extremely glad I had opted to travel the night before and, after the usual cholesterol-charged pile of grease that passed for breakfast, we made our way to the top of the ridge and joined the 2nd Field Regiment group. The FOOs were deployed forward and facing out to sea, the BCs about 100 metres behind them. The whole procedure was conducted by the HQRA staff who ran around the plateau directing everyone to their places. Once parked, I wandered over to the HQRA tent for a briefing. It was to be a technical day, largely for the benefit of the FOOs. There would be some stands for those not engaged in firing, covering such topics as close air support and the Global Positioning System. Our part of the exercise would last all day and the guns would then go through a two-day tactical deployment exercise starting on the next day. I was ordered to dispatch one of my FOOs to observe an MLRS shoot taking place to our north, some time in the afternoon, and on the morrow I was to take my tac party to the Pylon Line/Tarmac Road junction to RV with some engineers from GKN who would look over our new vehicles. I duly noted all this down, then wandered off to see John Buchanan and get the latest update on gossip.

John was half-way through his breakfast and sanguine as usual. He told me that Richard Farndale was up and running and had just reported being some 4kms away. The Battery was playing a blinder and setting the pace within the Artillery Division, and while I was sleeping soundly the previous night, 4 Scuds, probably the long-range Al Hussein, were fired into Saudi Arabia. One landed short in the sea and the others were left to land harmlessly in the desert 20 miles from Al Jubayl or en route to Riyadh and Dhahran. 'I didn't think I should wake you,' he added with a smile.

The day went well if slowly. The FOOs all had good shoots given by David Radcliffe which reinforced their confidence and at the end I was given a simple BC's fire plan which went well and without incident. The air stand organized by the Brigade Air Liaison Officer was particularly valuable and I left feeling very much happier about the control of aircraft. Call sign Three Three Alpha, Derek Hudson, left at midday to observe the MLRS shoot. He was the only FOO to date to be issued with M-Star, a new and extremely impressive locating radar. Earlier he had received a severe fright when a Tomahawk Cruise Missile had cleared his vehicle by less than 50 ft, presumably on its way to a target to our north.

It was a long trip back to the Battlegroup and dark when we arrived. As we parked up close to the Emperor, the Operations Officer dashed across and told me I was required at Brigade HQ for orders for tomorrow's FTX. With just my respirator and weapon I struggled into the back of the Colonel's Rover for what was to be a very long and bumpy cross-country journey. I was tired and very hungry and with a clear sky the temperature plummeted to below freezing. I had no time to grab anything warm and was still in my thin cotton desert combats, so I was not 100% receptive when I eventually sat down at the back of a tent to take down the orders for Exercise NESSUN DORMA. I was reminded that this means 'No one sleeps'.

As I sat scribbling, it dawned on me that these exercises were developing a familiar pattern: a move, individual battlegroup attacks, a dash to a phase line. Perhaps the intention was not only to fight the battlegroups sequentially but also the two Brigades, only one being in action at a time. What typified all the exercises was the inordinate use of control lines and code words. It was not until we reached the 'timings' paragraph of the orders that alarm bells began to ring. H hour, the start of the exercise, was to be 06.00 the following morning.

24 JANUARY 1991

It was past midnight when the three of us eventually left the Orders Group and groped our way to the Landrover. The night was dark and cold and I was very tired and very very hungry. Brigade HQ was situated in an area of undulating sand mounds each about 18 inches high. The sand had clearly formed these molehill-like features around vegetation which was now dead or very dormant, for all that showed above the sand was a sparse thatch of spindly twigs. There was one of these features every few metres which made driving in any direction both difficult and uncomfortable. The Operations Officer had brought with him a GPS to enable us to return to the Battlegroup. The Colonel was seated with the GPS held at arm's length out of the Landrover's window. He was directing the driver who was trying both to follow the directions and avoid the hillocks. An impossible task and very soon the Landrover bellied on one of the mounds and stopped dead. Our efforts to free the vehicle by revving the engine and spinning the wheels only made matters worse. We piled out and, in the darkness, started to dig. We got stuck twice more on the return journey and it was 01.30 before we finally reached the Battlegroup.

It was a reflection of the state of our training that orders had been given, crews briefed and the Battlegroup had crossed its Line of Departure by 06.00. We started with a Brigade Advance to Contact led by the 14th/20th Battlegroup. Enemy positions were dealt with as they were identified. At this point only the Royal Scots Battlegroup had any live firing, on Range Charlie. For the rest of us the exercise was dry, concentrating on movement and procedures. As we reached the far side of the range, in sight of the sea, I was ordered to send a FOO (Three Three Alpha) to conduct a linear shoot across what had now become known as Crab Island. This was a prearranged link in with the CRA's exercise being conducted to our south and went very well. Close to the coast the Brigade turned, regrouped and shook out into its assault formation, the Scots on the left, Hussars in the centre and Fusiliers on the right. It was now midday and the temperature had climbed to over 90°F in the shade, the hottest day so far. We were then ordered to advance along an axis as fast as possible.

What followed was like a massive mechanized cavalry charge, Challengers, Warriors, screaming engines and pounding tracks, throwing a sand cloud thousands of feet into the air. The steel fleet of over 200 armoured vehicles stampeded across the desert. It was the first time we had taken the Warrior up to full speed and she sat steadily on her tracks absorbing the undulations in the ground while my driver, Lance Bombardier Covill, kept his eyes glued to the dust cloud that was the Emperor. From inside the turret the view through the periscopes was exhilarating. Outside the sight of an Armoured Brigade at full speed must have been awesome. Perhaps I should have stopped and asked, for suddenly in front of us was a small hill, on top of which was a Bedouin camp. All the inhabitants of the area should have been 'relocated' before the range was built, but often the local people would return without being discovered. Tanks and APCs weaved frantically to avoid tents, camels, satellite dishes, chickens and children. What those Arabs thought can only be wondered at, though I do remember catching a glimpse of a grinning, toothless old man waving a Saudi flag as I flashed by.

Then, almost as soon as we had started, we had stopped. Hatches opened, heat poured from engine decks. The tanks swung round to face down ranges T1 and T2 to fire off the remainder of their training ammunition. It was a spectacular turkey shoot. For us Gunners the exercise was over and so was our work-up training. We were now officially ready for war. I ordered my FOOs to meet me at the REPLEN and, after bidding farewell to Mike Vickery and the 14th/20th, I made my way to the refuelling point. It was getting dark when our small convoy of four vehicles eventually set off to return to the junction of the Tarmac and Pylon Line Roads. On arrival we parked in a tight square about 100 metres from the road junction, fed ourselves and went to bed. Before finally dozing off I again lay and watched the twinkling lights of the circling tanker aircraft and their thirsty customers.

25 JANUARY 1991

We all arose later than planned to a dull but dry day. We had come to this prominent road junction to wait for the technicians from GKN, the vehicle manufacturers. The team, under Paul Harris, had been flown out to deal with the numerous teething problems we had been experiencing. In my own vehicle, communications had been a constant problem, not only with the outside world but also internally within the vehicle. The APES navigation system had been playing up with some crews and the TI sights with others. Such a situation was not wholly unexpected. The Warriors were new and had been rushed into service. It was state of the art technology for which our limited training had not fully prepared us and in my vehicle, a great deal had simply been bodged, as components that had not yet even been manufactured were bypassed using a cat's-cradle of cables.

Warrior crews wait by the road junction for the men from GKN. (AG)

The crews set about the vehicles, sorting and unloading kit, spring-cleaning and repacking and preparing for the GKN team. Sergeant Allen

banished me to the top of the turret, out of the way. Perched on the outside I was able to catch up on the inevitable admin and my own private correspondence. By midday the road junction was very busy with heavily laden convoys moving west, also the sky had cleared and the temperature had soared. I listened on the radio to the Battery being exercised by the CRA and to the order sending them back to their original deployment position astride the Pylon Line Road.

It was mid-afternoon before a somewhat dishevelled GKN team found us. They set about their task with enthusiasm, but they were missing some key people and some of the problems clearly could not be solved in the space of one quick visit. With some more bodging and exhortations to 'Try this!' they eventually departed just before dark with the promise to return the next day. I had to attend David Radcliffe's evening Orders Group, so I scrounged a lift in BC 23 Battery's Landrover, leaving the Warriors to make their own way down a now very rutted and waterlogged Pylon Line Road back to the guns. It was raining heavily when we arrived at A2 Echelon for the meeting. Before the proceedings started I interrogated our EME (the officer responsible for all our vehicle maintenance) as to the whereabouts of my 432 and, more importantly, Sergeant Radcliffe and his crew. He assured me it was at the ECP (Equipment Collecting Point) and all was well. It and they were now a Divisional responsibility and would be returned safe, sound and fixed in due course. Above all I was not to interfere with, or try to short-cut, a tried and tested system. Nothing he said reassured me, in particular his last statement.

David Radcliffe started his Orders with a further exhortation to ensure that everyone realized that, excepting some unforeseen about-turn by Saddam, we were going to war. He then went on to emphasize that the lives of everyone, both at the gun end and those we were supporting forward, would depend on everyone's ability to do their allotted job regardless of the difficulties. At the guns and at the OPs accuracy had to be paramount, as to kill our own side would be the most appalling tragedy. We had to get through on the radio, and we must do everything to ensure that our equipment worked and not just rely on our maintenance crews. He then went on to outline the move to KEYES before the Adjutant gave out the movement details.

The move west would be driven, primarily, by the availability of transporters, and already the 4 Brigade battlegroups were starting their move. The 2nd Regiment move would start with the harbour party on the 27th. All soldiers not travelling with a vehicle could expect to fly on the 30th. The last convoy would be the wheeled vehicles, leaving at 00.01 on the morning of the 30th. On arrival there would be a significantly increased threat as we would be in range of enemy aircraft and artillery. We were therefore to dig in quickly and there was to be no radio traffic or lights.

The Orders Group over, I grabbed a lift with Ray Harper, the Unit Training Officer and Steven Young, the 2IC, who dropped me off at the Battery. The Warriors had parked in their, by now, familiar slots and I was keenly aware that this patch of sand by the Pylon Line had become ours and it was like returning home. To welcome me, the rain fell out of the sky.

26 JANUARY 1991

The dawn rose bright and clear with every prospect of the day being a scorcher. Now back in our old 'homes', the crews set about the vehicle maintenance while I sat down with the BK and BSM to wade through the plethora of administrative chores. It was nearly midday before I was able to return to the Warrior, retrieve my bag of still wet washing and start about the process all over again. With luck it would dry before the next downpour. The BK, BSM and BQMS had worked wonders on this small patch of desert. Each day, to the continuing bewilderment of the US Marines, facilities had grown and improved. For the European, desert life meant prickly heat, foot rot and diarrhoea, mixed with a good dose of dust, flies and the occasional scorpion. Hygiene was our biggest problem. We now fed centrally whenever the situation allowed. Centrally cooked food meant that control could be kept on what was eaten and, most important, what happened to that food which was left over. Disposable plastic plates, knives and forks avoided the need to wash up and the long queue of soldiers lining up to be fed three times a day enabled the BSM and the SNCO management of the Battery to keep a weather eye on all. Strategically placed plastic drainpipes, sunk into the sand at an angle, provided pee shoots, which kept the flies down and removed the temptation to urinate close to the vehicles. These marvels of ingenuity were known as 'Desert Roses'.

My principal concern was Sergeant Radcliffe, his crew and their 432. I did not share our EME's confidence in the system. They were part of my Battery and I wanted personally to see them and to know they were well. I borrowed Lance Bombardier Witt and the PADS Rover and set off to look for myself. We journeyed north via the Regimental A1 and A2 echelons then on to the Brigade RV – all without success. Undaunted, I turned east and after another half-hour's drive came to the Divisional ECP (Equipment Collection Point). I was in time to see the last broken-down vehicle being winched onto a low-loader to be driven west. The NCO in charge of the ECP informed me that, along with the rest of the Division, all maintenance was moving to VII Corps' area, but that my own 432 had been repaired and sent back to the Regiment. Which Regiment? He did not have that gem of information but he went on to give me a dissertation on the problems caused when a vehicle belonging to 2nd Field Regiment has its repairs tasked and documented by the

1. M109 guns line up in the convoy marshalling area at Al Jubayl (AG).

2. Stuck in the sand (AG).

3. First recce with the Forward Observation Officers. *Left to right:* Captain Richard Farndale, Major Andrew Gillespie, Captain Graham Ambrose, Captain Derek Hudson (AG).

4. A 432 stuck in the dreaded Sabka (AC).

5. The first 'gas attack' (AG).

6. Command Post Two. *Left to right:* Lieutenant Hubbard, Gunner Sheppard, Lance Bombardier Worsley, Lance Bombardier Collinson, Bombardier Tilson, the author, Lance Bombardier Douglas (MH).

7. The view from the Divisional RV – a navigator's nightmare (AG).

8. 'The Emperor', having just arrived at KEYES (AG).

9. The 'Optimist' – with the author atop (PN).

10. An Orders Group: *Left to right* Major Al Wicks, Captain Alistair Ross, Major Andrew Gillespie, Major Godfrey Tilney, Lieutenant Colonel Mike Vickery (AW).

11. The artillery raids begin. The first round fired by The Rocket Troop.

12. Moving down cleared lanes from the Breach – tracks left and wheels right (AW).

13. Sergeant Allen and a terrified Iraqi at Objective COPPER SOUTH (AG)

14. Home from home – inside the Iraqi Command Bunker (AW).

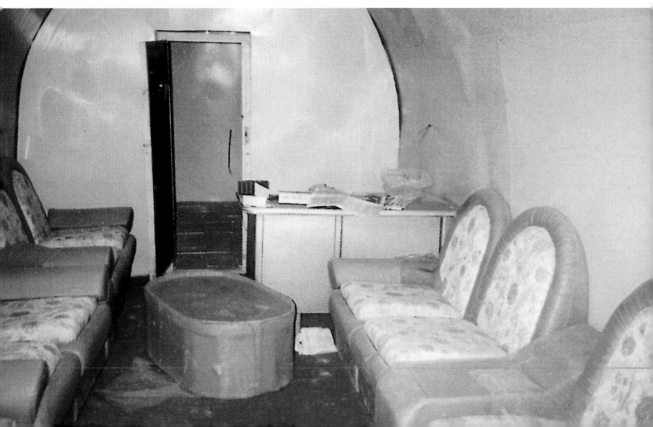

15. The remains of an Iraqi T55 tank at Objective BRASS (AG).

16. The turret of an Iraqi T55 tank (AG).

14th/20th. Matters were further complicated by the fact that it was a Command Vehicle and therefore had the highest priority, so would have been moved to the first maintenance unit that had spare capacity. I left to try to catch the Battlegroup before it moved west.

As I approached the turn-off which would take me to the Battlegroup, I spotted the now familiar silhouette of the Colonel's Land Cruiser. It was perched on top of an adjacent hill. I swung off the road and drove for about a kilometre across country to investigate. The vehicle was on the highest point, but as I crested the hill I saw on the far slope a 4-tonne truck and about twenty soldiers. "Time up," said the Adjutant, and a soldier stepped out of the Toyota, while another walked forward to take his place. A grinning Jonty Palmer explained that he had 'acquired' a car telephone from a friendly expat and they were making the most of it before they moved west and out of range of the only telephone transmitter. Each soldier got five minutes. He kindly let me have a go, and for a few brief moments I was able to speak to Annie.

On reaching the Battlegroup I had a long talk with Mike Vickery, seated outside his trailer caravan, drinking coke. We talked of the move west, the rejoining of my Gunner tac group and the world in general. The one thing he could shed no light on was the fate of my 432, the 14th/20th EME having gone ahead as part of their advance party.

Wearily I made my way home, first down the tarmac then, slowly and uncomfortably, down the long Pylon Line Road. It was dark when I left the Rover and wandered back to the Warrior. I was tired, hungry and not a little frustrated. I was greeted with the latest intelligence update and the news that the desert cinema was visiting tonight. The Intelligence news in the KTO (Kuwaiti Theatre of Operations) was encouraging. The report stated that all nuclear and chemical production facilities had been destroyed along with missile manufacturing sites. There were still a number of Scud launchers remaining, but the majority had been destroyed. Most important, of the 20,000 tons of supplies needed daily by the Iraqi Army, only about 2,000 tons was getting through. The much-feared Republican Guard divisions were enduring over 350 B52 sorties per day, air defence resistance was minimal and there was evidence that their command chain had started to collapse.

About an hour later, cheered by the Intelligence news, fed and watered, I sat with most of the Battery in a hollow square formed by 14-tonne ammo trucks, and watched the film Top Gun. Wonderful! There is a Spitfire pilot in all of us.

27 JANUARY 1991

I was woken at 05.00 by the GPO and BSM. When you are the commander of a unit in a war theatre, being unexpectedly woken at five is alarming enough; to be woken by two very key members of your team all but stops the heart. "We are missing a weapon!" I struggled out of my sleeping bag, dressed and made my way across to one of the guns. I was greeted by Sergeant Tunley, the gun commander. He had held his usual first-light weapons check and a rifle was found to be missing. The crew had buried a mass of rubbish the day before and were now frantically digging in the sand some twenty metres away. Across the gun position crews were checking and rechecking weapons. I was told that a detailed search of the gun and surrounding area had failed to find anything.

Sergeant Tunley was an extremely experienced and professional gun No 1. I took him aside and asked him how this could have happened. He was adamant that weapon checks were done religiously at first and last light and on every move. A check had been done the night before and all weapons had been accounted for. This was supported by the crew's second-in-command. Yet mysteriously a weapon was now missing. After two hours of hard digging and searching it was clear that the weapon was not on the position. I reasoned that we had about eight hours before I had to bare my soul to the system and admit all. If we were to find the weapon we must start with the soldier and work backwards.

After some subtle questioning from the BSM and some less than subtle threats from his No 1, he at last confessed that he had perhaps been less than diligent the night before when he himself had counted the weapons and reported them all correct. He also had a vague memory of leaving his rifle on the front engine decks of the gun prior to their last move. Men and shovels were loaded onto vehicles and the search party, under command of WO2 Windle, departed to scour the last deployment position. They were away nearly three hours but found nothing. Again the BSM took the young Gunner aside. It took some time, but eventually the true story emerged. He had lost his weapon some days earlier but had been too frightened to report it. He always sat on the right-hand side of the turret where the weapons were stored, so, with just a little subterfuge, he could make sure that it was always he that checked the weapons and gave the report to the No 1. It was only our imminent move west, and consequently the possibility that he might go to war unarmed, that had made him report that his weapon was missing.

I left to drive to RHQ to tell David Radcliffe personally. As I walked over to the mass of canvas and cam nets that disguised the headquarters I met Ray Fox, the QM, and told him my unhappy tale. He led me across to his own tent and showed me a bent, rusting, but still identifiable rifle. It had been found by a REME unit and had clearly been run over by a heavy tracked vehicle, probably one of our own guns. As the Regiment was the only unit exercising in that area, he had been waiting for one of the BCs to own up.

74

We were very lucky and yet again a lesson had been learnt. Sergeant Tunley took the whole incident very badly. A No 1 of the old school he took the greatest care and pride in his crew. They became his family and he felt he had been personally betrayed. It was a feeling shared by all those who had needlessly dug, searched and given up their valuable time. By the time I returned the BSM had already taken the precaution of removing the soldier from the Gun Line. I had him moved out of the Battery that day.

Excitement over, the Battery returned to vehicle maintenance and personal admin. Trucks loaded with as many men as could be spared were sent back to Al Jubayl's Camp 4 for showers. By mid-afternoon the sky was grey and overcast and the temperature was dropping by the minute. The wind was getting stronger and starting to lift the sand. By late afternoon the temperature was the lowest we had yet experienced and we were in the grip of a full-blown sandstorm.

28 JANUARY 1991

By now I had been forced to tackle the problem of space and equipment. We had to date been living, not only with what we had carried on the aircraft, but all the goodies we had crammed aboard our vehicles before they were loaded onto ships. In addition we had been issued extra equipment and clothing in theatre and this had again been supplemented by purchases from the PX, plundering of the Americans and parcels from home. In short, we were well provided for, if just a little overcrowded. This state of affairs could not continue indefinitely as we were about to move west and go to war. Ammunition racks would now have to hold ammunition, not kit bags. Comfort was about to become a luxury we could no longer afford. An examination of the likely war load of food, fuel, ammunition, water and chemical protection suits convinced me that we must get rid of everything not considered absolutely essential and we must do it now.

Overcrowding was not a problem unique to O Battery and the question of how to solve it had been raised repeatedly at CO's conferences by the BC's union. The Regiment's answer was to acquire a number of containers at 'Container City' in which unwanted kit could be stored. Already the BQMS had backloaded masses of equipment originally thought indispensable but which experience had shown to be of little use. Since the end of the formal work-up training a steady convoy of trucks had been shuttling back to Al Jubayl so that all members of the Battery could make a final visit to the showers, PX, telephone and container. Today was my turn for the round trip.

I left for Al Jubayl at 09.30, with Derek Hudson, Richard Farndale and all our own and much of our crew's kit, crammed into the BK's Landrover. Our route took us south down the Pylon Line Road, then west to join the main TAP Line road. It took us again past the workings where I had earlier enlisted the help of a bulldozer. Here much had changed and cam nets and Rapier missile launchers could now be seen between the neat rows of crushed limestone. The main road had also changed. It was now a pot-holed and very worn tarmac artery up which flowed an almost unbroken column of vehicles of every size and nature, all plodding one behind the other in a seemingly endless line. The road south was less busy, as trucks, mostly Arab civilian contractors, returned for another precious and no doubt highly profitable load.

After over an hour's driving we turned west for Al Jubayl, passing the American Tent City and the main police traffic control point. It was now very hot and as we passed the main refuse disposal site the wind was blowing clouds of paper and plastic bags across the road. Suddenly there was an ominous grinding noise and the Landrover coasted to a halt. We were still some 5kms from the outskirts of the town, but now off the busy military convoy route so it was some time before a 4-tonner stopped and offered us a tow. It was driven by Driver Taylor of 7 Tank Transporter Regiment, Royal Corps of Transport. He was heading close to Pearl Beach Camp, not the direction we wished to go, but useful none the less as it was now the base of our Regimental rear party. It took over an hour to reach Pearl Beach which was situated next to the sea, just outside the dock area, and a few kilometres from Archiroden Camp. We were later to discover that this concrete, hutted camp had been built for young Saudi bachelors to provide them with controlled, single-sex, holidays. It was now the main Royal Military Police post, transit accommodation for incoming BCRs (Battle Casualty Replacements) and home for the rear parties of 4 Brigade. The Bedford skilfully towed us through the steel chicane marking the entrance and left us on the side of the road opposite the police post.

The Royal Military Police had only a vague idea where each unit was supposed to be and no idea if any one was there. It took us some time to locate 2nd Regiment's hut and moments to ascertain that it was locked and empty. Fortunately fate was smiling on us. As we made our dejected way back to the RMPs we met the Assistant Adjutant of the Royal Scots. He did not know us from Adam, but on hearing of our plight offered to drive us to the containers in his own Land Cruiser. After a hurried telephone call to the Regiment, which we hoped would ultimately result in our recovery, we cross-loaded our kit and set off for Container City.

Container City lived up to its name - literally thousands of containers covering acres, and growing by the day. The BQMS had given me very specific directions, so we found our target, with 'O BTY' chalked on the side, with little difficulty. I unlocked the steel door to be greeted by a wall of boxes, suitcases and kit bags - the penalty one pays for being the last in the queue. We had to all but empty the container, toiling in the sun and heat, before we found our own bags and it was over an hour before we had repacked our belongings and reloaded the container. We then returned to Pearl Beach to await help.

"I would offer you a meal," said an apologetic Assistant Adjutant, "but they are very awkward about who they will feed here." I was tired and I was very hungry. I led my small party across to the cookhouse and joined the long queue of BCRs at the hot-plate. As we approached the food, a Catering Corps Senior NCO who had been standing scrutinizing the soldiers filing past the hot-plate, started to walk towards the unfamiliar group of one Major, two Captains and a Gunner. Before he got within speaking distance I gave him my much-practised "Don't even think about it" look and he peeled off to busy himself elsewhere. We ate a very enjoyable meal with the staff of the Royal Scots, cheered by the food and the news that a truck was on its way to collect us.

At 20.00 Staff Sergeant Fender, my REME Artificer or 'Tiffy' arrived with one of the 14-tonne trucks and a very short tow bar. Gunner Row-Cousins, the driver, hooked us up and, after the appropriate farewells, we started on our three-hour journey north. As we approached the edge of the town the sirens began to wail, signalling that a Scud attack was imminent. Row-Cousins' reaction was to put his foot on the floor and for the next thirty minutes I had to endure my second uncontrolled and terrifying journey of the campaign. On arrival at the Battery all I wanted to do was go to sleep. It was past midnight and very cold. I was greeted by a signal telling me that I was needed by the 14th/20th for an exercise in the new deployment area on Wednesday 30 January. I was to move west as soon as possible. Knowing my response, the BK had already assembled the management team and together we spent some time finalizing the movement plan of the Battery and our deployment options on arrival. I told the GPO to find me a Landrover, driver and rations. They were to be ready to move at first light and he was not to expect to see either of us until we were all in Assembly Area KEYES. Cheered by the news that over 100 Iraqi planes had fled to Iran, I hurriedly packed my own kit before snatching a few hours' disturbed and uncomfortable sleep.

29 JANUARY 1991
At 05.30 I draped my map across the bonnet of the PADS truck and with my driver, Lance Bombardier Witt, and the light of a torch planned my route. It would take us north to the junction of the Tarmac Road, then west to the TAP Line Road, north to MSR (Main Supply Route) DODGE and then westwards for hundreds of kilometres to area KEYES. At the end would be, firstly, the Divisional RV, then the Brigade RV and, finally, with a lot of luck, the 14th/20th King's Hussars Battlegroup.

The distance I estimated to be over 400 kms.

The journey started well enough and we made good time over the roads which were familiar to us. As we reached DODGE and new territory, we began to get a clearer picture of life on the Main Supply Route. Convoys were travelling bumper to bumper, at high speeds and with tired drivers. At regular intervals a wrecked truck, its load scattered all around it, punctuated the flat open expanse of sand and nothing which stretched from the sides of the road to the horizon. Some of the wrecks were horrific and clearly had resulted in the death of their crews, yet convoys sped past them without a second glance or any discernible drop in speed. British, French, American, Egyptian, Saudi and civilian trucks all vied for space on a road built to carry local traffic and the occasional oil pipeline team. In places the surface had completely disintegrated, exposing bare sand and providing countless missiles for wheels to hurl through windscreens. Even more alarming, in some areas the rhythm of wheels had combined with the soft, unstable tar to produce wave formations in the road.

After about two hours' driving, the flat sand landscape began to be broken by high, towering rock formations reminiscent of Clint Eastwood movies. I knew that, back at the Battery, vehicles would be moving down to join low-loaders and those crews not travelling with their vehicles would be getting ready to fly by RAF Hercules. I felt particularly sorry for Geoff Ravenhill who would somehow have to get

View from the road west to KEYES. (AG)

78

The move west – by
air and road. (AG)

our vehicles safely along this insane highway. At about 10.00 we spotted our first shop and pulled off the road to join several other vehicles at the 'Services'.

The shop was the focal point of a small village of about twenty old and dilapidated buildings, many of which looked deserted, I presumed due to the imminence of war rather than economic depression. The word 'depression' is not in the Saudi vocabulary. The shop itself was a single-storey building set some ten metres back from the main road on the T junction which marked the centre of this metropolis. Witt and I joined a line of US Servicemen queuing for the attention of the shopkeeper who dashed back and forth behind the low, very grubby, glass counter. There were sacks, boxes, bundles and trays everywhere. Rice, paraffin and beans rubbed shoulders with transistor radios and Desert Shield T-shirts. Other than the sand and distinctive Gulf aroma, we could have been in the Klondike.

My travels in Nepal had taught me not to eat anything that was not straight out of its skin, a tin or boiling oil, not to be fooled by sealed bottles and never to drink the water. In this far-away watering hole abiding by such rules did not leave one with much of a choice. However, I was determined not to go down with the Arab equivalent of the Katmandu quickstep. When my turn came I bravely purchased a can of Coke and a safe-looking Mars bar.

Our presence in the shop excited a degree of interest amongst the Americans, who, having driven direct from their own mounting base at Dhahran, had not yet encountered the Brits, indeed many did not even know we were in the Gulf. I parried a few good-natured 'Hi mans' and the odd 'How's the Queen', turned down a lucrative offer for my uniform, then wandered outside to consume my goodies. Witt and I were standing watching the traffic thunder by when a green US Army bus

**Convoys on Route
DODGE.** (PW)

pulled to a stop and disgorged its passengers, a contingent of National
Guard nurses, fresh from the States. They swirled by in a cloud of
chatter, long hair, make up and perfume. My head reeled. It had been
weeks since I had seen a female that remotely looked like a female let
alone smelt like one. I now understand why they used to put that stuff
in our tea. Slowly they filed through the shop and slowly the crowd of
nurses around our Landrover grew. For fifteen minutes Witt and I were
famous, the centre of attention and stars of the show. Then at the bark
of a command they were back on their bus and gone.

    We drove on until, without warning, we passed a small black and
white police sign on the side of the road which read '1 UK Armd Div RV
1km.' We continued on, not knowing what to look for but expecting
something impressive. As usual we were disappointed. The Divisional
RV consisted of a sign, a policeman and a motor bike. That was all. I
asked him for directions to 4 Brigade and he pointed to the horizon.
"Follow the tracks for 30kms until you meet a track running from right
to left. Turn left for 10kms and look around you." In this part of the
desert there truly was nothing but hard, coarse sand. No hills, rocks,
plants or animals. It was like being at sea. I later heard one of our North
American cousins describe this part of the desert by saying, "Here you
can watch your dog running away for three days." In the direction the
policeman pointed was not a road or even a track but hundreds of tyre
marks each making their own individual way in a common direction,
towards the horizon and out of sight. It was now midday, sunny, hot and
dusty.

    We set off across the sand, keeping the Landrover in the centre of the
mass of the tyre tracks. It was not long before we had lost sight of route
DODGE and the Divisional RV and were entirely alone. I imagine

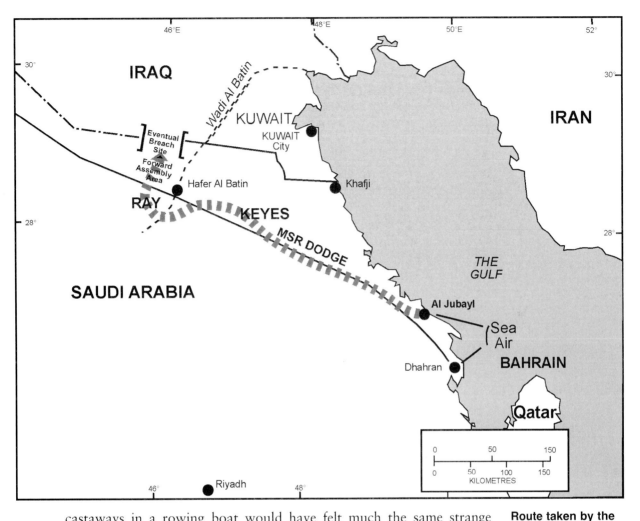

Map labels:
IRAQ
KUWAIT
KUWAIT City
IRAN
Wadi Al Batin
Eventual Breach Site
Forward Assembly Area
RAY
Hafer Al Batin
KEYES
Khafji
MSR DODGE
THE GULF
SAUDI ARABIA
Al Jubayl
Sea
Air
Dhahran
BAHRAIN
Qatar
Riyadh

Scale bar:
0   50   150
0   50   100   150
KILOMETRES

Route taken by the British Division prior to the ground offensive.

castaways in a rowing boat would have felt much the same strange sensation, for it was unnerving to be able to see, totally without interruption, to the skyline in which ever direction one looked. We drove on, mile after mile, until without warning we came to our second small sign, at the head of a T-junction. The junction was simply where the mass of tyre tracks turned left or right. The sign was marked with two arrows, indicating 4 and 7 Brigade RVs. We followed 4 Brigade's tracks until at a second junction we came to a clump of tents and vehicles that marked the entry point to the Brigade area. Sand tracks left this location like the ribs of a fan.

It was now 14.30 and a quick glance at the RMP map of the area showed that we had no hope of being with the 14th/20th by our planned 15.00. The map looked like a single sheet of brown wrapping paper with grid lines. It was devoid of all topographical features. The Brigade RV was marked at the very bottom of the map and the small circle with the

81

14/20H tactical sign was almost at the top. I asked for and was given directions to 4 Brigade MAIN HQ which we found with relative ease by following the densest line of tyre tracks.

The HQ was divided into three distinct areas, separated by a few hundred metres of sand. There was a main complex, a living area and an admin and parking area. Bulldozers had already piled a high protective sand wall around the main complex and were now busily working on the other sites. We parked the Landrover close to the sand wall and booked in with the control point at the entrance to the main complex. I made my way towards the dark tunnel formed by a double row of 432s, parked back-to-back, their rear doors open. Connecting them all was a series of purpose-built canvas penthouses which fitted securely around the doors of each pair of vehicles and linked into the penthouses of the vehicles on the right and left. This provided a light and weatherproof walkway between the armoured vehicles. Suspended over everything were vast desert camouflage nets. As I entered and started down the lane between the vehicles, I passed signs hung on the armoured steel back doors; Int, Maint, Tels, Ops, each with their own small staff working feverishly. From every direction came the all-pervading hum that was a mixture of human chatter, generator engines and radio traffic. I stopped outside the vehicle marked 'Arty Ops' and was greeted by John Buchanan and our own Intelligence Officer, Lieutenant Ben Sharp.

Our immediate need was sustenance and shortly Witt and I were crammed onto the 432's long bench seat, mug and sandwich in hand, getting the latest Intelligence brief. Nothing was new. For every indicator pointing to an inevitable ground war there was one proving conclusively that it would never happen. The Iraqis were, however, active in our sector. A glance at the brown, almost featureless map showed 4 and 7 Brigades deployed side by side with only a light reconnaissance screen from an American cavalry unit between us and the enemy. Somewhat alarming was the fact that the 14th/20th Battlegroup seemed to be on picket duty, deployed as it was forward of all the other divisional units. I also noted the goose eggs drawn on the map, indicating where the artillery units would be deploying on arrival. They were a long way back, too far back to be able to support the 14th/20th should we come under attack. Time was pressing and so, refreshed and replenished, we set off to join the Battlegroup.

I estimated that I would have to travel about 18kms north-east, through either the 3rd Fusiliers or the Royal Scots. It was impossible to read a compass from inside the vehicle and, with a shimmering horizon that was devoid of features, I could not pick a point and drive towards it. I would have been much happier if I had been routed the same way as the Battlegroup; I could have followed their tracks. Unfortunately for me they were not required to check in at the Brigade HQ and had therefore deployed directly from the east. I was a single vehicle, charting a new course, and if I missed my target the Iraqis would no doubt put me straight. I took a bearing off my map, translated it to my compass and pointed the Rover in the desired direction. We set off and after about 15 minutes that horrible feeling of isolation overtook us again. There was nothing, not even a large stone, from horizon to horizon. I did my best to keep on course by looking backwards and applying a correction if our tyre track appeared to waver from a straight line. I also used the vehicles trip and marked off each kilometre on my map to try to keep a record of the distance travelled. Occasionally we crossed tyre and track marks running at right-angles to our route and I had to fight the temptation to turn and follow them. We pressed on. The twilight of early evening was reducing visibility to a few kilometres and the sun was sinking frighteningly fast. Being caught out in the middle of nowhere, this close to the border, would be unsettling.

Bang on target, out of the gloom appeared a series of sand mounds and the familiar outline of Warriors. The 3RRF Battlegroup digging in. Their Motor Transport Officer pointed me in the direction of some tyre tracks and some 7kms later we pulled up beside a small huddle of command vehicles. This was RHQ 14th/20th King's Hussars. Away in the distance the shadowy shapes of single tanks could just be seen. There were no lights or noise anywhere. I made my way through the double blackout curtains and into the small complex to be greeted by Captain Neil Palmer, the Regimental Signals Officer.

The journey had taken us nearly 15 hours. Witt and I were exhausted but very relieved to have made it. After a bite to eat we settled down to spend the night in the Landrover. In the early hours of the morning we felt the consequences of being so far from the sea. The temperature plummeted to way below zero.

30 JANUARY 1991

I awoke stiff and cold to the sound and smell of frying bacon burger. Lance Bombardier Witt was up, bright and cheerful, and was cooking breakfast under the cam net at the rear of the Landrover. What other activity I could see was confined to the small group of Sultan command vehicles of RHQ, huddled together on the flat sand, some fifteen metres distant. I could see the Emperor, parked on its own a few hundred metres away. Shimmering on the horizon, at 10 and 2 o'clock as I looked north, were two of the squadrons. Otherwise there was only wide-open sand nothing, the other squadron and the company having yet to materialize from the morning haze.

Fed and watered, I wandered across to RHQ. No, they had not seen my 432 but they were confident it would turn up. I did not share their confidence. There was nothing I could do anyway, for today was the start of Exercise MUSSANAH STORM, the 1 (British) Armoured Division Command Post Exercise (CPX). I was soon seated in the back of the Battlegroup Commander's Land Cruiser and, together with the Operations Officer, Captain Alistair Ross, was bouncing along the increasingly rutted track towards Divisional HQ.

The exercise started with a briefing at 08.00. The CPX ground on all morning with no one in the Battlegroup required to do much more than say 'Roger out' occasionally. After lunch we went into practical (CFX) mode organized by the American 1st Infantry Division (Mechanized). This was to be the first rehearsal for what was to happen come the great day. All the British Division seemed to be there in some guise or other and so a real social atmosphere prevailed as we caught up with old friends and the latest news. We started by driving in convoy to look at, and then drive across, an American-made obstacle. It was a replica of the Iraqi defensive sand berm and was some 5kms long and orientated the same way as the real thing. As I sat in the back of the Land Cruiser, slowly moving in the midst of the Divisional column, I saw my first Apache helicopter. Dark and very sinister, it was flying a slow parallel path about 100ft off the ground and 500metres to our right. Occasionally it would hover, turn and appear to line up its weapon systems on the long line of vehicles meandering across the desert. It was presumably from the Air Cavalry Regiment, on picket duty to our north, there to act as a trigger should the Iraqis suddenly attack south. I was delighted to have them between us and the enemy; however, I was not so keen to have them use me for target practice. The thought of some hot-shot pilot's finger pressing a button just that little bit too hard and sending a missile my way gave me a distinctly uneasy feeling.

While all this was going on, back at HQ 14th/20th, a new engine for my 432 had arrived, from where we knew not. Finding no vehicle it departed, to an equally unknown destination.

We returned to the Divisional HQ at about 17.00 to great excitement. The Iraqis had attacked south near the coast and the Saudis and the Marines were engaged in a fierce fight. Information was at best sketchy, so, after the usual speculation, everyone settled down again to the demands of the exercise. Once it was dark we again drove through the US-made obstacle and, after a refuel at A1 echelon, returned to the CPX just after midnight. It had all gone extremely well and any reservations we had about working with the Americans had largely evaporated. Unlike the Marines, the US Division was from Germany, well motivated, in good order and we spoke a common language. There was a general feeling of confidence in the American Army's ability to deliver the goods. I instructed the signaller to wake me only if we were in imminent danger of being overrun and went to sleep in the back of the Land Cruiser.

31 JANUARY 1991

The morning briefing told us a little more of the drama unfolding to our east. It appeared, from what scant information we had received on the command net and the very full report from the BBC, that an Iraqi armoured brigade had captured the unoccupied small town of Khafji, some 12kms into Saudi territory. There had been a brief engagement with both the US Marines and some Saudi armour, but the Coalition had not yet got its act together to counter-attack. A look at the map showed that the town was of no strategic or military significance whatsoever, which was probably the reason that the Saudis had abandoned it in the first place. Equally, the Iraqi force was of no threat, being in a known location, isolated from its artillery and logistic support and devoid of air cover. The smart thing to do was to leave the Iraqis where they were. For certain that would not be the case, as Arab pride, politics and Coalition solidarity demanded that Khafji be retaken regardless of the cost.

The CPX droned on with the heat inside the green canvas command post rising steadily with the movement of the sun. Interest in the far from taxing procedural exercise waned as unconfirmed reports arrived of Iraqi tank movement to our west. At just after midday the Brigade was placed on 6 hours' notice to move. John Buchanan rang to tell me that they were working on plans to bring the guns forward if enemy movement could be confirmed. They would, however, be used to support the US Cavalry Regiment to our front, so in any eventuality I, together with my tac group, were to stay with the exercise. The one piece of good news he was able to give me was that my Warrior had arrived at the RV and had gone to get some 2.5 tonnes of Chobham Armour fitted. No more reports were received to spark movement or to fuel speculation and the CPX finally spluttered to a halt at 23.00. I returned to the 14th/20th RHQ tired and cold and struggled into the back of the Landrover. Lance Bombardier Witt was sleeping soundly under the cam net.

1 FEBRUARY 1991

The day was technically a rest day. For me, with only Witt and the Landrover, it certainly would be. The day was sunny and hot and I took the opportunity to sort out my kit and do some washing. I spent the bulk of the day in my flip-flops, my feet not having seen daylight for some time. Mid-morning, we lined up for our second Anthrax jab and, horror of horrors, a Bubonic Plague jab. Bubonic Plague is one of the most infectious diseases known to man and, although it can now be cured, it must be treated within 12 hours of the first symptoms or it is invariably fatal. While Plague was on the menu of biological weapons, its use by the Iraqis was considered unlikely. The real risk was to unprotected Europeans entering enemy trenches and dugouts where troops had been living for months in what was assessed to be very unsanitary conditions.

85

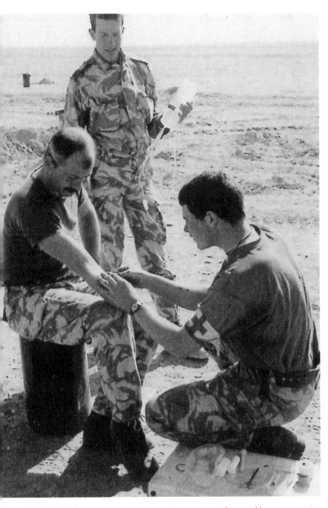

First Aid training...how to fit a drip. (AW)

Bubonic Plague being endemic to the region, the risk of infection was considered very high. With little chance of meeting the 12-hour treatment deadline, the jab was a sensible precaution. Once again they were deep-muscle and hurt like hell. Again some of the troops were pole-axed for about 48 hours with flu-like symptoms and again, fortunately, I was fine.

At 14.00 the Colonel and I went to the Brigade Orders Group. The continuing rumours of Iraqi movement in our area remained unconfirmed. There were, however, graphic tales of US A10 aircraft and C130 Gun Ships 'Puff the Magic Dragon' in action against the Iraqi front-line troops. Otherwise there was little news of consequence. At the end of the briefing I was introduced to Robert Fox of the *Daily Telegraph* who would remain with the Battlegroup until whatever was to happen happened.

In the east the fighting around Khafji was coming to an end. There were conflicting reports, but it appeared that the Iraqis had sustained heavy casualties. Once again the BBC was ahead of our own information system. General Schwarzkopf was in good heart, declaring to the World's airwaves that all was going to plan. The Air War had destroyed thirty-eight of the forty-five bridges on the supply routes from Iraq into Kuwait. Most encouraging of all was the report that Russia and the USA had put forward a joint peace initiative which, it was claimed, encompassed the whole of the Middle East.

In the evening there was another flap with, again, reports unconfirmed of Iraqi troop movement to our west. The Battlegroup being the most northerly deployed of the British force was reduced from 6 on 2 hours' notice to move. I considered that a bit sharp and rang 2nd Field's Operations room to tell them that my particular armoured force was supported by a BC in a Landrover. They agreed that if notice was further reduced they would send a 432 and crew forward; however, as the Americans to our front had seen nothing, such an eventuality was unlikely. In fact we were increased to 3 hours' NTM just after midnight. That was good enough for me and I and my very sore arm retired to bed.

2 FEBRUARY 1991

I rose quite early, aching from the cold and my cramped sleeping position in the Landrover. As soon as I was dressed I wandered the twenty or so paces to the Ops vehicle to get confirmation from the duty watch-keeper that we were still on 3 hours' notice to move. We were. All was well and so breakfast could be both leisurely and enjoyable. Having eaten, I joined all available staff for what was to become a daily ritual, the Intelligence update given by the Intelligence Officer, Captain Richard Pakenham-Walsh, 13th/18th Hussars. The news was encouraging. The Republican Guard Force divisions had taken the brunt of the night's air activity, in particular the Tawalkana Division had taken a pounding. The Division's score was now:

Tanks: 122 destroyed, 34 damaged, 66 remaining.

APCs: 59 destroyed, 3 damaged, 187 remaining.

Artillery: 12 destroyed, 14 damaged, 78 remaining.

The wider picture gave the same message of Coalition success:

Airfields: 24 out of 44 were damaged and a further 10 were non-operational.

Logistics: The main highways had been carpet-bombed. It was now assessed that supplies to the Kuwait theatre had been reduced from 120,000 to 80,000 tonnes per day. It was estimated that if supplies could be cut to 45,000 tonnes per day, then the Iraqi force could not sustain itself. Predumped stocks were, however, assessed as still being considerable.

Things were looking good, but I had heard too many 'Intelligence' briefings before ever to put money on their reliability. It did, however, raise morale. My priority for the day was to track down my 432. Witt and I headed south towards where we hoped the Battery was deploying. The first hour took us through what was now becoming familiar territory. First through our own A1 Echelon then past the Fusiliers, their Warriors spread out in company groups, rapidly being walled in with high banks of sand. The Royal Engineers must have been working through the night because the banking work was almost complete. We travelled on across the featureless desert, past 4 Brigade HQ, now a sprouting mass of aerials and cam nets peeking over the sand barriers, on to the Brigade RV, which had also grown. Around the original RMP tent there was now a Bath unit, Postal unit and, operating from three containers, a NAAFI. From this point we were reliant on sand tracks and pointed directions. Second Field Regiment was positioned well to the south of the Brigade, the batteries about 5 kms apart, deployed in a loose triangle with RHQ and the Echelons in the centre. We had to visit every Battery before we finally found The Rocket Troop.

The desert in which the Battery was deployed was still hard, lifeless sand, but here the surface had started gently to undulate. The guns, still in their box formation, were tucked, wherever possible, into the folds in

Royal Engineers building protective sand walls. (AC)

the ground, making them difficult to see until you were very close. Already a lot of protective engineering work had been done and two bulldozers were still hard at it. However, unlike the Warriors and the Challengers, which needed the sand for initial concealment only, the guns were being dug in to fight. Each pair of guns was parked, side by side, in deep gun pits which enabled the massive bulk of the M109 to be hidden below ground level, exposing only the turret and barrel. To the front and sides sand walls were erected and over the whole structure went a massive cam net. To the rear of the guns, in a similar construction, were the M548 tracked ammunition limbers, one per gun, while to the left and right, burrowed into the sand, were the crew living shelters. Construction was still at an early stage, but as I walked from gun to gun with the BK it was clear that the crews were glad to be doing something positive. They knew how vital this work might be.

I spent an hour or so walking round the position, talking to the crews. The conversation was a mixture of tales of the move up from them, what

Sergeant Radcliffe, Gunner Newell and the 432 Command Post. (PN)

I knew compared with what they knew of events and the 'It will be all right' speech from me. They were clearly in good spirits and I was heartened by how genuinely pleased they all were to see me. I finished my tour at the CP and, after a lengthy session with the BK and BSM on the inevitable administration, I drove the few hundred yards to the Battery echelon which was parked up waiting to be called onto the position once their pits had been prepared. There I found Sergeant Radcliffe, his crew and the 432, complete with new engine.

Sergeant Radcliffe's tale was a salutary one. He had been forced to stand idly by while one unit after another had attempted to marry up 432 and engine. He had been transported between numerous vehicle repair dumps, each time being forced to move west as part of the Divisional move just before the engine caught up. By dint of his own ingenuity he had found his way to the Battery and our own REME fitter section had somehow 'acquired' an engine and fitted it. That had taken him until the previous day and, knowing that I would visit the Battery as soon as I could, he had decided to stay put and await my arrival. We greeted each other with the question uppermost in all our minds, 'Do you have the mail?' Sadly none of us did. Our last delivery was back on the Pylon Line Road and we were all now desperate for some news from home. Investigation revealed that Richard Farndale had collected a mass

A 432 receives a new engine. (HM)

Chobham armour being fitted at Repair Point 7 Alpha. (AG)

of mail from the Brigade RV. Further investigation revealed that the four Warriors, having been dropped some 40kms short of their original RV by nervous Arab drivers, were now at Repair Point 7 Alpha. I gave Sergeant Radcliffe directions to the 14th/20th Battlegroup and set off for 7 Alpha.

The dust cloud hanging over 7 Alpha identified it from miles away, so our journey, if tedious, was easy. It was a repair and recovery area and broken-down vehicles of every kind mingled with low-loaders, wreckers, tracked recovery vehicles and their crews. The place covered acres and was a hive of activity. As well as repairs, 7 Alpha was the 4 Brigade up-armouring base. Warriors were lined up in neat rows in various stages of undress. Crews were removing the side panniers and bins, then, with the aid of a forklift truck, bolting heavy panels of Chobham Armour to the sides and the front. Every 15 minutes or so a Chinook helicopter would deliver more armour, suspended in nets beneath the twin rotors. It was this that was creating the distinctive dust cloud. All four of my Warriors had just left.

I made my weary way back to 14th/20th RHQ. We arrived about an hour before sunset and as I approached from the south I could see a freshly uparmoured Warrior parked up between the Colonel's and his 'wing man's' tank, making a tight tac group of three vehicles some two hundred yards from RHQ itself. As I pulled up along the sand wall surrounding the MAIN HQ I saw that my 432 was sitting inside the defensive perimeter but had not yet been inserted into the command complex. I was met by Sergeant Radcliffe who explained rapidly that he had my mail, food was ready and he would move the vehicle in slow time tomorrow. Oh, and by the way, I had ten minutes before the Orders

Group which would now be a daily fixture until further notice. I noted, ate, ducked under the canvas cover of the Operations vehicle and waded through an hour of vehicle reports, demands for spares and situation updates. There was little new information, indeed an air of calm seemed to have settled after the days of rumour and alarm.

I decided to base myself with the 432, but before I went to bed I wandered across to the Warrior and Sergeant Allen and his crew. They were all well and their move up had been straightforward and uneventful. In spite of the extra 2.5 tonnes now hanging on the Warrior, its performance was as impressive as ever, indeed it was now even steadier at high speed; it also now boasted an electrically driven 7.62mm Hughes Chain Gun. The gun was on the left-hand side of the turret, but both crew members could fire it using their foot pedals. Sergeant Allen explained that before it could be fired it had to be cocked and, as yet, we did not have a cocking lever. There were none in theatre. In lieu we had a socket and wrench from the tool kit. Wonderful! I made my way back to the 432, its penthouse and my sorely missed camp bed. I spent an hour or so reading the massive backlog of mail which seemed to have come from every one I knew or had ever known, and then went to sleep. Bliss!

An up-armoured Optimist and crew: Sergeant Allen, Lance Bombardier Covill, Gunner Lyons and Bombardier Wilkins. (AG)

3 FEBRUARY 1991

Sunday, a quiet day. Sergeant Radcliffe moved the 432 into the complex and then created a degree of alarm and despondency by starting to dig a shelter for the crew, complete with overhead protection. His efforts were first greeted with sceptical derision from the other crews, but he continued to dig stalwartly, pausing only to embellish his "what artillery can do to you if you are not prepared" anecdotes. One by one the other crews broke ranks and began to dig. I attended a Divisional planning conference at 09.00 with the Colonel and then parked myself with the Landrover and waded through the backlog of correspondence. The letters were as varied as they were numerous and all, in their way, most welcome. One was from an Ex-Battery Commander of The Rocket Troop. He had commanded in Libya and was passing on some 'Useful Tips.' The highlight of the morning was watching the OP crews have their jabs.

By midday a sandstorm was blowing and, although visibility remained reasonable, movement outside was uncomfortable. Now that all my vehicles were with me I ran into the first glitch of the logistic system. It was axiomatic that joining units arrived with their first-line scaling, the battlegroup being responsible for subsequent resupply. This system was now operating, but, to the consternation of the complete logistics chain, the battlegroups had formed before most of the ammunition had even docked. My first-line scale of 9mm and 7.62mm bullets, 94mm anti tank rockets, hand and smoke grenades was significant and beyond the resources of QM 14th/20th. My ammunition was some miles away at 2nd Field Regiment and was showing every likelihood of remaining there. By mid-afternoon the promised delivery had failed to arrive and so, being out of direct contact with echelon, I dispatched Witt and the Landrover back to 2nd Field but with orders not to attempt to return until daylight next morning.

After supper we played Monopoly while the sandstorm reached gale force. Derek won (again!)

4 FEBRUARY 1991

The day rose bright and settled, though the night's storm had left everything covered in a fine dusting of sand, which penetrated everywhere. Half-way through breakfast we were attracted outside by the excited chatter of voices. Other than the man-made sand berms, the desert in our area was completely flat and totally featureless. It resembled a calm sand sea, with one small exception. About 150 metres from RHQ was an area about twice the size of a snooker table. We speculated that this was a spot where some wandering nomad, some many moons ago, had stopped to feed his camels. He must also have spilt some of the grain for, over the last few days, to everyone's

The lone white donkey. (AG)

astonishment, this small patch of sand had turned green. Now, this morning, in the centre of the green shoots stood a white donkey. Where it had come from, how it had found the grass, was a total mystery. Had this been Ireland they would have built a shrine to the miracle. As it was not, and knowing no one would ever believe me, I took a photograph of the apparition and went back to my breakfast. The soldiers christened it 'Corporal Saddam'.

Having eaten, I stood outside and listened to the Intelligence update. Total Iraqi losses were now assessed as tanks: 476, APCs: 200, artillery: 339. The regular army divisions had been the focus of most of the recent air activity and 6 Division was 61% effective, 16 Division was 42% effective and 25 and 21 Divisions were 54% effective. The Tawalkana Division was down to 79% effective. This was strange considering the losses reported earlier. My suspicions about the reliability of our Intelligence confirmed, I wandered off for what was to be the first of many 'interviews' with Robert Fox.

Robert Fox was part of the accredited news pool. As such he was an official newsman with the backing of the Army and the protection of the Geneva Convention. As the post suggested, his stories and reports went back to a central pool for access and use by all the media. Accreditation provided him with a uniform, protection, transport, NBC kit, indeed all the comforts of home and, most important, information. In return he went where he was told, did what he was told, his copy went through the military censor and he was under the wing of a minder. If the balance was right it should work to the mutual benefit of all parties. That was the theory anyway. Robert had been assigned by the news pool to the 14th/20th Kings Hussars Battlegroup. He was a war correspondent without a war. He was bored.

Bespectacled, sandy haired and amiable, Robert's answer to his editor's never-ending demand for news was an article on The Rocket Troop. Mindful that, in media terms, 7 Brigade had already stolen the limelight and within 4 Brigade the artillery were likely to remain an unglamorous and well-kept secret, I took what I thought would be my only opportunity to put the Battery and the Royal Regiment on the map. After an 'in depth' interview followed by much thumping of typewriter keys, the article was on its way.

At midday Witt returned with the BQMS and our first issue of operational ammunition. It was very nearly a truck full, but not enough. The realization that 2,000 rounds of belted 7.62 ammunition takes up half the turret but represents only four minutes' fire came as something of a shock. Ten hand grenades per man seemed reasonable until we had to try and stow fifty somewhere on the vehicle. There is a finite number of places suitable for the storage of live grenades. With the 'Q' came more mail, this time a parcel from Peter and Avril Grimwood, a couple I had met beside the pool in Penang, Malaysia. The parcel contained soap, a few goodies and a brief note hoping that I would 'enjoy the shampoo.' A quick smell and a long taste ensured that if this 'shampoo' went to my head it would not get there via my hair.

Today was also the start of Exercise DIBDIBAH DRIVE, a 1st (British) Armoured Division Formation Training Exercise. Mike Vickery had been away at a VII (US) Corps symposium and returned mid-afternoon to give orders. Before we sat down he asked me if I would take Robert Fox as a permanent member of my Warrior crew. As there was not the room in a tank my vehicle was the only practical option if he was to go into battle. I reluctantly agreed. Sergeant Allen was not amused. As a Northern Irishman he was not a great lover of the Press and saw this newsman as extra baggage, an extra mouth and an extra worry. It was one of Sergeant Allen's many tasks to ensure that the vehicle, its crew and all its equipment would get me around the battlefield. A journalist was not welcome and he didn't care who knew it.

It became very clear at the Orders Group that this exercise was in fact a rehearsal for 1 (British) Armoured Division's breach crossing. We were to practice the following:

1. A long move to a Staging Area.
2. The occupation of the Staging Area.
3. The firing of the breach fire plan.
4. The move from the Staging Area to the breach.
5. The transit of the breach.
6. The deployment into 1 Infantry Division (Mechanised) area.
7. The move out of the bridgehead.
8. An advance to contact.

The Chief of Staff painted the exercise picture, the fictitious scenario that would give meaning and life to our activities. The Brigade Commander gave our Mission as 'To rehearse the transit of the breach and the forward passage of lines with 1 Infantry Division (Mechanized).' He

94

then went on to give a general outline of events. In the exercise setting we had advanced into the future and 1st (British) Armoured Division was already in TAA (Tactical Assembly Area) RAY. The Brigade would now depart from RAY on routes BLACK, WHITE and GREEN and move to Staging Areas S1, S2, S3 and S4. The 14/20H Battlegroup was to go to S3. From S3 we would be led forward by US Military Police and guided through the breach. On exiting the breach we would be picked up by our own recce and Royal Military Police and taken into the small Staging Area. On orders, we would pass through the forward American troops (a Forward Passage of Lines), cross our Start Line and 'break out'.

For over an hour I sat taking down orders and peering at maps and diagrams. The orders went through the complicated and detailed instructions necessary to execute the Mission. The recce group would move first, to prove the routes and to be in position ready to receive the main body. Battlegroup Tac HQ would move as a single packet, less the two tanks, One One Bravo (The Emperor) and One One Charlie, which would move on transporters, to save fuel, and would rejoin in the Staging Area.

We were given a series of CPs (Critical Points), which when programmed into the navigation system would get us to the start of route BLACK. We were to be at the Start Point at 18.10 where we would join the Brigade Liaison Group, then be led down route BLACK by the Americans, to emerge at the Release Point at 19.56. All timings were critical. From there we would be collected by our own recce and led into S2, tracks on the left, wheels on the right. Behind us, at staged intervals throughout the night, the Battlegroup would undertake a similar move, a long drive, a Start Point, down route BLUE and into S3. Last packet in at 23.21 hrs.

The Emperor being prepared to move from KEYES to RAY.
(AG)

With no tanks, Battlegroup Tac HQ consisted only of my Warrior. Now without his tank, Mike Vickery opted to travel with me. Mindful of how critical navigation would be and of Sergeant Allen's skill with the SATNAV, I graciously let the Colonel travel up in the turret while I dozed in the back with my two signallers and a bemused journalist.

We were now carrying two extra passengers and all their kit. It was cramped. I sat at the rear opposite Robert Fox and jousted for leg room. By the base of the turret, on either side, sat Gunner Sean 'Killer' Lyons and Bombardier Brian 'Pip' Wilkins. Up in the turret Sergeant Steve Allen was giving directions to the driver, Lance Bombardier Alan Covill. Collectively they made up the crew. We were moving on radio silence, but all three sets were on stand-by and, in partnership with the massive diesel engine, pushed the temperature in the crew compartment to an almost unbearable level. We made good progress initially, entering route BLACK smack on time. We were now in the hands of the US Military Police. The speed down route BLACK was 15 kph, both to conserve fuel and, ultimately, to avoid producing a dust cloud that might herald our intentions. The Warrior clearly was not happy at this speed, for the engine alternately screamed and struggled as it changed up and down the gears. We sat, hot, hunched and uncomfortable, sometimes trying to chat or eat and drink but constantly watching the time. When our due time at S2 came and went I asked Sergeant Allen for a SITREP. "The Yanks are lost," came the terse reply from Mike Vickery. We eventually made it about an hour late.

When the back doors finally opened, I tumbled from the oven into the blessed coolness of the night air. We were in a column of vehicles, at the rear of 4 Brigade HQ to be exact. In the moonlight I could see, to my left and right, the shadowy outlines of other columns. This was Staging Area 2. I spent some minutes walking up the column to stretch my legs and find out what was going on. Crews that had arrived earlier were already sound asleep, and when the Brigade watchkeeper told me that he would wake everyone as soon as he was warned of Orders I went back to the vehicle and told everyone to get to bed. I slept on the roof, knowing from experience that I would have to get up long before the crew. As I lay in my sleeping bag, staring at the sky, I just had time to wish the twinkling aircraft lights good luck and safe return before I fell asleep.

5 FEBRUARY 1991.

I was awakened by the guard shaking my foot. "Orders in 15 minutes, Sir." It was still dark, the stars shone and I could feel the near-zero temperature on my face. Below me in the vehicle the crew slept on. I jumped down onto the soft sand and headed up the row of vehicles.

The Orders when they came were largely confirmatory, given by the Brigade Chief of Staff using a large map hung on the Command Post door. The exercise scenario had the artillery fire plan in support of the American attack well under way with all the British artillery in action. Friendly progress and enemy reaction was unclear. 4 Brigade was at one hour's notice to move. On orders, we were to move forward across line CHERRY (the front edge of the Staging Area) and, guided by American Military Police, we would cross phase-line VERMONT and be led on to WISCONSIN (the entrance to the obstacle). We were to pass through the obstacle down lanes cleared by the American engineers and marked using large orange letter boards. In our case, tracks on route K, wheels on route L. At the end of the obstacle, line COLORADO, we would be met by our own recce and guided into our FUP (Forming Up Position) behind the Battle Hand-over Line, NEW JERSEY. That was the plan. If we were to do it for real, it would provide the Iraqis with the perfect opportunity to shell or gas the hell out of us.

It was daylight when I returned to the crew. They were up and breakfast was on. I ate, briefed them and settled down for what I knew would be a long wait. About mid-morning the two Tac HQ tanks arrived and we were replenished with fuel; during this I had cause to climb onto the roof of the Warrior. The sun was out but the heat of the day had not yet distorted the visibility. Stretched out across the desert, in great columns, was the 1st (British) Armoured Division. It was an awesome and spectacular sight. Away to my left was 7 Brigade with its preponderance of tanks and to my right our own Battlegroup in its squadron and company lines. In my own line was 4 Brigade MAIN HQ and the Tac HQs of the Brigade's three battlegroups. Because we had arrived last, we were behind both the Royal Scots and the Fusiliers. We Tac HQs would move as a single group, only rejoining our individual battlegroups in the FUP.

It was an exercise. There was no live ammunition and no guns really firing. It was all pretend, the activity being acted out on the ground and on the airways. We were attempting to rehearse what could be one of the most hazardous operations of war, a formal Passage of Lines; the passing of one major formation through another, possibly in contact with the enemy. This particular manoeuvre was further complicated by the differences in nationality of the two forces. It was difficult, dangerous and relied on rigid drills and procedures for success - the reason why we were rehearsing.

If a ground war was ordered, the American 1st Infantry Division (Mechanized), 'The Big Red One,' with the aid of a massive artillery barrage, would forge a breach in the Iraqi obstacle belt and widen it into a breach-head some 15kms wide and 18kms deep. Once firm and the lanes had been cleared and marked, the British Division would transit the breach, regroup and break out. This would be made doubly difficult if we had to fight our way through and then out of the breach. The secret of success lay in command and control. To achieve this, the formation passing through sent its command elements to colocate with the receiving units' HQs. Our own Brigade Commander, with his Tac HQ, was already forward with the American Brigade HQ. We in turn would link up with the Task Force whose area the Battlegroup would pass through, getting an up-to-date situation report on events, friendly force and enemy locations, artillery targets and, ultimately, take over the battle.

It was not until 13.00 that our column, led by a US police detachment in a HMMW V, crossed line CHERRY and started to make its way towards the breach. We moved in a tight packet at the end of the column, Challenger, Challenger, Warrior. As per the Standard Operating Procedures for crossing breaches, we had our NBC suits on, with respirators ready close by. Sitting high in the turret I could see to my left and right long, snaking columns of vehicles all making their meandering way towards their designated lane in the obstacle. I was very quickly struck by the distances involved. I had pictured from the briefing diagram a short move, down a lane and out the other side. This clearly was not to be. We travelled for nearly an hour, losing sight of the other columns in the shimmering heat. Eventually we stopped short of a sand wall with a bulldozed gap, lots of white and orange plastic tape, and Americans. We waited. Clearly something was wrong. I saw, way ahead at the front of our column, some of the Brigade staff leave their vehicles and go into a huddle with the US Police. The message eventually made its way down the line. The MPs had got lost. We were in the wrong place. It would take some time to sort out. On the basis that if you can do nothing, don't interfere, I sat in my turret and contemplated the meaning of life.

"Sir, give a starving man a decent meal, Sir." I looked down to see two US soldiers looking up at me. One was holding up a box of MREs. "Any chance of an exchange, Sir?" If an army marches on its stomach it was fortunate for the Americans that they had a lot of transport. British rations, the much-maligned Compo, was bulky, heavy, difficult to cook, nutritious, delicious and filling. The American MREs, Meals Ready to Eat (the three lies in one/Meals Rejected by Ethiopians) were slim, light-weight, easy to cook, reasonably edible, but had no bulk whatsoever. The Brits liked them as they made convenient mid-morning and evening snacks. The Americans loathed them for they left them half-starved. Consequently our own MREs (Meals Ready to Exchange) were in great demand. Having confirmed with Sergeant Allen that we were carrying surplus rations (as usual) and been briefed on the current exchange rate, boxes of rations changed hands in the true spirit of international harmony, but distinctly in our favour (as usual). The boiling vessel was filled, the bags dropped in and it was meal-time. For me, meatballs in tomato sauce followed by crackers and peanut butter.

Movement at last! Mike Vickery waved me over to the Emperor and told me that, if we were to salvage anything from this fiasco, we would have to find the right lane and the smart answer was to head off independently. We set off, running parallel to the obstacle belt until we came to the next manned breach. Here we were greeted by a stunningly attractive female American Military Police Officer who directed us to a small huddle of British 432s parked to the left of the transit lane. They were part of the traffic control system and could do little other than confirm that the 14th/20th Battlegroup was safely through the breach and eagerly awaiting our arrival in the Forward Assembly Area. Ignoring US directions, which would have sent us directly through one of the minefields, we left to rejoin the exercise.

We were with the Battlegroup just long enough to be told that we were to practise the breach crossing again, only this time in the dark. A long sweeping route finally brought us back into the Brigade HQ line in our original Staging Area. Here we were refuelled and sat down to await nightfall.

It was a long, cold and very dark night punctuated regularly by massive flashes in the sky to our north. The air forces were hard at work. We were not due to move forward until 04.30, so I caught what sleep I could on the roof of the Warrior. From my left and right came the noise of armour on the move, but I had no way of telling if it was vehicles arriving or departing. One fear was that, once we had broken out from the breach, we would meet such strong enemy resistance that we would be forced back. We would then be faced with the problem of withdrawing in contact back towards the American defended breach. The scope for fratricide was enormous, so we needed some very clear identification marks. As withdrawing vehicles would approach with their guns towards the enemy, it was decided to place a red light on the back of each turret to be illuminated during the transit, break-out and, if necessary, the withdrawal. This had an added advantage for me as I did not have a thermal sight, so was reliant on my much less capable Image Intensifying sight. The red torch shone as a clear white dot on my otherwise green screen, making following the tanks easy.

6 FEBRUARY 1991

At 04.30 we moved off, in column, in the darkness; I presume behind an American guide. I travelled for the first part of the journey down in the turret, the hatch securely closed and my face glued to the green flickering world that was my night sight. Suddenly there was darkness. The sight had broken. I pushed the large butterfly switch to its optical position, but, other than the odd pinprick of red light, I was blind. I opened the hatch and pumped my seat until I could just see over the armoured shutter protecting my periscope. It was bitterly cold and inky black. To my left Sergeant Allen, eyes glued to his sight, was passing the occasional direction to the driver who could probably see better than anyone. A glance below and behind me showed the rest of the crew fast asleep. I closed the hatch, sank back into the turret and started to doze.

Clearly a lot of lessons had been learnt. A move, breach transit, reorganization and replenishment and an advance to contact came to a successful conclusion at midday. For our part it meant simply following the vehicle in front. The advance had been designed to bring the British Division back close to its Concentration Area. It was only a short distance from our Release Point, through our REPLEN, back to our leaguer. Breakfast was the last of the MREs. The weather was fortunately sunny. We had spent the whole exercise in our NBC suits and were now black from the charcoal which had flaked from the inside. Strip washes and laundry kept most of us occupied all afternoon. Ration packs were delivered, supplemented this time by some eggs and bread rolls. Bliss. Orders were at 16.00 followed by a disastrous curry and then bed by 19.00. I had had about six hours' proper sleep in three days. My ears were sore from the unrelenting pressure of my head-phones and they rang from the incessant noise. Worse still, my back ached constantly. In spite of my exhaustion, I was a long time getting to sleep.

7 FEBRUARY 1991

A sunny, relaxed, make and mend day for the 14th/20th. Not for the Gunners! I had to be at the A1 echelon to hear the Brigade Commander talk to 2nd Field Regiment. I borrowed Mike Vickery's Landrover and, with Robert Fox, set off to collect my three FOOs. Finding a Warrior within an armoured squadron is easy as there is only one. Trying to find Richard Farndale in the midst of a well-spaced and dug-in infantry company proved an unexpected problem. It took ages and caused us to arrive late. David Radcliffe was not impressed and told me so. Brigadier Christopher Hammerbeck talked to all the Officers of the Regiment. He spoke of the likelihood of war, about what to expect and the importance of preparing ourselves mentally for what might lie ahead. I particularly remember he laid great emphasis on writing a last letter home, to be held safely and sent to our loved ones should we be killed. There and then I determined that I would do no such thing. I could not imagine myself able to put on paper any words that would adequately express my feelings to Annie and the children. Besides there appeared a degree of defeatism in the gesture and in times of real desperation the knowledge that I had left such a letter might just be enough to make me give up. The Commander then toured each Battery in turn, talking to the crews.

Commander gone, I spent much of the remaining day on the inevitable admin matters with the BK and BSM and walking round the position with the GPO and Robert Fox. At C Sub we were greeted by a small crowd led by one of the Gun Line Section Commanders, WO2 Ian Mullin. They were admiring a curvaceous, skimpily clad siren painted on the side of the gun barrel and discreetly hidden by a square of hessian. Enquiries revealed that she was called Pauline Van Gogh. Finally, with my rounds complete and everything tidied away, I ordered the Battery to parade so that I could speak to them for perhaps the last time.

The BSM seated them all on the sand and called for quiet. I remember thinking how many we now were. I had not wanted to say anything and had always hoped this moment would never come. We were going to war and, as their Battery Commander, I felt duty bound. I had thought long and hard, made copious notes, and, like Wellington, had hoped to be inspirational. As it was I never so much as looked at my notes. This was my Battery and the words came straight from the heart. I told them how proud I was of their achievements and of how they had welded together as a team. I told them that as their BC I had only ever set myself one aim and that was to bring them all home safely. I told them that Britain was not in danger, that their families were safe and therefore this was not a war for heroics. We were here to do a job and to do it to the best of our ability. By doing so we would win. I reminded them of their

The Battery Commander of 'O' Battery briefing the Battery. (GM)

101

past, that we had a proud tradition and that the spirits of the Rocket Troopers would be watching over us. I told them that above all else they must look after each other. The next time they fired, not just our own troops, but I and the Battery's FOO crews would be up there with their fire. They must be fast and they must be accurate. I joked that if they had skid marks in their pants, then we at the front would have motorways in ours. They laughed loyally. I ended by wishing them luck and God speed.

At 19.30 the Officers of the 14th/20th Battlegroup and their guests assembled at the Regimental Aid Post (medical tent) for a formal dinner. On 9 February a notice in the social section of the *Daily Telegraph* announced:

SERVICE DINNER IN THE DESERT

'A dinner on the eve of action was held by the officers of the 14th/20th King's Hussars at a forward operational location in the Eastern Saudi Arabian desert on Thursday.

Amongst the guests were the officers of attached formations to the 14th/20th King's Hussars Battlegroup from the Queen's and No 2 Company the Grenadier Guards, the Royal Engineers, 'O' Battery (The Rocket Troop) of Second Field Regiment, Royal Artillery, and support elements of the REME and the RAMC. The 4th Armoured Brigade was represented by Major Julian James, the Parachute Regiment, the Brigade Chief of Staff .The loyal toast and the toast to the Colonel in Chief, the Princess Royal, were proposed by the President of the Mess Committee, Major Richard Shirreff, 'B' Squadron Leader. The traditional toast of The Rocket Troop to the King of Sweden was proposed by the Battery Commander, Major Andrew Gillespie. The menu was Boeuf Wellington from the Compo Field Rations, and the beverage non-alcoholic beer, in conformity with standing orders for deployment in the Gulf.'

I have been blessed with many magical moments in my life. This was one of them.

8 FEBRUARY 1991

We were now settling into an ordered routine, constructively busy rather than a headlong scramble to get everything done by yesterday. Lance Bombardier Witt collected me in his Landrover and I spent the morning at the Gun Position and collecting mail and additional kit for the OPs. The Commander Royal Artillery was due to visit the Battery at midday to look at how we planned to load the gun turrets with equipment and ammunition. The Battery position was now fully ready with all engineer

Guns dig in. (AG)

work complete. The guns in their deep protective pits now had their ammunition waiting, ready for use.

Once I was satisfied that the BSM and GPO had produced the most sensible solution, I left them to field the Brigadier and returned to the 14th/20th. A sports day had been arranged and most of the crew had taken part. Major David Taylor, the Paymaster, was there, as was David Coulter our Padre. They were both in good spirits and we spent some time collectively putting the world to rights. The latest joke was that 'The Irish Government has sent 1,000 troops to the Gulf, but the Mexicans don't know what to do with them.' No doubt the same joke, in various national guises, was doing the rounds throughout the Coalition. Any light relief was most welcome.

We found a live gerboa, a real desert rat, in the tent – great excitement!

155mm artillery ammunition being loaded onto M548 limbers. (AG)

9 FEBRUARY 1991

I had to rise early as the 432 and its crew had to go to Divisional HQ for a two-day communications exercise. That meant that I had to transfer my home some 200 metres to the Warrior. Before they went I washed out all my combat kit. The crew could REPLEN at Division where there was never a shortage of water. It was only when it drove off that I realized quite how attached I had become to that armoured metal box and its small patch of desert. It really had become a home from home.

Mike Vickery, myself and the squadron leaders were required at Brigade HQ for a series of briefings, given by the component parts of the Brigade. The topics included the use of armour (given by 14/20H), deliberate breach (3RRF), armoured infantry (1RS), Passage of Lines (Chief of Staff), and casualty evacuation (5 Field Ambulance). A useful morning and we arrived back at the Battlegroup at 13.30 in time for the start of the sports competitions which had carried over from the previous day.

Late afternoon, the BQMS arrived with some new M-STAR locating radars and the PRC 344 radios which would enable the FOOs to talk directly to aircraft. He only just got away in time, as by nightfall we were in the teeth of an atrocious sandstorm. It was with sand beating against the tent walls that we sat down for the evening Orders Group. In addition to the reports on vehicles, people and equipment from myself and the other majors, the Colonel outlined the training for the following day. It included LAW 80 (Light Anti-Tank Weapon) with the infantry, medical drips and a test of the new secure radio fits. These fits had just been installed to allow secure speech. The drawback was that only the very top management had it and when in use it cut out all the other stations on the Battlegroup radio net. Useful, but only in dire emergencies. Only call signs Zero, One One Alpha and One One Bravo could initiate secure speech and this would be done using the code word 'Two Alpha'. The privileged few then had 60 seconds to switch to secure. In this high-tech world it was very 'Micky Mouse' but better than nothing. The Orders ended with the exhortation to burn all classified papers, personal letters, etc, in case they fell into enemy hands. Diaries, photographs, cameras, etc, were to be back-loaded. I decided to return or destroy all my letters but to keep my camera with me. I reasoned that if I survived a ground war it would be nice to have some pictures to look back on. If I was captured a camera would be the least of my worries.

With no penthouse tent, sleeping conditions with the Warrior were pretty spartan although the crew had made themselves as comfortable as possible in a tank tent tied to one side. However, I had to be readily available and therefore findable, 24 hours a day. Bed for me became the short crew seat in the back of the vehicle. As I lay listening to the hum of the radios and the roar of the sandstorm the temperature plummeted.

17. British MLRS – Multiple-Launch Rocket System – firing (PW).

18. A bomblet strike on an Iraqi T55 tank at Objective BRASS (AG).

19. MLRS firing at Objective TUNGSTEN (PW).

20. Blue on blue – Spartans of 10 Battery, Royal Artillery (AG).

21. Commander Andy Forsyth RN, Captain of HMS *Manchester*, with members of the Battery (AG).

22. A few Iraqi guns at the Divisional Collection Point (AG).

23. Iraqi MTLB destroyed by American A10 aircraft as it led a 2S1 battery towards Kuwait City (AG).

24. Oil wells burning close to Kuwait City. The photograph was taken at midday (AG).

25. The road to Kuwait City (AG).

26. Wreckage of the British Airways 747 at Kuwait City Airport (AG).

27. The 'Highway of Death' – the Basra Road (AG).

28. The Basra Road (AG).

29. The Basra Road (AG).

30. The true horror of war (PW).

31. Leaving the Desert – C130 'Fat Albert' Hercules (AW).

32. Gunners Richardson and Newell celebrate victory (LEP).

10 FEBRUARY 1991

Dawn rose clear and sunny with no hint of the storm that had raged throughout the night. It was, however, stupefyingly cold. There was a distinct sparkle to the sand and a sheen of white frost lay on my sleeping bag. Fortunately time spurred me on as I and all the FOO parties had to be at 2nd Regiment for a talk on how we were going to use air power, should we go to war. The only transport readily available to take all the crews was an 8-tonne truck, so it was a long and uncomfortable journey to A2 Echelon. Each Battlegroup now had a Tac P, a Tactical Air Control Party. In our case he was an ex-Queen's Own Highlander volunteer from the Territorial Army, Captain Tristram Carter. The talk was given by the Brigade Air Liaison Officer and filled in many of the gaps in our knowledge. The Tac P and the newly issued PRC 344 radios would significantly improve matters. Air strikes could be requested via the Tac P or sent direct to the AWACs aircraft and then to the pilot. Any hope of having dedicated air controllers up with the leading troops was, however, impossible as they travelled in slow, vulnerable Sultans; no other vehicles were available. Even so, the briefing left us all very much more confident in our ability to use Air. With some 2,100 strike aircraft in theatre, 1st (British) Armoured Division could expect some 300 sorties a day. Pairs of aircraft would take off at 8-10 minute intervals, all with prearranged targets. They would join the 'stack' under control of an AWACs Airborne Command and Control Centre (ABCCC). If not tasked within ten minutes the aircraft would automatically fly on to their original target. If, however, the ABCCC received a request for air support from a Tac P or FOO it would allocate aircraft from the stack and order them to switch frequency and talk direct to the ground station. We were told to plan on a 'flash to bang' time of about half an hour. The aircraft and weapons load would be dependent on what was available at the time, but as likely as not would be A10s with Maverick missiles and cluster bombs or F16s with laser-guided ordnance.

A parcel was waiting for me when I arrived back at the Battlegroup. It was marked 'British Embassy, Riyadh' and was from Ginnie Sincock, the wife of the Defence Attaché. It contained a couple of films, a book, some tea bags, some tapes (Paul Simon and Elke Brooks) and, best of all, some fresh dates from her garden. That evening Witt collected me and took me back to A2 to watch the family video sent out from Münster. The video had been made by Captain Peter Doyle, our families officer, and its arrival had been awaited with great expectation. For me the journey to A2 was a three-hour round trip while some from the gun batteries had walked miles in the dark for the viewing. As we sat expectantly in the darkened tent most must have thought, as I did, that perhaps we were seeing our loved ones for the last time. As we peered

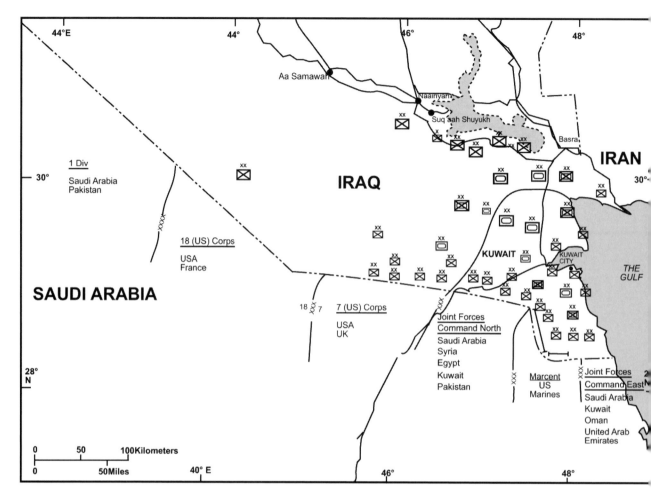

Force deployment prior to the ground offensive.

intently to catch sight of a wife or a child there was a succession of giggling women, some refusing to say anything, some with a garbled message or worse, and some with their hands over their faces saying 'I don't want to be filmed.' There was a brief clip with John, my son, but only a brief glimpse of Annie and my daughter Katie at the back of the crowd. I will never forget the awful, almost overpowering feeling of disappointment that descended in that tent when finally the video ended. Many sat around in depressed silence, others just walked off into the darkness.

11 FEBRUARY 1991

There was now a feeling everywhere that we were going through the calm before the storm. Everyone was firmly bedded into a desert routine but there was only so much planning and maintenance that could be done, then it was a matter of filling time. Monotony and tedium were in themselves exhausting. The order to paint black chevrons on all the

106

vehicles therefore came as a welcome relief. All Coalition vehicles were to carry the identification of a vertically-pointing chevron on the back and on the sides and a forward-pointing chevron on the roof. The shape had been chosen for its ease of identification through both optical and thermal sights. We would in addition carry an orange dayglo panel on the roof to aid identification by helicopters. Mid-morning the Brigade Commander came and addressed the officers of the Battlegroup. I thought he spoke well, emphasizing the need to get our own personal acts together, write letters home and then to give whatever was to come maximum commitment and effort. Success or failure would depend on the quality of individual leadership. He then toured the squadrons with the Colonel to talk to the boys. As it was sunny and therefore good drying weather I got my own act together by washing my socks, underpants and combat kit.

For most of the evening the Brigade radio net was out of order, effectively isolating the Battlegroup. When it did eventually come back on air the first message was for me. There had been an explosion on my Gun Position at approximately 17.00. Everything was under control and there were no serious casualties. I was not to visit the Battery until after the GOC's briefing tomorrow. Still unable to talk to the Battery and with no further news from Brigade, I went to bed with a deep sense of foreboding, frustration and impotence.

12 FEBRUARY 1991

I spent all morning with Mike Vickery and the Operations Officer at Brigade HQ. It was a long morning made worse by my anxiety to get down to the Battery. However it was soon clear why I had been ordered to attend. There was no longer an air of 'maybe'. Everyone now spoke of 'when'. The preamble to the GOC's formal briefing was brisk and workmanlike. We were going. Every man was to take 5-10 litres of water with him through the breach. The NBC kit we had been issued with was all there was. 'We go with what we have got' was now the cry. NBC warning and reporting must enable us to react quickly and effectively. Assess, then act. Send everything in clear. The Orders Group then thinned down to the key Brigade players to be briefed on the operational plan.

The plan as it unfolded was bold and imaginative and fitted all our work-up training and scenarios. The briefing, carried out using a sand model built outside, served to put meat onto the bones of what we already knew or had guessed. Even so it was still a shock to be briefed on going to war. Exercises, no matter how realistic, are, after all, only exercises. This was all somehow very different. It was real!

The Air War, we were told, was now in its third phase battlefield preparation and the destruction of Iraqi ground forces. At G Day minus

6 days, the artillery war would commence. Coalition artillery units would move forward, fire at predetermined targets and withdraw. On G Day, XVIII Corps' 82nd Airborne Division and 101 Air Assault Division (the Screaming Eagles) would be helicoptered forwards to seize vital crossings on the River Euphrates and establish Forward Operating Base COBRA, thus isolating the enemy troops in Kuwait from their main supply lines from Iraq. On the ground a total of four corps would attack. XVIII (US) Corps, with 24th Infantry Division, 3rd Armoured Cavalry Regiment and the 6th (French) Daguet Division would secure the west flank. The Egyptian, Syrian, Pakistani, Kuwaiti and Saudi forces of Joint Force Command North would assault northwards into Kuwait. The Marine Expeditionary Force and the Arab forces of Joint Force Command East would attack up the coast. The objective of this first day was to convince Saddam that the Coalition's main effort was directly north towards Kuwait City. The most powerful Corps, VII (US) Corps, would not attack until G Day plus 1. It would be the real main effort and would attack the Iraqi Republican Guard.

VII (US) CORPS COMMANDER'S INTENT

'I intend to conduct a swift, violent series of attacks to destroy the Republican Guard Force and minimize our own casualties. Speed, tempo, and a co-ordinated air-land campaign are key. I want Iraqi Forces to move so we can attack them throughout the depth of his Formations by fire, manoeuvre, and air. The first phases of our operation will be deliberate and rehearsed. The latter will be more Mission, Enemy, Terrain, Troops and Time dependent. We will conduct a deliberate breach with precision and synchronization resulting from precise targeting and continuous rehearsal. Once through the breach, I intend to defeat forces to the east rapidly with one division as an economy of force and pass three divisions and the armoured cavalry regiment as point of main effort to the west of that action to destroy the Republican Guard Force Divisions in a fast-moving battle with zones of action and agile forces attacking by fire, manoeuvre and air. Combat Service Support must keep up because I intend no pause. We must strike hard and continually and finish rapidly.'

General Fredrick M Franks Junior
Commanding VII (US) Corps

So VII (US) Corps, of which the 1st (British) Armoured Division was part, had drawn the short straw. It had the mission of destroying the Republican Guard Force divisions and thus Saddam Hussein's power base. All was described with sweeping hands and much waving of

108

pointers. We waited expectantly to hear our mission. When it came, the mission given to the British was to 'Attack the enemy's tactical reserve in order to protect the right flank of VII (US) Corps.' This was not welcome news. Whilst their equipment was not as modern as that with the Republican Guard divisions, it was still very effective and in vast quantities. Worst of all, these were regular troops, combat-hardened from eight years of war with Iran and whose officers had advanced on merit and experience rather than by favour. In short, they were an extremely powerful and potent force. There must have been many hearing the orders that day who considered that, among holders of short straws, once again the British had drawn the shortest of them all.

The General Officer Commanding the British Division, Major General Rupert Smith, outlined the Corps Concept of Operations. We would undertake a swift and violent advance with the aim of tempting the Republican Guard Force divisions to move from their defensive positions so that they could be destroyed from the air and ground. Deception would play a vital role. Strategic deception was well advanced with the enemy unclear on the Coalition's resolve or intentions. Operational deception was also proving effective with the enemy denied the means to gather information on our movement and deployment. Operational deception would now be supplemented by the increased use of radio and Electronic Warfare. At the tactical level a specialist unit known as 'Rhino Force' would be deployed. Details later.

The General then explained how the 1st (British) Armoured Division's operation would be conducted. It would be done in four parts or phases:

Phase 1:
a. The move of the Division to Tactical Staging Area KEYES. (Now complete)
b. Continuation training and final preparations in Area KEYES.

Phase 2:
a. The move of the artillery and the in-loading of a large logistic base code-named ECHO.
b. A Divisional Formation Training Exercise, part of which would involve the move of the Division from Tactical Staging Area KEYES to Tactical Staging Area RAY.

Phase 3:
a. The move of the Division from RAY to its Forward Staging Areas.
b. The move of the Division through the obstacle belt to its Forming Up Position at the front of the breach.

Phase 4:
The break-out. This could happen in one of three ways dependent on the tactical situation on the ground. The likely options were:
a. A successful breach operation by the Americans and no Iraqi

opposition immediately forward of the breach – 7 Brigade would move first.

b. The Iraqis have committed their tactical reserve to counter the Coalition action in which case we were likely to meet strong opposition close to the exit from the breach – 4 Brigade would move first.

c. The Iraqi defence is so strong that the Americans fail to get through the breach – 4 Brigade would be ordered to continue the breaching operation and then break out.

On top of our mission, the Phase 4 options did little to gladden the hearts of those of us in the 4th Armoured Brigade. Fortunately I did not have time to dwell on my likely fate. The General went on to give his personal feelings. It would be chaos. It was meant to be that way because we would be the ones creating that chaos. Accept it! Victory would go to the side which best managed the chaos. Plans would change, they must. Changing a plan is not necessarily a bad thing. It means we are reacting to events. We must constantly act in order to stay inside the enemy's decision cycle. In each circumstance make a value judgement as to what action you must take and then take it. Decide quickly and communicate it calmly. He reminded us all of his own maxim, FIDO (Fuck It, Drive On). The GOC then answered a few questions before the meeting broke up. The only question he was unable or unwilling to answer was where we were on the countdown to G Day.

It was mid-afternoon before I finally made it down to the Battery. I was greeted by Nick Greaves and the BSM. Between them they related the previous day's events. An M548 tracked cargo vehicle was being used to load ammunition into the turrets of a pair of M109s. The two guns, side by side with about twenty metres between them, were in their protective pits with their camouflage nets fully deployed. The M548, with two Unit Load Containers (34 rounds of 155mm bomblet, plus propellant charges), had been parked close to the rear of the guns and the crews were in the process of manhandling the shells and charges out of their storage tubes, carrying them the short distance to the guns' rear door, then stowing them in racks within the turret - a difficult and exhausting task in the soft sand and heat. While they worked, smoke was seen to be coming from the engine louvres of the M548 which then burst into flames. As the alarm was given and the flames spread rapidly to the gun cam nets, the crews fought frantically to get the nets off and to move the guns to safety. The M548 then exploded, hurling detonating bomblet rounds right across the position. The noise could be heard across the whole Divisional area. Within minutes rescue crews and helicopters were on the scene. Casualties! One M548 a total loss, one scorched but still serviceable M109 and my BK, Geoff Ravenhill. Geoff, while helping with the rescue, was hit in the shoulder by a 9mm round from a sub-machine gun that had cooked off in the driver's compartment. Fortunately two doctors were close at hand and a RAF Chinook helicopter, which was flying overhead, landed and flew him to hospital. The round had mercifully missed the bone and we would know within two or three days when he would be well enough to rejoin us.

My walk around the position brought home to me just how lucky had been our escape. The scene was one of utter devastation. Broken and deformed chunks of metal were strewn over hundreds of metres. Not one piece of the M548 was more than about eighteen inches across. The largest lump, the engine block, lay twisted and blackened amidst split and half-exploded rounds. One

The M548 explodes.
(KW)

The badly burnt M109. (AG)

The engine block of the M548 – all that remained. (AG)

round had split open like a pea pod to reveal the rows of charred but still deadly bomblets. Sergeant Webber, the gun commander, and Sergeant Johnson who commanded the ambulance, were the real heroes of the day. They stood grinning at the rear of the charred gun as I arrived. Irrepressible as ever, they proudly held up the almost unrecognisable remnants of the set of webbing that had been hanging on the gun's back door handle.

I spent a long time walking round with the BSM and talking to the crews. Many were clearly shaken but perked up when I explained that the Iraqis had this happen to them every day. If clouds do have silver linings then for us this near-disaster served to confirm that our luck was still holding and for the few who still did not fully believe, it finally ended their exercise mentality. Events now were serious, dangerous and very real.

It was late when I finally returned to my own crew. They were anxious to hear my news and listened attentively as I tried inadequately to describe the scene at the Gun Position. No sooner had I finished than it was the evening Orders and I was required to repeat my performance for the Battlegroup management. It was past midnight when I clambered onto the Warrior seat that doubled as my bed, the day's events still tumbling through my mind. I lay staring out the back door into the darkness. Occasionally a flash on the horizon served to remind me that the Air Forces were going about their relentless business.

13 FEBRUARY 1991
Today was supposed to be a make and mend day. I started by briefing my two HQ crews, Tac and MAIN, on the overall plan for battle with the warning not to mention anything in letters home. I spent the rest of the morning catching up on my own correspondence. Now that the chevrons and the marking policy for all the vehicles had been decided,

112

the crews felt able to add their own personal touches. Names appeared on the tanks, each beginning with the squadron's letter, A, B etc. Not to be left out I decided that all the Gunner vehicles would carry a name beginning with O. I chose my own and by midday the Warrior had 'OPTIMIST' in 6-inch black letters on the front and sides. I was very pleased with my choice, feeling it suited the brave, dashing image we wished to portray even if we didn't feel. Clearly others liked it, for I learnt after the war that a picture of the 'OPTIMIST' had been syndicated to half the world's press. Typically not to the British.

The three FOOs also joined in the name game:

Call sign Three Three Alpha, Captain Derek Hudson, 'ODIN'

Call sign Three Three Bravo, Captain Richard Farndale, 'ORION'

Call sign Three Three Charlie, Captain Graham Ambrose, 'ODYSSEY'

Such is the miracle of modern technology that back home the following article appeared in the *Daily Telegraph*:

We're in the killing business this time says artillery chief

By Robert Fox with O Battery, The Rocket Troop.

'Along the battle lines between the allied and Iraqi forces the great guns, in Wilfred Owen's phrase, are about to open their mouths and curse. American and British artillery in the next few days or weeks will engage in the biggest operation since the Second World War.

In the forthcoming ground offensive, artillery on either side, which before the war began was reckoned to be of equal weight, will play as big a role as any arm - including tanks. The British field howitzers and multi-launch rocket systems make up virtually a third brigade in Major General Rupert Smith's 1st Armoured Division. The M109 self-propelled howitzers will be used closer to the front-line troops and tanks than in their traditional NATO role.

'The difference this time is that artillery is in the killing business, not just suppressing the enemy over a wide area' says Major Andrew Gillespie of O Battery, 2 Field Regiment, Royal Artillery. 'We have a quantity and quality we just haven't had before.'

Major Gillespie recognizes the strength and quality of the Iraqi artillery, more than 3,000 heavy pieces before war broke out, but he thinks that might be exaggerated. Some Iraqi howitzers have a range of up to 20 miles.

'I am not bothered about them outranging us - they've got to find me first and allied targeting is better. The bang required to fire the charges for such distances are so wearing on the gun crews that they become totally punch-drunk within an hour or so.'

Major Gillespie commands one of the most colourful of all the batteries in the Royal Artillery - The Rocket Troop. Raised in 1807, the troop was to fire the rockets of William Congreve, who believed his rockets, packed with shot, would have a devastating effect on a battlefield packed with lines and squares of infantry. Unfortunately, the

War Department was not so enthusiastic and the Troop was only deployed first with the personal guard of Crown Prince Bernadotte of Sweden, for the Battle of Leipzig in 1813. Some 200 men carried the rockets, built on the lines of the Guy Fawkes version with long sticks, in panniers attached to their saddles.

The battle was in its second day when the Troop Commander, Captain Richard Bogue, persuaded Bernadotte to allow him to fire. The Prince gave leave for the officer to follow his course of action, declares the official account.

The effect of the first salvo was devastating. Within minutes 3,000 French surrendered to The Rocket Troop, 'after giving three hurrahs.' Bogue himself was shot in the last action of the battle.

To this day, The Rocket Troop wear the blue and yellow of Sweden to commemorate their role in maintaining Bernadotte on his throne.

The toast of the Battery is to the King of Sweden, drunk last week in alcohol-free lager from a grenade tin at a mess night with the 14th/20th Hussars.

The Rocket Troop has supported the Hussars since 1911, when they met up in Poonah in India, and again in Egypt throughout the 1930s. As Battery Commander, Major Gillespie will follow behind the tank of the Hussars' Battlegroup Commander, Lieutenant Colonel Mike Vickery.

'I have to live in his pocket as my main role is to provide close support fire for his troops on the ground. Others will provide the counter-battery depth fire to suppress the enemy's artillery.'

Major Gillespie is preparing the eight-gun teams of his battery for battle. Each team mans an American-built M109 self-propelled 155mm howitzer - a relatively old design.

'It's got the same engine as a Greyhound bus,' explains the Major, 'Not quite as comfortable but stops as often - though not for the same reason.'

In their hides and shell scrapes, the crews relax after an arduous day and night exercise.

At C Sub (as each gun is called), the crews are putting the finishing touches to their emblem 'Pauline Van Gogh,' a voluptuous, skimpily-clad siren generally covered by a discreet patch on the barrel. A bombardier believes that the critical part of his armament is the latest ammunition he will be firing, in particular the new round which drops bomblets on the target at a range of 10 miles.

Traditional high explosive rounds can also be set to explode at varying heights above the ground spreading the blast and shrapnel over a considerable area of defences and trenches.

At B Sub, the crew prepare for a 'shoot and scoot' exercise - firing a few rounds before motoring to a new position before the enemy can find them. Rounds for the two machine guns are laid out on the ground like long necklaces, every other bullet tipped with red to indicate tracer. 'We've got forty-four grenades, four for each man,' boasts a young Gunner.

More deceptive in their ease in the midday sun are the Gunners at E Sub, who are lounging in armchairs they 'liberated' at Al Jubayl.

Most vital, but least publicized section, is the A2 Echelon, the main

114

quartermaster's stores of the 2nd Field Regiment. The Quartermaster himself, Captain Barry Moore, is giving his men last-minute instructions on how to defend their forward positions against enemy raids.

'If you see a fire fight on the right flank - don't go and join in just because it looks interesting. Stay where you are to guard the full arc of fire.'

Captain Moore's echelon has a strong representation of experienced NCOs. 'They're needed to keep a steady head' he says, 'And their routine is going to be tougher than most. They'll have to drive all kinds of ammunition, fuel and food from eleven at night to five in the morning to each battery, possibly under fire, and get the dead vehicles back.'

He insists his men sleep whenever they can, and 'Don't stand around chatting.' He is assisted by Sergeant-Major Patrick Burns, the Master Cook, who is now confined largely to cooking Compo rations. 'Luxuries like eggs have run out. Basically it's the same menu but they'll need to eat as much as they can. The biggest problem is getting enough liquid.'

Captain Moore and Sergeant-Major Burns now say they have got all the equipment they can for the men of 2nd Field Regiment and The Rocket Troop.

'Anything else will be 'issued in theatre' as the phrase goes and I suppose the last item to be issued in theatre, of course, will be the enemy,' says Captain Moore.

The three OP Warriors spent the morning at A2 Echelon having their Osprey Thermal Imaging sights and their APES navigation systems checked over. On their return, and after the usual make-do lunch, we all motored about 800 metres to a makeshift range to test fire our small arms and the Chain Guns. I had not heard the Chain Gun fire before. Inside the turret there was a deep whirring sound as the electrical motor spun the system, feeding the belt of ammunition up into and past the breech. Outside, it made a sharp clattering noise reminiscent of a small boy dragging a stick along iron railings. Satisfied that all was as it should be, we motored back. We were met by the BQMS with another large pile of mail and our Body Armour. Earlier, I had been warned that the Battery would not be issued with enough armour for every man. I had therefore ordered that priority should go to those at the guns who would be outside the turrets when in action and to those at the sharp end who might have to leave the Warriors and fight on their feet and who would sit in turrets above the line of the Chobham armour. That meant withdrawing some sets which had already been issued. It was not a popular decision, so I was relieved when the BQMS told me that he was confident we would receive sufficient sets to equip everyone before the ground war started. The other news was that Geoff Ravenhill was being flown back to the UK. He would be replaced as soon as possible by an officer from the Battle Casualty Replacement pool - Captain Paul Keleghan.

With the mail came a small brown 'Jiffy' bag with German postage stamps. It was from Herr Peter Arndt, the historian of the Hanoverian Regiment that had fought alongside The Rocket Troop at the Battle of The Nations in October 1813. To wish us luck in whatever was to come, Peter had sent a small flat piece of pine wood. It had been cut especially from a tree at Taucha, outside the city of Leipzig, the scene of The Rocket Troop's great battle.

By early evening the temperature had changed from oppressive heat to bitter cold. After the routine evening Orders Group I made my way over to the 432. The crew had built a Trivial Pursuit board, having brought only the cards with them from Germany. After three successful games in a row, I was banned from playing. I whiled away the rest of the evening sitting on the engine decks watching the flashes to our north and the flickering glow to our east which, I surmised, were the Kuwait oil wells burning.

14 FEBRUARY 1991

The night was bitterly cold, made worse by a pre-dawn reveille. We had to be at Brigade HQ for orders at 08.30. We sat in our customary Orders formation, the three battlegroup Commanders and the Gunner CO in the front, with the three BCs behind. The orders were for Exercise DIBDIBAH CHARGE, the 1st (British) Armoured Division exercise which would put us through our final tactical paces and at the same time move the Division closer to its final launch point. In his opening speech the Commander told us that the primary aim of this exercise was to refine drills. We were to practise the passage of lines of two Brigades, a Brigade attack co-ordinated by Divisional HQ, and counter-penetration. Throughout, we were to operate our radios on the lowest power and we would move onto absolute radio silence for the final move. This, we were told, was critical to the deception plan. The Brigade Intelligence Officer gave the enemy situation and the state of Friendly Forces. The Commander gave the Division's Mission as 'To move from KEYES to RAY.' It would be in three phases as follows:

Phase 1. The move of the Artillery Group.

Phase 2. Ex DIBDIBAH CHARGE for 4 and 7 Brigades.

Phase 3. Consolidation of the Brigade in RAY.

For the exercise the mission given to 4 Brigade was the now familiar 'To destroy the enemy's mobile tactical reserve in order to protect the right flank of VII (US) Corps.' In essence we would move to a FUP (Forming Up Point), cross a Line of Departure and attack an objective. We would then undertake subsequent operations. The Brigade would advance with 14/20H leading and the other two battlegroups in their usual left and right rear formations. The Battlegroup's mission was to destroy the enemy on objective GOLD in order to allow 7 Brigade to pass through us and on to further tasks. H hour was to be 16.00. Such timings allowed little room for error and we dashed back to get the battle preparation started. The Warrior crew only just managed to complete the 18,000 km service before we left at 13.00 with the Emperor to join Brigade Tac, crossing the Line of Departure at 17.00 after a long drive. Before moving off we were ordered into our NBC suits, not popular in the still-blistering heat.

The night attack started well enough but soon dissolved into chaos. As we manoeuvred to form up behind our line, recce reported long columns of vehicles moving to our front, directly across our assault axis. There then followed a tirade of radio messages. Who were they, where were they, what were they doing, why were they there? It eventually transpired that they were a US Army logistic column, halted, we knew not why, on their way to we knew not where. The result was a delay that eventually led to the virtual abandonment of that phase of the exercise. Quite early on in the hiatus I found myself, with all the other tac groups, alongside the Brigade Tac HQ. Robert Fox and I were soon seated on top of the Optimist, mug in hand, whiling away the time. David Radcliffe spotted us and wandered over. Almost as if by prior arrangement MLRS batteries started firing, lighting up the distant sky. It was both eerie and fascinating and the three of us sat on the Optimist's engine decks and watched, in silence, our own deadly firework display. The MLRS were American. I later heard the Commanding Officer of the British MLRS, Lieutenant Colonel Peter Williams, refer to the awesome power of the weapon system as, 'The British Army's very own grid square removal service.' As if for a finale, there was a blinding flash high and away to our rear. I turned and was just quick enough to see what looked like an enormous sparkler in the sky. I learnt later that a Scud, fired at the nearby installation known as King Khaled Military City, had been intercepted by a Patriot missile.

15 FEBRUARY 1991

By 05.00, what little activity there had been, ceased, and I felt confident enough to stretch out on the roof of the Optimist and get some sleep, thankful now for the extra warmth of my NBC suit. I was woken at 07.00, stiff, sore and very cold. I was required at Brigade for orders. Cold and hungry, I sat through the briefing. We would advance, block, then withdraw before counter-attacking. By the time we had returned to the Battlegroup and orders had been issued, the sun had climbed and the heat had become overpowering. Still in our NBC suits, we moved off. We advanced over open desert until recce reported a contact. Battle procedure then went into full swing like a well-rehearsed drill. A FOO moved up to start the adjustment of the artillery fire and the nearest squadron deployed to form a fire base. While the rest of the Battlegroup moved to an assembly area, the Colonel and I moved up to assess the situation and make our plan.

Plan made, orders issued, I took control of the fire plan, issued it to the artillery Fire Direction Centre, gave the FOOs their tasks and briefed the Battlegroup over the air on the artillery plan. Meanwhile tac had moved to take up its position immediately behind the assaulting troops. We sat, engines running, waiting for H hour. At the planned minus time the Fire Direction Centre reported that they had commenced firing on the fire plan. A fraction before H hour, Mike Vickery looked over from his turret and I gave him the customary thumbs up.

"Hello all stations this is Zero Alfa, move now. Out."
We rumbled forward, the FOOs lifting the fire in front of the assaulting troops. As we closed on the objective the leading tanks broke left and right leaving the few intimate support tanks to see the infantry onto their quarry. By the time Tac HQ reached the position, the infantry had debussed into the trenches and their Warriors were providing fire support from their main armament and chain guns.

It was nearly midday and swelteringly hot. The charcoal from the inside of my suit came away and mixed with sweat to form a black film over my hands and face. While the final reorganization took place to my front, I lolled exhausted, half-out of the turret. I was tired, dirty, very hot and my ears hurt from the constant noise and the pressure of my head set. I looked back over the Optimist's rear hatches and to my delight saw The Rocket Troop, led by Lieutenant Matthew Hubbard, drive past. They were in a loose file formation about 50 metres apart with some 100 metres between vehicles. I was greeted by cheery waves and the odd good-natured jibe. The fact that the artillery was moving ahead of the

Guns of The Rocket Troop drive past. (AG)

battlegroups and would be in action before them, was clearly a source of great satisfaction. I watched them disappear into the heat shimmer with a real sense of loss.

A halt for maintenance was called at noon, just in time for us all to tune into the BBC World Service news. I stood with the rest of the crew at the front of the Optimist, listening intently to the whistles and crackles of the small radio balanced precariously on the smoke discharger.

"The Iraqi Revolutionary Command Council has agreed to UN Resolution 660 and will withdraw from Kuwait."

Disbelief, then euphoria! I really did not know whether to laugh or cry. After all the training and mental anguish, there would be no war after all. From nowhere small hip flasks and covert alcohol stocks appeared. 'I was keeping this for the end of the war but we might as well have it now.'

The euphoria did not last long. As the conditions for the Iraqi withdrawal came across the air-waves it was clear that they would be unacceptable and that war was inevitable. A feeling of gloom and despondency descended on everyone. It was broken only by the receipt of new orders and the requirement to move. We were to withdraw in contact and then break clean. That was the exercise scenario anyway. In reality it would cover our movement west and then north to Assembly Area RAY. At a given point en route we would go onto radio silence thus enabling 14 Signal Regiment, part of the Rhino Force deception organization, to play recordings of our exercise as they moved east. This, it was hoped, would convince the Iraqis that the British Division had moved back to its original location by the sea.

We started our move at about 15.00 and joined a long, slow-moving snake of vehicles heading directly into the sinking sun. I sat high in my seat, musing on the day's disappointment and watching the sand flying up from the Emperor's tracks some 20 metres to my front. After about an hour and a half the column came to a lone 432 and turned due north. As we passed and tracked right, a blackboard on the side of the 432 said 'RADIO SILENCE.' The last transmission I heard was Battlegroup MAIN reporting that Sergeant Radcliffe's 432 had broken down with fuel injector problems. I called down to the signallers dozing in the heat of the back of the Optimist, "Switch off the sets." If anyone wished to contact me, they could write!

We arrived at our new home, Grid NS 670740, just as the sun was setting. The Warrior and the two Challengers parked in a tight defensive triangle and while some struggled with the cam nets others started to dig. We were only 14 kms from the border and well within Iraqi artillery range. Light, noise and radio discipline was tight. We were now on three hours notice to move. About an hour later I heard the sound of tracks and went out expecting to greet Battlegroup MAIN HQ. It was Sergeant Radcliffe and the now healthy 432. They had arrived ahead of the packet that had left them behind. As I manoeuvred the vehicle into position I resisted the temptation to ask him by which route he had come. I knew better than that.

16 FEBRUARY 1991

We were now very much at the sharp end and, just in case anyone had failed to grasp this fact, the Battlegroup stood-to at 05.30. Helmets, body armour, trenches, NBC suits, the works. The morning Intelligence brief gave us our first real information on the Iraqi attack at Al Khafji. Alarmingly, it had taken only fifteen minutes for the Iraqis to locate and fire upon Coalition artillery, much quicker than expected. It was now assessed that their NBC kit was poor and would not permit them to fight in a chemical environment for long. Their rations appeared adequate, but food was looted from the Saudis and stores in Khafji. Some tank crews deserted when they came under fire, particularly from the air. The majority of tanks used were the older T55/59, some of which did not have radios. All in all it was quite encouraging, although no one placed much store by Intelligence briefs.

The rest of the morning was spent packing the vehicles. With water rationed, clothes washing had all but stopped and, with temperatures now soaring into the 80s, drinking water was at a premium. By midday all work outside had to be abandoned as we found ourselves in the teeth of a ferocious sandstorm. At 14.00 the BBC reported that the Revolutionary Command Council had announced, via Nicosia, that it was willing to withdraw if, among other things, the Allies would pay for the damage done in the air war. The Bush reply was apparently curt and to the point.

The first artillery raids were due to start tonight but the wind was a problem. The Gun Position Officer, Lieutenant Nick Greaves, gave his orders for the raid and I, like all the other BCs, was ordered not to go with them. Ironically, if the politicians were able to sort the mess out and avoid a ground war, the gun batteries could be the only people to have fired in anger. There has always been a friendly rivalry between the OP and gun end. If the gun crews were the only ones to see action then they would be insufferable back in Germany.

With the wind and driving sand dictating our activity level, the evening Orders Group was a subdued affair. After the usual round of vehicle and weapon states, Intelligence updates, etc, Mike Vickery went through the salient points from the last exercise. In future, if we were jammed on the radio, we would flick to the alternative frequency at each half-hour point. Once forward of the breach, if we could not get through we were to switch to 50 watts, the maximum power. The secure BID 300

'The Management'
ready for the artillery
raid: Lieutenant
Hubbard, Staff
Sergeant Dines,
Sergeant Chauhan,
Lieutenant Greaves,
WO2 Steadman,
Sergeant Fullick.
(MH)

radio installations, which were a Heath Robinson affair at best, had been causing serious problems by going to permanent transmit. The answer, it was announced, was to switch to Narrow Mode before plugging in the grey cable. We, to my knowledge, only had black cables, but it was encouraging to hear that the boffins were at last sending instructions in terms we could at least half-understand. There would be no issue of flame-proof Nomex suits, NBC suits would have to do, but flash-proof face masks (immediately christened Nicki Lauda hoods by the troops) would be coming. The Paymaster would be doing his rounds and we were to give to him all letters, diaries, address books etc that we did not wish to destroy. Overall, morale was high, buoyed by the news that the artillery raids had been given the green light and the knowledge that as we sat in our pent-house, along the whole length of the front, artillery units were now deploying in anger.

17 FEBRUARY 1991

Another maintenance day, warm and sunny, but still very windy, so sand was everywhere. The news was that, although they had deployed, the British guns had not fired. No reason was given. All very puzzling! Rumour control had it that the area of deployment had not been fully cleared. Of what? By whom? The Intelligence brief could add nothing further. The Americans had cut over twenty 100-metre breaches in the sand walls in the 'neutral' area as part of their preliminary operations, but had suffered a disastrous 'blue on blue' in the dark. First reports indicated that an Apache helicopter had destroyed two vehicles, killing some of the crew.

Much of the morning was spent in the 432's penthouse tent. Here CO, 2IC, BC, Operations Officer and the chief watchkeeper, Captain Andrew

Gossage, talked through the breach crossing plan. After a gritty lunch, Mike Vickery and I drove to Brigade HQ to try to find out what was going on. The midday World Service bulletin had reported that the Iraqi Foreign Minister, Tariq Aziz, was in Moscow on a last-ditch peace mission. Was all this activity linked to the cancellation of the raids? David Radcliffe was in good spirits, but knew nothing either. The guns were now firmly under command of the CRA and so, like me, he was out of the information loop. He knew that raids had taken place in other sectors, it was only the British guns that had not fired and they had been issued with orders for a second deployment today sometime. He was also certain that we were still very much on course for the ground offensive. None the wiser, we returned to the Battlegroup. By now the sky was overcast and it had started to rain.

Just before the evening Orders Group we received word that fresh rations had arrived at A1 Echelon and so promptly despatched a foraging party. Earlier, the driving rain had given way to drizzle. With less wind noise I had attempted to make a tape recording to Annie and the children, to dispatch with the Paymaster. Just as I finished, disaster struck. I dropped the machine in the sand. Two hours of solid cleaning failed to get rid of the scratching and grinding from the mechanism.

The evening Orders Group did nothing to enlighten any one as to what was happening. We were once again living for the hourly World Service news broadcasts. Spirits went up and down with each broadcast and it was becoming a real strain. Orders over, I made my way back to the crew. The fresh rations had been a bit of a lottery but welcome none the less; beef-burgers and some bread but mostly pork chops and sausages. The optimists chirped that they were clearing the larders at Al Jubayl in order to feed Moslem prisoners, while the more pragmatic Mancunian wits retorted that it was simply our last meal of pork before we were captured.

18 FEBRUARY 1991

Yet another maintenance day. It was scorching hot and the guns again did not fire. Conflicting reports from Moscow simply added to the confusion and discomfort. Mike Vickery told me that we were at G -3 but that G Day had now been delayed. The official reason was that the moon was not bright enough, but the real reason could only be guessed at. I spent the morning briefing the crews on the Operational Plan but omitted any reference to G Day. The best I could tell them was that the plans had been made, everything was in place and that we now sat waiting for the politicians to say 'Go.'

The early evening saw the arrival of the BQMS with the last consignment of Body Armour. He was able to report that 32 Heavy Regiment (M110, 8 inch guns) and 39 Heavy Regiment (MLRS) had fired at 1400, but that, although O Battery had deployed forward as

Vital maintenance – 'track bashing'. (AW)

ordered, they had again not fired. No explanation had been given and the strain of going forward into no man's land and not firing was starting to tell; we received the news that Lance Bombardier Lilley had caught his hand in a breech and his fingers had been severely damaged.

I wandered back to the 432 despondent but looking forward to sampling the fresh rations and the mound of mail I knew the BQMS had dropped off. The food was well up to expectations and as we ate, the crew took it in turns to read Robert Fox's article from the *Daily Telegraph* which had just arrived. He sat eating, awaiting our comments with expectation. It was Bombardier Wicks who delivered the critical blow: 'Colourful! We're not colourful. We're legendary.' From that point on, in every article, Robert referred to us as the 'Legendary Rocket Troop'. I had to take a lot of stick from my peers but would not have changed it for the world. As well as family and friends there was a pile of letters from Joyce Hopkins, a friend of my mother-in-law. She was a teacher at a school in Camberley and the children in her class had written us letters. Again, I distributed them amongst the crews with strict instructions that they were each to pen a reply. To set a good example, I selected one at random for myself.

Later in the evening, when everyone else had gone to sleep I stretched out on the Optimist's back seat and read through my mail. Letters from Annie about the children, from friends and family and finally my letter

123

from the school. I read it over and over again. Here was a letter from a little girl that could be my little girl. I hoped to God that my daughters would never write such a letter.

St Peter's Junior School
Yateley
Hants
8th February 1991

Dear Soldiers,

My name is Vanessa, but my family call me Jayney. You can call me Jayney. My Daddy was in the Army in REME. He died six years ago in a car crash. When I see pictures of all of you on the television it reminds me of my dad.

At school my favourite subject is English. I enjoy school and being with my friends.

We are having terrible weather down in the South East for a change. I can't wait till March because I am going to a Whitney Houston Concert and in April I'm going to the Isle of Wight trip with the fourth year. I am eleven. I'm going to a New Kids on the Block concert.

I'v got a great mum whose name is Liz Aitken. My mum is in personnel and works very long hours. I miss her a lot when she is at work.

I'v got a pussy cat called George and I feed another cat who I have adopted and I call her Twiggy. I did have two gold fish but my cat ate them.

I go caravaning most weekends with my nanny and granddad. At the moment my granddad is in Northern Ireland. He has travelled all over the world.

I am going to phone the Gulf Helpline and one of the people I help may be one of your wives or girlfriends.
GOOD LUCK

From
Vanessa Aitken

19 FEBRUARY 1991

Our lives were now dictated by the BBC World Service hourly reports. From gloom to glee to gloom each broadcast. I determined to stop listening but did not have the will power. The tension was awful and the heat blistering. Today was the hottest day yet. This morning I finally put to bed the last of my administration. There was not much to do now that we were effectively divorced from the Battery. With no direct communications, we were reliant on the Q's visits and odd snippets from Artillery HQ at Brigade. Lance Bombardier Lilley was flown out today. His hand had not been crushed in a breech as had originally been reported, but had been severely injured by contact with the engine's high-speed fans. At midday a water tanker appeared, not the promised Bath Unit, but a lot better than nothing. It enabled us all to have a shower and re-distribute the dirt in our combat suits. Morale soared.

The afternoon was taken up by the Orders Group. Mike Vickery confirmed what had become common knowledge, that G Day was on hold. No date had been set, but he thought that the Brigade would get at least 48 hours' notice. The current guess was that G Day would be 23 or 24 February. One reason why the artillery raids had been delayed was the possibility that the Americans had advanced too far on some of their probing attacks and there was a rumour that Commander VII Corps had given Commander 1st Mechanized Division a formal dressing down for jeopardizing surprise on G Day.

The Intelligence update stated that the enemy's combat effectiveness had been reduced to the following percentages: Tawalkana Division 70%, Hammurabi Division 84%, Medina Division 63%, 12 Armoured Division 68%, 17 Armoured Division 79%, 52 Armoured Division 70% and all front-line infantry divisions were down to less than thirty tanks each. Considering how long the much-vaunted air forces had been attacking them, to a simple soldier the Iraqis seemed to be holding out pretty well.

It was assessed that the Republican Guard Force divisions could be holding chemical warheads and that their MTLB tracked troop carriers could have an active Infra-Red sight with a range of approximately 500 metres. Wire and illuminating mines had been discovered much further west than had previously been expected. There was also a report that a US 8-inch gun battery had fired on a raid, moved, and the vacated position had been hit by Iraqi Counter Battery Fire. A British Sound Ranging Base had produced a 10-figure fix and A10 aircraft had been dispatched. The enemy gun position had been comprehensively destroyed. On the logistics side, it was now assessed that they had seventy-five days of stocks left, but at war rates these would last less than ten. All this was cheering enough, as was the promise that the Bath Unit would open at the Brigade RV at 08.30 on 21 February, and be there all day.

The evening BBC broadcast brought the news that President Bush had rejected the 'peace initiative'. No one was surprised. As I sat in the back of the Optimist, the next batch of pass words and numbers arrived. We had long ago given up on the number system, there being no non-English speakers closely deployed. The words-in-the-sentence system, however, stretched the imagination to breaking point. The latest list would be a real challenge:

    19 Feb   Pizza. 7, Duty. 10
    20 Feb   Suitcase. 9, Socket. 4
    21 Feb   Footstool. 3, Jumper. 7
    22 Feb   Rabbit. 9 Vendor. 5
    23 Feb   Moisture. 8, Packet. 1
    24 Feb   Photo. 2, Palace. 5
    25 Feb   Orbit. 10, Grammar. 6
    26 Feb   Bearskin. 4, Soap box 2
    27 Feb   Kindness. 6 Infield. 8
    28 Feb   Damper. 1, Affair. 3

Finally, as dusk appeared, the BQMS arrived with a replacement Raven Image Intensifying sight for the Optimist, which was fitted promptly and satisfactorily. The evening was most uncomfortable. As well as the general feeling of despondency which had descended, the temperature was high, the humidity oppressive and there was absolute stillness in the air. It was eerie. The atmosphere was charged with static electricity, radios crackled, hair stood on end and, on the tips of some of the antenna, St Elmo's fire gave a ghostly glow. I retired early and lay on top of my sleeping bag, watching the flashes from the distant artillery raids through the open back door, sweating profusely and trying to sleep.

20 FEBRUARY 1991
I must have fallen asleep for I remember waking up with a start. It was 04.00 and initially I thought we were under artillery fire. The noise was deafening: air, sand, debris. Tents crushed flat, cam nets ripped from their stays. I struggled from my bed. The heavy steel back door of the Optimist was now flapping as if made of cardboard. I managed to clamp it, and climbed out into a hurricane-force wind. But this wind was like no other. It was not blowing across the desert, it was blowing down upon us, crushing tents, nets, anything not made of armour. Flashes illuminated the chaos around me, and then they came, like something from H.G. Wells' *War of the Worlds*. Bolts of ball lightning; striking, then running along the ground. I don't know how long it lasted but the whole experience was first terrifying then captivating. Back in the safety of the Warrior, I lay and watched this amazing natural spectacular. Then it rained. How it rained. Like the monsoon. For hours. Soaking, drenching, saturating.

The dawn revealed the state of our battering. The small tent on the side of the Optimist was awash, yet miraculously the 432's penthouse had withstood the ordeal. Everywhere disgruntled soldiers were draping sodden sleeping bags across tank barrels or over hot engine louvres. As it was the only outpost of order that morning, I had breakfast with the 432.

I did not have the luxury of sitting around and surveying the scene. As soon as I had eaten, the Colonel, 2IC, Intelligence, Operations Officer and myself set off in the Land Cruiser for HQ 1/41 Infantry Battalion of 3 Brigade, 1st Infantry Division (Mechanized), US Army. The hours we had spent rehearsing the Passage of Lines would now, hopefully, bear fruit. The 1/41 were the Task Force of the 'Big Red One' through which the Battlegroup would pass prior to breaking out of the Breach Head. It would require careful liaison and this was our task for today. Directed only by the SATNAV, we headed north, crossing miles of open desert, a dangerous occupation so close to the front line. As we approached the American unit's HQ, Godfrey Tilney, who was driving, drove into the only puddle for miles around and promptly got stuck. To the amusement of the rapidly gathering American Army, a M113 APC (Armoured Personnel Carrier) was hitched up and pulled us out. Not a very auspicious start.

After my experience with the American Army in Germany and more recently the US Marines, I had viewed our move to VII Corps with some trepidation. I need not have worried. The 1/41 MAIN HQ was a tight formation of M577s (the command variant of the M113) joined by canvas walkways around a central tented area - a forest of aerials and a

The recce to the 1/41 Infantry Battalion. The US Army to the rescue.
(AG)

127

cacophony of humming generators. We were greeted warmly by the Battalion Commander, Lieutenant Colonel Jim Hillman, shown into the central briefing area and each introduced to our opposite number. There then followed a very sound and professional briefing. It covered their plan for the breaching operation, the move of the 14th/20th Battlegroup through to NEW JERSEY and their support for our break-out. They were full of optimism. They planned on leaving VERMONT at 07.00, reaching COLORADO by 11.30 and being on NEW JERSEY by 16.30. I was both relieved and impressed. Everything about this unit had an air of competence and professionalism. The American Artillery Officer had plotted all the known enemy gun positions within range. He had allocated target numbers and would give me a very comprehensive 'state of play' as I passed through. The Americans would have no artillery forward of line UTAH so their support to us would be restricted. He would keep control of the supporting fire until we were clear of our Line of Departure then hand over control to me, thus ensuring no 'blue on blue' from the artillery at least. Over a lunch of cold MREs, we learnt something of our Corps Commander. He was General Fredrick Franks, a no-nonsense Vietnam veteran with one leg. I liked what I heard. A veteran would understand what it was like for those up at the sharp end. Better still, spoilt for choice as the Americans certainly were, their selection of a man with one leg meant that General Franks came highly recommended. Later Jim Hillman gave us the details of the friendly fire attack on two of his vehicles. It had happened on the night of 17 February when an Apache helicopter had mistakenly engaged a Bradley and an M113. It was a fascinating but tragic tale. We then bade farewell and left to allow him to attend the memorial service for two of his dead soldiers.

From the Americans we made our way across a still very damp desert to HQ 4 Brigade. We reported on our visit to our respective heads, but there was little that they could tell us in return. There was confusion as to the state of the peace negotiations, with the Russians now appearing to be acting as brokers between the Iraqis and Americans and Saddam giving his 'Mother of all Battles' speech. They could however confirm that we were holding on G minus 3.

By the time the Land Cruiser had returned us to the Battlegroup it was late afternoon. The hot sun had worked its magic on soldiers and sleeping bags alike and the place looked a little less like a refugee camp. The boys were all in good spirits and were eager to hear my news. As darkness descended we were again being buffeted by strong winds and driving rain.

21 FEBRUARY 1991
At 10.00 hrs, in the artillery penthouse tent and for the first time since 1945, the 14th/20th King's Hussars held formal orders to go to war. At

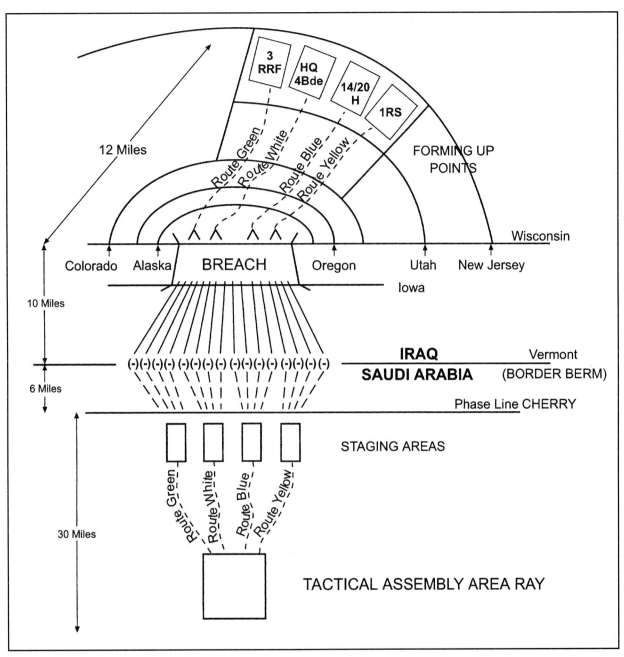

The following labels appear in the figure:

3 RRF

HQ 4Bde

14/20 H

1RS

FORMING UP POINTS

12 Miles

Route Green

Route White

Route Blue

Route Yellow

Wisconsin

Colorado   Alaska   BREACH   Oregon   Utah   New Jersey

Iowa

10 Miles

6 Miles

(-)(-)(-)(-) (-)(-)(-)(-) (-)(-)(-)(-) (-)(-)(-)(-)

IRAQ   Vermont

SAUDI ARABIA   (BORDER BERM)

Phase Line CHERRY

STAGING AREAS

Route Green

Route White

Route Blue

Route Yellow

30 Miles

TACTICAL ASSEMBLY AREA RAY

the front was a blackboard with the tac map. We sat in our now familiar places, me on the right, then the squadron leaders and company commanders with the FOOs behind. It was a sombre occasion. The Commanding Officer welcomed us all and told us that these orders were for the removal of Iraqi troops from Kuwait by force, Operation DESERT SABRE.

The Minefield Breach.

1. SITUATION

a. Enemy Forces.

In our likely area of operation the enemy is deployed in three belts, a forward defensive line, a tactical reserve and a strategic reserve. The front-line troops are primarily low-quality conscript infantry and deployment from east to west is 27th, 25th, 31st, 48th and 26th Divisions. Behind the 25th and the 31st, at a distance of 50 to 75 kms, is the tactical reserve of the 12th and 52nd Armoured Divisions comprising well-trained and well-equipped regular troops. Their task is almost certainly to plug any gaps in the front defensive line. Behind again and in greater depth is the strategic reserve of the Republican Guard; Saddam Hussein's elite forces and his power base. Their task is to defend Iraq and to counter-attack into the coalition forces.

The Iraqi obstacles belt in our area is believed to be thinner than is the case further east but it is still formidable with high sand berms, wire, trenches and revetments. Special Forces are known to be operating behind the main breach area, probably to deter Iraqi soldiers from deserting the forward positions.

There is only one report of NBC and that was unspecified and in the area of 25 Division. The Air threat remains mercifully low.

b. Friendly Forces.

(1) We are part of 3rd US Army:

The Army Commander's plan is to advance with 2 corps leading, XVIII Airborne Corps forward left, VII (US) Corps forward right.

(2) XVIII Airborne Corps:

Comprising the 82 Airborne Division, 101 Air Assault Division and the 24th Infantry Division, their Mission is to prevent east-west movement along the Iraqi line of communication in order to isolate the enemy in the Kuwait Theatre of Operation.

(3) VII (US) Corps:

The Coalition's initial main effort. Their Mission is to destroy the Republican Guard Force divisions. This will remove the force protecting Kuwait and destroy Saddam Hussein's power base. The Corps will move on G +1.

(4) Flanking Formations:

On our left boundary is XVIII Corps and on our right boundary is Forces Command North comprising: 2 x Egyptian Divisions, 2 x Saudi Brigades, 2 x Kuwaiti Brigades with 1 x Syrian Division in reserve.

7th (US) Cavalry Division will be in support of Forces

Command North. Their Mission is to block the lines of communication north to south in order to isolate Kuwait City.

2. VII (US) CORPS.

a. Mission. To destroy the Republican Guard with maximum force and maximum speed.

b. Execution. The Mission will be achieved in the order:

(1) 1 Infantry Division (Mechanized) secures the breach in the Iraqi main defensive line.

(2) 1 (British) Armoured Division passes through the breach to destroy the enemy's first tactical reserve in order to protect the Corps right flank. Concurrently 2 Armoured Cavalry Regiment is to move to seize objective COLLINS.

c. Main Effort. The Corps' main effort is the breach operation then the break out of the British Division.

3. 1 (BR) ARMOURED DIVISION

a. Mission. To attack through 1 Infantry Division (Mechanized) to destroy the enemy tactical reserve in order to protect the right flank of VII (US) Corps.

b. Concept of Operations:

(1) G Day. Move on orders from RAY to the Staging Areas (SAs).

(2) On orders, transit the breach and break out. 3 x scenarios are likely:

(a) No enemy opposition immediately forward of NEW JERSEY – 7 Brigade will move first.

(b) Powerful enemy force closing on NEW JERSEY so we will have to fight from the Forming Up Position – 4 Brigade will move first.

(c) The Americans fail to secure the breach – 4 Brigade will assist. Once clear of breach, they will advance as quickly as possible to destroy enemy.

4. 4 ARMOURED BRIGADE

a. Phases applicable to 14/20H

(1) Phase 3a. Move from RAY to Staging Area 3. Artillery bombardment starts.

(2) Phase 3b. Move from Staging Area 3 up to the breach entrance under the tactical control of 1 Infantry Division (Mechanized).

(3) Phase 3c. Move through the breach and 3 (US) Brigade (Forward passage of lines) to the Forming Up Position. Tac HQ to co-locate with 3 (US) Brigade/1/41 Task Force.

(4) Phase 3d. Fight out of breach past Phase Line NEW

JERSEY. D Squadron to be prepared to detach to 3RRF Battlegroup.

(5) Phase 4. Defeat enemy tactical reserve.

(6) Phase 5. As part of VII (US) Corps reserve, assist in the Corps main effort in destroying the Republican Guard Force divisions or other tasks as ordered.

5. 14/20H BATTLEGROUP

a. Mission. To conduct a forward passage of lines through 1 Infantry Division (Mechanized) to destroy the enemy's tactical reserve as soon as possible.

b. Execution:

(1) Tasks: A, B and D Squadrons and the Queen's Company:

(a) Phase 3a. Deploy Harbour Parties on orders.

(b) Phase 3b. Move through the breach on orders.

(c) Phase 3c. Move through 3 (US) Brigade on orders.

6. COORDINATING INSTRUCTIONS

a. Timings:

1. G Day. Not Yet Known.

2. H hr G +1. Start of VII (US) Corps' offensive.

3. L hr. Start of 1 (British) Armoured Division's offensive.

4. M hr. Break out.

5. Battlegroup is now at 3 hrs NTM.

6. All Arms Air Defence: Weapons Hold.

b. Bypassing. Positions occupied by enemy forces but without any offensive capability may be bypassed.

c. NBC. MEDIUM. (A chemical or biological attack is likely. Full suits to be worn with respirators immediately available.)

7. SERVICE SUPPORT. Later...still being produced by the Brigade Staff.

8. COMMAND AND SIGNALS:

a. Tac HQ is to deploy on G-1 and to co-locate with 3 (US) Brigade MAIN.

b. MAIN HQ is to move with the Battlegroup to the Forming Up Position.

c. STEP UP HQ is to co-locate with the American 1/41 HQ until we leave the Forming Up Position.

d. Emissions: 3A to Phase 4, 3B onwards for HF.

8. MOVEMENT ORDER:

a. Movement:

(1) Phase 3a. All tanks are to move by transporter. All the other tracked and the wheeled vehicles are to move under their own steam.

(2) Phase 3b. Move from Staging Area 3 through the breach

entrance, tracks down lane K, wheels down lane L. The RV grid for the recce will be given in Staging Area 3.

(3) Phase 3c. Move from the breach exit to the Battlegroup RV at Grid NT864494 which is at the rear edge of FUP BLUE.

b. Timings:

(1) G-1. Battlegroup Tac and Recce move.

(2) G 09.00. Harbour parties cross the Start Point on route BLUE.

(3) L+269. First tank lift. (A Squadron, 11C and one tank from B Squadron) and 3 x Armoured Repair and Recovery Vehicles (ARRV).

(4) L+653. B and D Squadrons move by transporters.

(5) L+870. Wheels plus any remaining tracked vehicles move.

(6) L+1115. All complete in the new location.

The orders took over three hours with questions and explanations. Everyone had to understand what we were trying to do and their part in the grand scheme. Each of the key players contributed their penny's worth, Intelligence, Operations, the Echelon commanders. I spoke on how the artillery would be fought. I explained that the artillery would be the Division's third manoeuvre force. That the Brigades would be fought sequentially with the weight of the firepower supporting the in-action Brigade. This meant that the out-of-action Brigade would consequently have very little, if any, artillery firepower. I tried to get over the scale and power of the artillery massed in their support. I spoke of the shattering effect of the new L15 air-burst round and the devastating effect MLRS and the bomblet round had on armour. I ended by giving them my own personal mission as their BC; that the 14/20H Battlegroup would never have to go anywhere that a shell had not already been, and that I would see to it that we never had to dismount our infantry in anger.

The evening BBC broadcast brought the news that Saddam had accepted the Soviet peace proposal. Iraq would withdraw 75% of its forces from Kuwait in the next four days if the Allies also withdrew and all UN sanctions were lifted. There was no reply as yet from Washington or London. For the first time the ground swell of opinion in Battlegroup HQ was for going ahead and getting the war over. I confess that I still hung on to every thread of hope, no matter how unlikely, that it could be settled in some other way. I was cold, tired and my brain was approaching overload when I eventually curled up on my seat and attempted to sleep. It was raining and all along the front the guns were in action.

22 FEBRUARY 1991

The news was encouraging. London and Washington appeared to be considering the latest peace proposals which, according to Iraq, had the 'support of the whole world.' After breakfast I finished marking up my maps and did a final check on my kit. At 10.30 the Battlegroup received a Warning Order. It calmly announced that today was G-2 and that the three Battlegroup Tac HQs were to move to co-locate with 4 Brigade's Tac HQ tomorrow. The Recce Group, including the engineer Spartan and the REME Samson vehicles, were to move north to join HQ 3 (US) Brigade to conduct rehearsals for the breach crossing with US scouts. Just in case any certainty could be attached to this announcement there was the caveat that dates and times could be slipped by political pressure being brought to bear. They could also be slipped as both the British and American forces were not yet 'logistically mature'. What did that mean? Nobody knew. It was, however, a positive order, it moved us closer to war and, expected though it was, it came as a shock.

On the basis that the war was on until told otherwise, the Battlegroup carried on with its planning. At the evening Orders Group we talked through how we would refuel in the Staging Areas and how we would move from FUP BLUE to NEW JERSEY. Much would depend on the tactical situation for this would decide which brigade moved first. Assuming the worst case, the US 1/41 would mark lanes from the FUP using blue chemical lights attached to poles. We would move in two columns, A Squadron and the Queen's Company in the right-hand lane, B and D Squadrons in the left. All would move as close to the markers as possible to reduce the mine hazard. We would only shake out once we were 1,000 metres plus of NEW JERSEY or were forced to do so by enemy action. We talked through many options. In the event that 4 Brigade moved first it was likely that we would be ordered into a blocking position, forward of the breach, in front of the Iraqi 46th Division. Our task would be to hold the enemy to enable 7 Brigade to manoeuvre behind us and then counter-attack. Another option on the planner's board was called Option DIANA. Here the entire British Division would attempt to block the enemy's tactical reserve long enough for an American helicopter force to attack into their flank. Studying the maps, and knowing how their helicopters had performed to date, this was not a popular option. Mike Vickery ended by telling us that the consensus of opinion upon high was that the deception plan was still working and that the Iraqis genuinely did not know where we were. I wondered who they thought had been shelling them.

After the orders I had a final briefing with the FOOs and issued DF (Defensive Fire) lists and allocated Fire Plan numbers. When I emerged from the tent it was late afternoon, the sky was clear and it was hot. The BQMS had delivered some laser protection goggles but sadly no mail. The lack of mail was now becoming a problem. I had been quite lucky but some of the crews had received nothing for weeks now and with war looming the lack of contact with loved ones was acutely felt. The

Captain Paul Keleghan gives orders to the guns. (MH)

evening morale booster from the BBC announced that President Bush had given the Iraqis until 8 o'clock the next evening to withdraw. I spent the early evening with the crew of the 432 then talked through our plans with Sergeant Radcliffe. After I had eaten I sat with Robert Fox and pondered the meaning of life over numerous cans of 'delicious malt beverage'. The guns were firing again, the air forces were working overtime and it was raining. I was going to war. What sort of hell would my family now go through? Gloom!

Meanwhile, unknown to me at the time, Captain Paul Keleghan arrived at the Battery from the pool of Battle Casualty Replacements; he replaced Captain Geoff Ravenhill as the BK.

23 FEBRUARY 1991

A bright and sunny day, which was not matched by our moods. We were up early to keep our appointment with the refuelling tanker at 07.30. The Battlegroup recce and the Step Up HQ vehicle, Zero Charlie, departed at 08.15. After a leisurely breakfast I did the final checks of fuel, water, oil, rations, ammunition. Every nook and cranny of the Optimist had something crammed into it - bottled water, mars bars, hand grenades. At 13.00 we held Battlegroup orders. Mike Vickery opened by telling the assembled multitude that it was almost 100% certain that we would be going to war and the likely option was for 4 Brigade to lead out of the breach. The timings we should now plan on were:

1. G +1. 10.00hrs. Battlegroup firm in Staging Area 3.
2. G +1. 16.30hrs. Americans firm on NEW JERSEY.
3. G +1. p.m. Move to FUP BLUE.
4. G +2. 02.00-03.00 Attack Iraqi 46th Division.
5. G +2. Morning/midday attack Iraqi 50th Division.

In the Staging Area we were to run up all systems and there would be a final brief on transiting the breach.

Orders over, to much waving and a few lumpy throats, the Battlegroup Tac HQ left for the Brigade RV. We motored steadily across the flat, featureless desert, travelling in a straight line, guided by the SATNAV. The Emperor led the way, with One One Charlie and the Optimist following on behind. Occasionally we had to stop to let convoys of wheeled and tracked vehicles cross our path. From my position high in the turret I could see these long columns moving as if on some invisible highway. Clearly the level of activity was increasing rapidly, both on the ground and in the sky. The distant rumble of guns firing could at times be heard over the steady beat of the Optimist's engine and, for those who recognized it, there was now a taste of cordite in the air, mixing with the now familiar smell of unburned aviation spirit. It took some time to reach the Brigade RV, and we were the last of the tac groups to arrive. The RV was nothing more than a grid reference that could be set into the SATNAV. There was nothing physically there on the ground. There was nothing anywhere. The RV now comprised the fighting HQs of the 4th Armoured Brigade: the Commander's tank, David Radcliffe's 432 and the three Battlegroup Commanders and their BCs. In all, three tanks, one 432 and five Warriors. We were greeted warmly and spent a few precious moments catching up on tittle tattle. Pleasantries over, we gathered around Nomad, the Commander's tank, for an update briefing. Soon we were on our way again, this time following the herds of vehicles heading for war.

Co-located with H.Q. 1 Infantry Division (Mechanzed) – 'The Big Red One'. (AG)

Robert Fox digging in. (AG)

The Main HQ of the 'Big Red One' consisted of a huddle of M577 tracked APCs, draped in nets and sprouting a bewildering array of aerials. One hundred metres or so away was a small group of Jeeps, HMMW Vs and a Range Rover. We stopped about 100 metres short and went into our own huddle. As I struggled on the turret roof to untangle the cam net, I looked down to the rear of the Optimist and saw Robert Fox digging manfully. He was not the only one. Everywhere I looked people were preparing for war. Any last lingering hope that war would at the last moment be averted vanished. Clearly we were well past the last safe moment. As it got dark and we settled down to wait it started to rain. The Brigade Commander and David Radcliffe had to go to Division that night for orders so David offered to do a last mail run. I sat in the back of the Optimist and by its dim light I wrote to Annie. What do you put in a letter to your wife which you know she won't get until after you have been to war, and maybe after you have been killed?

137

I was too cold, wet and frightened to be either philosophical or even romantic. I wrote what I felt:

> *By the time you read this it will be all over. I don't look on it as the start of the land war, but the start of my journey home. I will be home safe and sound, don't worry. I love you and the children terribly, particularly tonight. I am determined to be home soon.*
> *With all my love,*
> *Andrew*
> *xxxx*

At 20.00hrs the deadline came and went and somewhere, dry, warm and very safe, President Bush gave the green light for war. Inside the Optimist we made the best we could of our lot. Plans changed constantly. Map updates, overprints, frequency lists continued to arrive. Eventually, as I was preparing to catch some sleep, fully clothed with my respirator by my head, the order came that we were to move at 07.00.

OPERATION DESERT SABRE

(1(British) Armoured Division's operation)

24 FEBRUARY 1991

I was shaken awake at 05.30 by Mike Vickery. It was raining hard. He briefed me as I lay fully clothed and shivering in my sleeping bag. G Day was confirmed. G for Go. The war had started. The Battlegroup was to go to one hour's notice to move at 06.00. There was now a real possibility that our L Hour, the move to Staging Area 3, would be brought forward from 14.00 to 10.00 on G +1, but this had not yet been confirmed. We would move at 08.15. He then disappeared into the greyness of the dawn leaving me to ponder over the events that were now driving my life. At 06.00 I could endure the cold, damp and discomfort no longer and got up. Outside the rain had stopped, but all around was evidence of the night's downpour. Cam nets hung limp and heavy and everywhere soldiers were stamping about and flailing their arms in order to get some warmth back into their bodies. I was just in time to hear the BBC's news of the assaults against the Iraqi defensive line, XVIII Corps' dash to the River Euphrates and that a 24-hour news blackout had been imposed. Around me the Americans were already on the move. Columns of vehicles, mostly wheeled, snaked past the main HQ complex and disappeared into the morning gloom. Although I could hear nothing I knew that along every sector of the front but ours the war was raging.

We were lined up, on time, for our move forward to join 3 Brigade's Tac HQ. However, we were not the only people moving in that direction that morning and it was as the end vehicles of the 'mother of all traffic jams' that we made very slow progress forward and it was not until 16.00 that we finally reached our destination. We were greeted by the news of spectacular successes both by the Airborne Forces to our west and the

The Americans move out. (AG)

139

Arab and Marine forces to our east. While I had been bumbling along at the end of my column, plans had been changing rapidly. The original plan was for VII (US) Corps to attack the breach on G +1. The British Division would also move on G +1, moving about 20 km northwards from the Assembly Area RAY into their Staging Areas, right behind the Americans, in order to be ready to pass through the breach and then to break out. However such was the pace of events that the American 'Big Red One' had been ordered to attack on G Day. Their operation had been heralded by a Corps fire plan in which sixty batteries of M109 guns had fired. Add in the 8-inch, MLRS, B52s and any one else who had wanted to join the party and it was not surprising that Iraqi resistance in the breach area had been less than formidable.

By the time we reached 3 Brigade's Tac HQ, 1 and 2 Brigades had already successfully completed their part of the operation, were through

The author ready to go. (AG)

140

the first line of Iraqi defences and firm on COLORADO. In order to keep pace the British had been ordered forward at 14.00 and at 20.00 we received the news that the Battlegroup had successfully transited route BLUE and was now secure in the Staging Area. After such news we expected events to move on apace and NEW JERSEY to be secured imminently. We were very surprised therefore to be told that the Americans had decided to halt their breaching operation during darkness as they did not believe that their state of training would enable them to carry out a night assault. This was confirmed by the announcement that 3 Brigade had an H hour of 06.00, 25 February, to start the final phase of the breach and were to be secure on NEW JERSEY by 12.00.

3 Brigade's Tac HQ consisted of a small clump of armoured command posts nestled behind one of the few topographical features in the area, a slight sand hillock. We parked up close enough to do business but far enough away to avoid any artillery fire which the HQ's bristling array of radio masts might attract. With the news that our war was on temporary hold, the only thing we could do was sit tight, make ourselves as comfortable as the situation would allow and tune into the BBC. We slept as best we could that night, at NBC BLACK with respirators by our heads.

25 FEBRUARY 1991

At 04.00 a Warning Order was received from 1st (British) Armoured Division. It read:

WARNING ORDER

FRIENDLY FORCES:

1 Infantry Division (Mech) firm on COLORADO. Attacking 25 Feb 0600 with 3 Brigade to be on NEW JERSEY by 25 Feb 1200. 1 Brigade to be on NEW JERSEY by 25 Feb 1200. 1 Brigade is to clear on to Grid NT8641.

Flanks: 2 Armoured Cavalry Regiment now firm on Phase Line MELON with recce 10km forward to continue attack at 0600. 1 Cavalry Division to continue feint attack in their sector. Arab Coalition forces expected to attack 25 Feb 0600 through breaches made today.

MISSION: No Change.

EXECUTION: Orders to follow. Forward HQ at 05.00. Order of march through breach will be:

Artillery Group including 16th/5th Lancers, then 7 Brigade then 4 Brigade. Order of March out of FUP will be 7 Brigade, Artillery Group, 4 Brigade.

CO-ORDINATING INSTRUCTIONS:

No move expected before 25 Feb 0800. 7 Brigade at 30 minutes NTM from 25 Feb 0730. 4 Brigade expected to move at 25 Feb 1030.

Considering the time frame there was little point in staying where we were. We broke camp at 05.30, wished 3 Brigade good fortune and set off in the rising dawn to rejoin the Battlegroup. It was a long but uneventful journey requiring us to move back in a sweeping arc so as to approach the Staging Area from the rear. It could not have been achieved without the miracle of SATNAV. As we moved through the myriad of tracks, still clear in the sand despite the night's heavy rain, out of the morning haze appeared great shadowy columns like sleeping snakes. As we drew closer we could see that these were made up of vehicles, one behind the other in neat single file, some over 1,000 metres long. Between each column was some 500 metres of open sand. The columns were divided into wheels and tracks. These were the battlegroups of the British Division, lined up alternately 4 Brigade and 7 Brigade. It was an awesome sight made tactically possible only by the Coalition's total control of the sky. It would have been a dream target for the enemy's artillery if only he knew it was there. It was also the perfect chemical target and it would not have taken the brains of an Archbishop to figure out that behind such a breach must be troops waiting to pass through that breach. We were still probably out of effective chemical range but the breach could be very different.

We made our way across the ends of the many columns until we found the tail of the 14th/20th and turned to drive alongside the tracked vehicles. As the Emperor, One One Charlie and the Optimist made their way up the line, crews in the middle of washing or their breakfast, gave us a warm welcome and the occasional 'Where have you been then?' Almost at the head of the line we swung into the gap left for us and parked up in front of MAIN HQ.

The Battlegroup line up. (AG)

We were greeted warmly by Godfrey Tilney and Sergeant Radcliffe. The news was very positive. 3 Brigade's attack was going well and a call forward of one of the British brigades, hopefully 7 Brigade, was awaited.

At 10.00 I looked across to my right and saw the long column of tanks of the Queen's Royal Irish Hussars start to move. Jubilation! 7 Brigade was moving first and that meant that the breach was successful and there was clear air beyond. At 10.30 we were placed at 30 minutes' NTM and at 11.00 came confirmation that the Americans had secured NEW JERSEY.

I whiled away the morning as best I could, sometimes sitting musing with Robert Fox as we watched the columns of armour disappear into the shimmer or wandering to the back of the Operations vehicle to where the secure radio was the only source of information. At 12.20 M hour for 4 Brigade was confirmed as 13.15. By 13.00 we were mounted, engines running, ready to go. If a chemical attack was to happen it would likely as not be during the transit of the breach. The American attack and the move of 7 Brigade must have given the Iraqis enough warning to finally get their act together to hit 4 Brigade. I sat nervously on the right-hand side of the Optimist's turret. My seat was pumped up to its highest position, the hatch open and secured flat behind me. In front of me the armoured shutter protecting my night sight and optical periscope was in the half-down position, giving some protection, yet still

HQ 14th/20th King's Hussars at the head of Line 2. Tanks of 7 Brigade start to move forward. (AG)

143

enabling me to see. On the outside of the dome-shaped turret, next to the shutter and immediately above where my head would be when we closed down, was a strategically placed sandbag. In times of crisis one clings to straws. All around me were the tools of my trade and the paraphernalia that makes life in the confines of a turret bearable. In the space to my front left, where the breach for the 30mm Rarden Cannon should have been, was my enormous and unwieldy tac map in its plastic case. Next to it and inches from my nose was my respirator. I was dressed in NBC underwear, a cotton desert combat suit, a charcoal-impregnated NBC suit, body armour and helmet. It was a dank, overcast day, but, even with the hatches fully open, the temperature inside the Optimist was rising.

A minute before the appointed hour the hatches on the Emperor clanged shut. It was the signal for us all to follow suit. To the sound of escaping hydraulic fluid, I dropped my seat and secured my hatch in one practised movement. As we settled into the twilight world of the turret, our ears momentarily popped as the fans built up the over-pressure which hopefully would stop anything nasty from entering the vehicle. 'Back door shut?' A muffled confirmation came from the bowels of the vehicle. At M hour the Emperor and One One Charlie moved and the Optimist followed, keeping a respectful 50 metres behind. We were moving in column, A Squadron in the front, then the tac group and then the rest of the Battlegroup. Leading the whole fleet I presumed, because I could not see them, was an American Military Police guide. I hoped that they would perform better than during the rehearsal. Through my right-hand periscope I could see a column of wheeled vehicles moving in parallel with me, some 500 metres away. I had no feeling of time but I learned later that it was 13.45 when A Squadron technically entered Iraq on their way towards the breach.

In the back of the Optimist sat a very frustrated journalist. He was taking part in every correspondent's dream but all he could see was the swirling sand from the tracks through the 6 by 4 inch panel of armoured glass in the back door. All he could hear was my commentary on the tannoy. We seemed to have been motoring for some time when at last I saw the enormous sand berm which marked the start of the breach. All along it great chunks had been bulldozed out so that from a distance it looked like a child's toothy smile. As we grew closer to our designated breaching point I could see an American Abrams tank, its crew seated up in the turret, picketing the entrance to our lane. There were two signs that I remember, a large red marker board with the letter K designating our safe lane and a small sign hanging on the back of the tank. It read 'Remember soldier, every piece of your equipment was built by the lowest bidder.' An opened-up tank crew with a sense of humour. Things must be going well.

144

All the time I kept up a running commentary for the benefit of the crew in the back. Robert Fox was later to quote me in a report:

'The track is now winding away to the right, through what seems to be the main berm, Major Andrew Gillespie shouted down from the Optimist's turret. It looks much less formidable than I expected. The Americans have a Command Post. Everything, enemy vehicles, bunkers and trenches, has been bulldozed flat by the Americans. To the horizon I can see columns and columns of British and American convoys. The artillery is starting to fire from either side of us.'

Our transit of the breach was uneventful. Lane K was about 15 kms long and one tank wide. The lane had been cleared of mines by American Engineers and marked by fluorescent pickets. Being narrower than the Challengers, the Warrior had a lopsided journey, the right-hand track down in the ever deepening groove while the left-hand track rode high on almost virgin sand. Evidence of the battle to force the breach was everywhere - burnt and destroyed vehicles, flattened and bulldozed bunkers. The artillery fire plan for the breaching operation must have been truly awesome. In all over 11,000 rounds and 60,000 bomblets were reported to have been hurled at the defending forces. Few can have survived. A final sand wall marked the far extremity where we were met by our own recce and taken forward to our Forming Up Position (FUP). As we were led forward, the Artillery Group which had moved ahead of 7 Brigade, began to fire from all around us - MLRS launchers, M109 batteries, flashes, dust clouds, noise. We wove our way between gun positions, supply convoys, Americans and British. Chaos! At 15.50, A Squadron reported firm in FUP BLUE with the Battlegroup's MAIN HQ firm at 16.40 at grid NT 869505. The arrival of 4 Brigade into the Staging Areas also heralded the departure of 7 Brigade. They had an H hour of 15.15 and now only their logistic tail was left waiting to move. The weather was dull, cold and it was starting to rain.

Tac HQ parked up in a small compact group close to the MAIN HQ of the 3rd (US) Brigade. At 15.18 Battlegroup MAIN had received orders while still on the move via the secure SCRA radio system. They

An American Abrams tank. (PW)

confirmed our original orders and gave us an H hour of 19.30. The 14th/20th Battlegroup would lead the 4 Brigade advance out of the breach-head. We would move on route HAWK, the axis of which was formed by 3 SATNAV way-points.

On our return from the

American HQ there was a short Orders Group at the front of the Emperor to update every one on the 'Cunning Plan'. The latest intelligence on our first large objective, BRASS, indicated that the enemy was deployed as follows:

Western end:
A mechanized infantry battlegroup of two companies of MTLB APCs and a company of T55 tanks.

Central and Southern:
A large armoured battlegroup of some thirty tanks, four MTLBs, and a large number of unidentified vehicles positioned behind sand berms and orientated south.

Eastern end:
A large number of artillery and logistic positions.

The area of BRASS had been divided into three so that it could be attacked sequentially by the Brigade's three battlegroups. The strongly held central and southern position would be the 14th/20th target. This immediately prompted the question as to how many vehicles made a 'large number'. No answer was forthcoming. Mike Vickery went on to explain the need for the British Division's logistics to keep close behind the fighting troops and therefore 4 Brigade had first to clear through COPPER SOUTH and BRONZE in order to secure a firm location for the Divisional Administration Area. The 14th/20th would clear COPPER SOUTH and the Royal Scots would clear BRONZE. There was, however, every indication that neither position was occupied. BRONZE and COPPER were both on a barely discernible dome-shaped feature called Al Haniya on our maps. BRASS, however, was our first proper objective as it was certainly held by the Iraqis and to drive home the point the Colonel handed me a FRAGO (Fragmentary Order) showing the suspected enemy deployment on BRASS.

All around us was a hive of frenetic activity. The last remaining logistics packets of 7 Brigade were now moving out to be replaced by those from our own 4 Brigade. The nearby artillery batteries were coming out of action in order to join the great move. A frenzy of running troops, shouted orders and revving engines. As darkness descended the Tac HQ moved to join the rest of the Battlegroup behind our line of departure, NEW JERSEY. It was too dark to see but I knew that I was left rear of the Emperor with One One Charlie, the wing man, stationed right rear. As Tac HQ we were in the centre of the Battlegroup which had now shaken out into its standard formation for an advance to contact - A Squadron forward left, B Squadron forward right, the Queen's Company rear left and D Squadron rear right. The two forward squadrons were in a box formation with their outside rear troops echeloned out in flank protection. On the back of every bustle there now

146

shone a red torch. I placed ours inside the turret, shining back through the central rear periscope. As we approached the dreaded hour, final preparations were completed and the weather deteriorated to torrential rain. About 19.00 Mike Vickery came across with the news that all the satellites were down and he had just heard that 7 Brigade had stopped in the desert to await their reappearance, which would not be until about 21.30. A glance at our own SATNAV confirmed the situation. We talked over our options and what we should do.

Unlike 7 Brigade, time was not on our side, but unlike 7 Brigade my FOO vehicles had the APES navigation system that was not dependent on satellites. With an FOO with both of the lead squadrons I felt it was worth the risk. Much as I feared going to war I had a greater horror of sitting exposed behind NEW JERSEY. Mike Vickery decided to go on our H hour and then disappeared into the darkness to finish his own preparations. I walked slowly round the Optimist. With the bustle behind the turret crammed with rations, spare NBC suits, cam nets and water and with twelve Jerry cans of fuel hanging on the side, it looked very unmilitary. I kicked a road wheel for luck and then hauled myself up and into the turret. I hoped that this was not for the last time.

At precisely 19.30 the 14th/20th King's Hussars Battlegroup pushed forward out of its FUP as the lead element of the 4 Armoured Brigade advance. At 20.00 A Squadron reported that they were plus of Phase Line NEW JERSEY. We were at war. We moved on route HAWK. Our plan had been to navigate like a fleet at sea, using the satellite way-points. The satellites being down we now relied totally on my FOOs.

We moved through inky darkness accompanied by a strong blustery wind and driving rain. I sat high in my turret letting the cold air and water balance the heat that welled up from the engine and banks of radios below me. I knew that over on my right the Royal Scots Battlegroup would be preparing to move on their axis, TARTAN, and likewise the Fusiliers on my left. The suitably appropriate name for their axis had escaped me at the briefing. The Drone pilotless aircraft had reported COPPER clear, so, although I was apprehensive, I felt I had plenty of time to allow myself to get properly frightened. Suddenly the nets were alive with reports of unidentified vehicles moving across our front. We stopped. I peered into my Image Intensifying sight desperate for a glimpse of the activity that was so clear in the tanks' Thermal Imaging sights. A green shadowy blur was all I saw. Through my head-set came Mike Vickery's voice demanding to know if these were Gunner logistic vehicles. I clicked my radio net selector switch on the harness hanging around my neck and challenged my Fire Direction Centre. They had no idea. Their guns and logistic tail were following hard up behind the 14th/20th so it could only be 7 Brigade's artillery out in front of us. I crept slowly forward, along with the Emperor, until in the green of my sight I could make out the nose-to-tail line of artillery limbers. Slowly I traversed the turret, using the power traverse mechanism on my right-hand side. The turret moved, there was an acrid smell of burning and the turret stopped. The clutches on the electric motor had burnt out. I now only had the hand crank.

It took about 40 minutes before we were disentangled and advancing again. It had been an alarming experience because it was so unexpected. I do not know if the drivers of those trucks, trying to keep station in the darkness with nothing more than their eyes and a twinkling convoy light, knew that an armoured battlegroup had nearly driven into their side, or worse. We moved slowly and cautiously forward once more and some 15 minutes later I heard Alan Collett, BC with the Royal Scots, report that they were embroiled in another column of trucks.

We travelled on in darkness and relative silence. Occasionally, like sheep dogs, one of the FOOs would bark an instruction for his squadron to move left or right. Slowly the satellites emerged over the horizon enabling the tanks to regain their navigation. At 21.15 A Squadron reported crossing the 93 Easting and at 21.51 the 00 Easting. The GOC reported he was moving ahead of us but would be going firm at NT 942568 until 02.00. All these snippets of information I plotted on the enormous tac map that spread across my lap. Occasionally Sergeant Allen would call across the co-ordinates from our own SATNAV and so the line of plotted lumocolour dots marched slowly but inexorably towards the large ring with COPPER SOUTH written across it. Still a long way to go. No need to get panicky yet.

I was shaken from my doze at 22.34. The report of 'Contact' jolted the whole crew. A Squadron, moving forward left, had detected heat sources of what could be men in the open at Grid PT 085565. Again we stopped, expectant in the dark. I could see nothing through my sight and with my head proud of the hatch, could barely make out the shape of the Emperor no more than 20 feet away. It had stopped raining but the darkness was still total. Minutes later the contact was confirmed by B Squadron who had moved up parallel with A on our right. They reported infantry and APCs about 1,200 metres away. The initial fear was that this contact was Div HQ's Tac or an artillery recce party. There then ensued a frantic series of conversations on the Brigade command and artillery nets to try and sort out the situation. As I sat, high in my turret, staring vainly into the darkness, awaiting a reply to my questions, I looked up to see an array of tiny twinkling lights.

As I watched, captivated, the first tracer rounds fell all around us. Suddenly my ears rang to a sharp clang as a round struck the turret just inches behind me. In nano-seconds my seat was dropped and the hatch slammed shut. Across the turret Sergeant Allen was already down and had switched on the over-pressure fans to protect us from chemical attack. Through the II sight and my right-hand periscope the darkness was torn by criss-crossing white lines as bullets and rounds flew everywhere. My sight momentarily blanked out as the 120mm main armament on the Emperor spat a long sheet of flame into the desert darkness. The airwaves were full of reports and orders. On the artillery net I heard Hewlan Morgan, CPO of my own Battery, report that they were under fire and that two of the guns had been hit and that the turrets, loaded with live ammunition, had been penetrated. Being right behind the Battlegroup they had taken the full force of the enemy's first salvo, probably fired wildly and in panic in the general direction of our noise. Great flashes lit up the horizon as High Explosive Squash Head tank rounds impacted on their targets. Reports came in of armoured movements and incoming machine-gun fire. The voice of Mike Vickery rang in my ear,

"Echo One Zero this is Zero Alpha, give me some light."

I ordered Derek Hudson, the FOO with B Squadron, to put light about a kilometre forward of his position. Derek must have been working on just that as, seconds after his acknowledgement, I heard his fire mission go down. After a short pause the voice of the Adjutant, Captain Sebastian Muntz, on duty in the Fire Direction Centre, reported that all guns were either out of range or deploying in support of 7 Brigade's operation. I changed frequency and tried to speak direct to O Battery, but got no reply. I was later to learn that they had reacted to a report of tanks moving in their direction and were at that moment deploying for anti-tank fire.

Being a battlegroup based on a tank regiment, the 14th/20th had no integral mortars. I spoke to Alan Collett, BC with the Royal Scots, only to be told that they had run into a large enemy artillery concentration and their mortars were already deploying. It was now raining again, further reducing the visibility of the TI sights. Dave Marshall with the Fusiliers offered up his mortars but they were currently some 20 kms away and with a range of only 5 kms would be some time coming to our aid. It was a very despondent BC that reported back to his Battlegroup Commander.

The fire-fight raged, the tanks using their TOGS and the recce troop providing some brief white light from their 76mm guns. Tank main armaments sent great plumes of flames stabbing out into the darkness followed almost instantly by a blinding flash in the distance as a vehicle disintegrated in a ball of fire. Between the tank rounds, stabbing streams of red-dotted tracer arced through the night from the coaxial machine guns. The enemy fought back and, at one point, the doodlebug-like splutter of an anti-tank missile passed directly over our heads. Confusion also reigned. A report from the Royal Scots Battlegroup of Iraqi tanks moving away to their north was soon matched by a report from B Squadron that armour was moving to their south. The situation only became clear when Derek Hudson heard a FOO with the Royal Scots call for a 'Fire Mission 3 Batteries'. A glance at his APES navigation system showed that the target was less than 100 metres from his own position. The two Battlegroups had almost collided and it was only by very prompt action over the artillery airwaves that the first 'blue on blue' was prevented.

26 FEBRUARY 1991

At 00.20 the artillery Fire Direction Centre reported that 16 Field Battery of 26 Regiment had one gun ready with illuminating rounds. I immediately reported our state to the Colonel who ordered me to continue. Some 30 seconds after Derek Hudson gave the order to fire, the area was bathed in white, moonlike light from the artillery flare hanging beneath its parachute. It was a sobering sight. The British Challenger tanks, in line, facing rows of burning and burnt-out vehicles. Everywhere white-flag-waving soldiers came scrambling out of trenches, gesticulating frantically. It is incredible to think that many in the British Army still believe that we can fight totally without artificial light, relying entirely on technology. Without white light the enemy cannot surrender and our infantry are largely impotent.

The illuminating round burst over Grid PT 120515. One of the Challenger tanks drove forward and stopped about 30 metres from the nearest Iraqis. As he lowered his gun barrel they knelt down; as he raised his gun barrel they all stood up. A traverse left moved the crowd to the left, a right movement produced a move to the right. There then ensued a couple of minutes of theatre that would have been at home in a Monty Python movie, as the tank commander tried in vain to direct the prisoners. As we sat pondering our next move, machine-gun fire erupted from the end of the defensive line in front of me, sending a stream of fiery dots through the sky and impacting amongst the British vehicles. As I peered through my II sight I saw firstly all those trying to surrender throw themselves on the ground and then the bodies of the machine gunners go spiralling into the air as a tank round tore through their bunker. Finally Captain Henry Joynson, B Squadron's Battle Captain, drove forward in his 432 to take the surrender of the terrified Iraqi troops.

Prisoners were a problem we had expected but never really rehearsed. They were to be an echelon problem but our echelon was a good way behind. I heard Mike Vickery order the infantry company forward and when I informed him that I did not yet know for how long I could maintain the artillery light, he ordered them to switch their headlights on. Almost immediately afterwards, Nomad halted alongside me. I confess I was surprised to see the Brigade Commander this far forward and seemingly acting as a single tank. As both the Emperor and Nomad

moved forward I felt a draught on my legs. Looking back over my shoulder and in the glow from the burning vehicles, I saw Robert Fox standing outside the back door of the Optimist. It was only by screaming at him to get back inside that I was able to catch up and not lose contact. By 00.30 16 Battery had managed to bring two guns into action and the FOO had moved the rounds back to Grid PT084565. The illumination went on until past 01.00.

A T55 on Objective BRONZE. The first engagement took place in the dark. Photograph taken after the ceasefire. (AG)

While the pantomime of the prisoners was being enacted the squadrons had pushed outwards to secure the area and to ensure we were not surprised by a counter-attack. At 00.45 B Squadron reported up to nine vehicles moving NE to SW. These were quickly engaged and destroyed, as were a second packet moving up behind. 00.55 A Squadron reported fifteen vehicles moving away to the NW. They engaged, but at maximum range and to little effect. Shortly afterwards the firing died down and it appeared that the enemy had either had enough or had withdrawn. The sky now glowed from the light of burning vehicles and the artillery shells.

The position appeared to have been occupied by a Signals (Electronic Warfare) unit of about company strength with a strong guard force and a transport echelon. They were equipped with a variety of APCs and tanks (mostly MTLBs and T55s). In all about 300 prisoners were taken. It had been a short but intense engagement. Our first blooding. Leaving the RSM and the Queen's Company of the Grenadier Guards to deal with the prisoners, we moved quickly back onto our axis. The infantry were not long in dealing with the problem. Once the now very pliant and obedient prisoners had been disarmed, their weapons were placed in a large pile and a Warrior driven over them. Now harmless, they were ordered to walk westwards. Well not quite! Out of the darkness we heard a Grenadier Guardsman inform the prisoners that to save them walking to the POW cages, they would march. This was followed by the sound of a Guards rifting. 'Shunn! Right turn. Left, right, left, right, swing your arms you idle Arabs.' Just when they were starting to think that things could not get any worse. Personally, it was twenty-one years since I left Sandhurst but I still had to fight the Pavlovian response to stand to attention in my turret.

It was not, however, until 03.15 that we had re-formed into our march formation and were moving again. We still had to clear COPPER SOUTH for the logistic units and were now well behind our planned schedule. Having been surprised by the enemy in an area our intelligence had reported clear, we advanced with caution. However, we made good progress and I was starting to doze in the soporific heat of the turret when, at 04.15, I was again jerked awake by a Contact Report. Call sign 42 of B Squadron reported a large lorry, on its own and stationary at NT 170582. The report was answered with the curt order to engage. The tank fired. It struck the ammunition truck which detonated, sending a massive column of flame hundreds of feet into the air. As we closed on the burning truck the squadron reported multiple hot-spots on their TOGS and deployed into battle lines. T55 tanks, dug into the sand with only their turrets showing, were soon being detected and destroyed. The Colonel and I moved forward to join the squadron and soon the Emperor was engaging, scoring a hit on a T55 turret at a range of 2,800 metres. A fuel tanker exploded in a spectacular fire-ball which momentarily both lit up the battlefield and blanked out my night-sight.

The Challengers fired from the short halt, moving, stopping, firing, moving on again. The enemy tanks returned fire and the air was rent by the sonic boom of rounds passing close overhead. I was clearly vulnerable and in a bad position to provide light or any other support. I therefore ordered us out of the battle line to a point some 400 metres back but still on the axis. I was again allocated 16 Battery from 26 Regiment for illumination which I assigned to Graham Ambrose. He was with A Squadron and they, with the Queen's Company, were swinging around from the left. By 05.30 they were involved in a rolling shoot. The infantry moved quickly behind the tanks taking prisoners by the light of the artillery rounds (Grid PT187605). Central in the battle I ordered the driver to keep a couple of bounds behind the lead troops.

Down in the depths of the turret I fought my battle from my map and on the radio, oblivious to everything else. It was only when I heard the order to reorganize that I looked up and out through the periscopes. It was 06.00 and just daylight. We were stationary. All around me was the devastation of the night's battle – burnt-out and still burning lines of armour, still in their sand holes, many with their guns pointing away from us, unable to traverse due to the sand wall. Those who had tried to flee suffered no better. Shattered APCs and annihilated logistics vehicles lay testament to the futility of their actions. I opened up my hatch and stiffly eased myself up. As the first rays of morning sun bathed me, I realized that the driver had either lost contact or fallen asleep from exhaustion for we were totally alone on the battlefield.

I scanned the horizon, desperate to see one of our own tanks.

T55 and MTLB at objective COPPER SOUTH. (AG)

Nothing! The night's rain had only blurred the tracks but there was such an array I could make no sense of the patterns. I dreaded having to come up on the radio and ask Mike Vickery for his position, so, cautiously, we motored forward towards the densest mass of burning vehicles. I reasoned that they were the most recently attacked and were therefore probably on the Battlegroup's main axis. Cautiously we moved between the hulks. Occasionally an Iraqi would spring from his hiding place and wave his arms frantically. I was high in the turret, my loaded and cocked sub-machine-gun clearly visible. I would aim the weapon and, as confidently and fiercely as possible, point over my shoulder. Without exception they scuttled off, relief written all over their faces. I cannot recall how long it took us to find the main force, but it was with considerable relief that we finally parked alongside the Emperor. Mike Vickery gave me a cheery wave and I waved back as if I had been away on some vital mission.

The battle for the Al Haniyah feature was over. I quickly briefed the FOOs and sent a SITREP back to the FDC, including the news that, in spite of the ferocity of the night's battles, we had taken no casualties. We were parked in the middle of a substantial enemy position. It was clear of tanks and APCs but was pock-marked with low sand walls surrounding what appeared to be the entrances to deep dugouts - dark, black, square holes. A few hundred yards away the infantry were persuading the Iraqis to leave their shelters and surrender. Mike Vickery climbed off the Emperor and stretched his legs. We were clearly going to be here for some time, so I gave the order to dismount. About 50 metres

153

Iraqi HQ at Objective COPPER SOUTH.
(AG)

behind us was the entrance to one of the dugouts with our track marks clearly indicating that we had driven right over the top. Sergeant Allen and I walked back to the half-collapsed hole to be confronted by a terrified Iraqi. Sergeant Allen marched him off to join his colleagues in the care of the Queen's Company.

We appeared to be in the centre of a heavily defended command complex and this was confirmed just before 07.00 when B Squadron, over on our right, reported the capture of an Iraqi brigadier. The Commander of 52 Tank Brigade surrendered with all his brigade staff. Investigations revealed an underground complex of staggering proportions. Some 4 metres underground was a command centre, living accommodation, offices and kitchens. Fully lit and carpeted, they were a marvel of military engineering. In one office was found a safe which was immediately liberated and a degree of 'force' applied to the door. It contained a mass of brand-new Iraqi currency. Our own Intelligence later estimated that the position consisted of the Brigade HQ protected by a tank company of eight T55s and a company of MTLB infantry carriers. Many of the Iraqi positions consisted of deep scrapes in the sand, with first a tank, barrel pointing forwards, then an APC parked immediately behind. Many tanks had been destroyed because they were unable to traverse their guns rearwards, obstructed by the APC. Others had been rendered useless, unable to fire because they were blinded by their burning APC. In all some 150 prisoners were taken.

As we remounted to move out, Brigadier Hammerbeck found a T55 that had escaped earlier attention. Being unwilling to fire at it with so many unprotected troops close by, Jonty Palmer, the Adjutant, destroyed it by dropping a hand grenade through the commander's hatch. I had travelled about 200 yards when the tank's magazine exploded, rocking the Optimist violently and all but sending me crashing to the bottom of the turret. As we reformed back onto our axis and waited for the lead

154

squadrons to report ready, we came across a battery of South African-made G5 guns, abandoned, but in perfect condition. They were well-dug-in with massive stocks of ammunition, yet appeared not to have taken part in the battle. We were under pressure to clear COPPER quickly so that second echelon troops could occupy. We could do nothing more than report and move on. We were now well behind schedule, very tired, and the weather, after a promising dawn, was again deteriorating. Our objective was now BRASS. Up to now we had fought short sharp engagements, mainly with the tanks. Objective BRASS would be a battle fought primarily with massed artillery, what Joseph Stalin had called 'The God of War'.

As we once more shook out into our march formation and headed towards our next pivot point, way-point Charlie, the Colonel gave orders for a change in formation. D Squadron, which had throughout the night been in reserve, moved up to relieve B Squadron now tired and low on ammunition. The perfectly executed manoeuvre was carried out like a ballroom dance movement.

A brief chance to stretch one's legs. The author and a T55 at COPPER SOUTH. (AG)

A typical wet desert scene – dawn at COPPER SOUTH. (AG)

Objective BRASS was believed to be held by an Iraqi armoured brigade and would therefore require a brigade assault. (Military wisdom had until now always decreed that an attacking force needed a 3 to 1 superiority to succeed). The brigade attack would be sequential. The Royal Scots Battlegroup would attack first into the infantry-held positions, the 14th/20th Battlegroup would then assault down and through the armoured centre and then the 3rd Fusiliers Battlegroup would take on the artillery and logistics before moving on to clear the small area marked as STEEL. The plan enabled the full weight of the Divisional Artillery to support each attack in turn. The Royal Scots were due to assault the western end of BRASS with an H hour of 07.30, but they also had been held up by two separate engagements during the night and so their H hour was delayed until 09.30. As we moved across the desert towards our own assembly area I heard Alan Collett's Fire Plan being sent down to the Fire Direction Centre. It went in familiar neat packets and, as is the practice with all artillery Fire Orders, each transmission was faithfully repeated back. Listening to the radio traffic it was difficult to believe that this was anything more than just another exercise on the ranges. I remembered receiving the orders for the attack on BRASS. Nothing complicated or dramatic, just a single sheet of paper

A quick O Group: Lieutenant Colonel Vickery, Lance Bombardier Covill, Sergeant Allen and the author at Objective COPPER SOUTH. (AG)

showing the assessed enemy positions. In the top right-hand corner was 'FRAGO 10/91 241200C Feb 91'. In the top left hand corner was written, 'No move North of 63 Northing.' There was then a series of broad felt-penned arrows and boundaries. Finally, scrawled down the side in the same thick felt pen, was 'Task Org: No change. Sequential attack: 1RS, 14/20H, 3RRF.' It was signed JG James, Major, Chief of Staff. That was all it now took to launch us into battle.

As the sun rose and warmed the wet ground, thick white mist descended, cutting visibility by the naked eye down to as little as 500 metres. The 14th/20th stopped some 3 kms short of Way-Point Charlie and shook out into their assault formation. We would now wait for the Royal Scots to complete their attack. The mist was like a protective blanket and the three vehicles of Tac HQ nestled close together. It was a welcome last chance for crews to stretch their legs and do any final personal admin. The Fire Plan in support of the Royal Scots Battlegroup now sent, there was an opportunity for me to complete my battle preparation. The planning and orders for our main attack had been done in the final assembly area where I had been given the Intelligence assessment of the enemy's deployment on BRASS. Our sector was about 7 kms by 10 kms. The enemy were orientated facing south, clearly a reserve to support the forward defensive position. The area was criss-crossed with high sand walls protecting dug-in tanks and infantry. We would attack from the north with two squadrons leading and, approximately half-way down the position, dogleg half right in order to keep central to the enemy's centre of mass. The third squadron would provide flank protection on our left, hopefully sanitizing the main force from the artillery and other units still to be attacked by 3RRF. The infantry would be the mobile reserve, able to move rapidly to assist wherever necessary. The plan relied on advancing behind massive artillery fire.

I spoke to David Radcliffe, who was well aware of the plan, and asked for an allocation of artillery. I was both heartened and staggered by the response. For the 14th/20th King's Hussars Battlegroup attack on the armoured heart of BRASS we would have the M109 guns of 2nd, 26 and 40 Regiments and a portion of the MLRS and M110 guns of the American 142 Field Artillery Brigade, Arkansas National Guard. To top it all I was allotted two air sorties. Our expected H hour was now to be 10.30.

Not wishing to get involved with the hazards of close air support I chose the armour centred around what would be our pivot point half-way through our attack and, through our Tactical Air Control Party, ordered a Time on Target air strike of 10.00. On the main attack I reasoned that control would be the most difficult problem, so I divided the target area vertically down the middle, allocating two Gun

4 Armoured Brigade's attack on Objective BRASS

Regiments to one side and a Gun Regiment and the American Brigade to the other. Within those sectors I further subdivided, putting the full force on the nearest targets to our break-in sector, but then alternating units so that we could step forward, effectively moving behind a wall of fire. I would start the fire plan but then pass control of the fire in each sector to the leading FOOs. We would fire a deadly mixed cocktail of bomblet, airburst and ground burst ammunition. My Fire Plan was sent without incident and duly acknowledged well before the Royal Scots' attack. Preliminaries over, I sat on my turret hatch in the cold, dense mist to await the first reports of '*Shot*' on the Royal Scots' attack.

Just before the Royal Scots H hour the Battlegroup was shaken by the sound of gunfire. Unknown to us, in the poor visibility, we had deployed between two M109 Regiments. Considering the tension we were all under it was a severe shock. Mike Vickery had the greatest shock of all. He had been conducting a 'Shovel Recce' beside the Emperor when the guns had opened fire. Still in a state of undress, he roundly cursed St Barbara and all her followers. Indignity is no respecter of rank. Great flashes in the fog showed that the MLRS were also in action and, although we could see none of the targets, we felt the ground shake from the impact of the fire. With Mike Vickery close at hand I was able to relay the Royal Scots' battle as it unfolded on the artillery net, a running commentary on the morning's event - the crossing of the Line of Departure, the advance, the enemy opening fire, the FOOs dismounting, entering and fighting through the trenches and all orchestrated by fire orders. As the battle started to draw to a close we mounted, awaiting a final confirmation of our own H hour. One by one Alan Collett released the artillery regiments and one by one the Fire Direction Centre reported them ready in support of my Fire Plan.

"*Hello Three Three this is Zero, Regiment Two, ready, over.*"

"*Three Three, Regiment Two, ready, out.*"

I knew that back at the gun batteries, computations were being completed and orders given. The 'Number One' with each gun would have all the firing data to hand, each bearing and elevation carefully logged. Ammunition would be unloaded, fuses screwed tight, charges prepared and all stacked ready.

"*Regiment One, ready, over.*"

"*Regiment One, ready, out.*"

I knew also that back at The Rocket Troop the CPO would have announced that they were about to fire for the 14th/20th, their Battlegroup, their tac crews. Drills would be that tiny bit slicker, checks even more exact. I could picture the Gun Line Section Commanders racing between their guns, compasses in hand, a final check that all was well.

"*American Brigade, ready, over.*"

"*American Brigade, ready, out.*"

At 10.15 we moved, wheeling round through 90 degrees like a fleet at sea, to head due south, stopping just behind our Line of Departure, a road made of oil-sprayed sand. I had determined that my Battlegroup would not be committed to battle until I was confident that the artillery had done everything possible to destroy the enemy and so prevent our own casualties. We were working to an H hour of around 10.30 but we would go when the Gunners were ready. My fire plan was therefore 'On Call.'

"Regiment Three ready, ready on Fire Plan UK 4300, over."

"Ready on Fire Plan UK 4300, out."

I clicked over to the Battlegroup net:

"Hello Zero Alpha this is Echo One Zero, we're ready, over"

"Zero Alpha, Roger. Go for it."

I switched back to the artillery net. It all seemed unreal. Here I was about to start a major armoured battle. On my left and right the assaulting force was spread out as far as I could see - the Challengers in line abreast across the desert, poised and waiting like living creatures, all guns pointing forward, grey plumes of smoke rising from the back decks as the drivers raised the power on the massive Condor engines. The visibility was improving rapidly. Inside the Optimist the hatch clamps were given a final tighten for luck, the fans switched on, and on my left-hand side Sergeant Allen fed the belted ammunition into the breech of the chain gun. On my lap were the tools of my trade, my tac map and Fire Plan proforma. We sat expectantly in the eerie half-glow of the turret lights and what little daylight found its way through the periscopes. Everything was ready. Please God don't let anything happen to us, and don't let me foul up. A deep breath,

"Fire, over."

I was surprised at the voice that gave the order. It was clear, steady and calm.

"Fire, out."

As the Fire Direction Centre reported *'Shot on Fire Plan'* the horizon now emerging to our front erupted. Safe inside our steel cocoons our world shook as for 10 minutes the might of the Divisional Artillery plus the American Brigade delivered more firepower than was at El Alamein onto the forward positions of Objective BRASS. At 10.40 I reported to Mike Vickery that I was confident we were able to go. It was answered with,

"All stations this is Zero Alpha, move now, out."

As one, the 14th/20th King's Hussars Battlegroup moved forward towards the mass of dust, smoke and fire. My plan was to lift the fire onto the next row of positions when we were about 1,000 metres short, giving 500 metres for the visibility to clear before the tanks closed with the enemy. As I crossed the Line of Departure I passed control of the

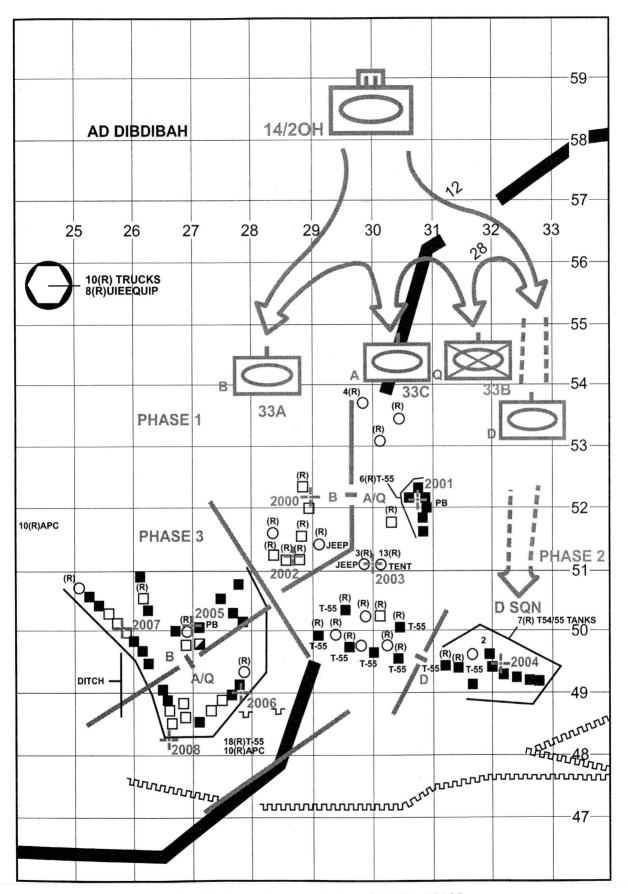

14th/20th King's Hussars attack on Objective BRASS

artillery fire to the two forward FOOs.

"Hello Charlie Charlie Six this is Three Three, you have control, out."
As we closed, travelling at maximum speed, I heard Derek Hudson check the fire in his sector and order it onto the next serials of the Fire Plan. I waited expectantly for Graham Ambrose to do the same. Suddenly there was chatter on the fire orders net. Not fire orders but tittle tattle. I don't know who it was but they were perpetrating the most heinous crime imaginable in the Royal Artillery. Graham Ambrose's voice cut the air,

"Three Three Charlie, Check Firing, over."
No reply from the Fire Direction Centre and the inane chatter continued.

"Three Three Charlie, Check Firing, over."
A note of desperation was now in the voice and I pictured A Squadron heading, like the fateful Light Brigade, at full speed towards a wall of artillery fire that was not going to lift. I tried, but could not get through. I screamed at the crew to switch the radio to the full 50 watts output, only to be told I was already on it. I was about to flick onto the Battlegroup Command Net and talk directly to the squadron leader and tell him to stop when Graham got through and I heard the Fire Direction Centre confirm check firing on that serial. While this was happening Sergeant Allen had kept the Optimist close in beside the two tanks of Tac HQ. Our small tight group charged headlong towards the dust which marked where the artillery had impacted. Suddenly to our flank a tank fired, sending a round screaming over the top of both the Emperor and the Optimist. A picket, not marked on the intelligence map and therefore outside the artillery footprint. I screamed a warning to Mike Vickery who stopped and put a round straight through the turret. It exploded sending the saucepan-shaped top spiralling into the air. Corporal Redgrave, the Colonel's gunner, was on form today. Before we moved again, I spotted a BRDM about 1,200 metres away hurriedly trying to deploy its Sagger anti-tank missile. A quick warning and a second round from Corporal Redgrave destroyed that also.

We were now moving through a world of dust, fire, smoke and carnage. As the artillery bombardment moved forward, the Battlegroup moved behind. Through the centre of BRASS we travelled, kilometre after kilometre. Shattered hulks and still-burning vehicles were everywhere, marking the path of the barrage. Burning ammunition detonated, throwing great chunks of blazing metal skywards. Challenger tanks, now moving as pairs or individuals, would stop and engage targets deep in the smoke, visible only to their miraculous TOGS sights. At the way-point we wheeled on the dogleg and headed on to what we hoped would be the end of the position. In those areas not under the artillery footprint, Iraqi soldiers, singly and in small groups were frantically waving white flags, unsure what to do as the armoured stampede bore down on them. As we continued forward and the last serials of the fire plan were executed I again took control of the artillery. Suddenly we were out of the dust into bright clear air. In front of us, at a range of about 1,500 metres, was a line of eight Iraqi T55 tanks untouched by the artillery and now frantically trying to turn their guns to engage us. Our group of three vehicles charged towards them at high speed. Through my right-hand periscope I could see the sand spewing from the Emperor's front sprocket. I knew the other tank would be close by.

We closed rapidly with the enemy, 1,000 metres, 800 metres, flashes in the distance and then their first salvo streaked over our heads. Tank rounds. A high pitched scream, like an express train, was followed by the pressure wave of the sonic booms. I yelled at the driver to "weave, weave," only to be yelled at in turn by two agitated tank commanders. Still we closed. The Challengers were now firing. One after another the T55s were hit. Some burnt, some exploded, some seemed to rise up momentarily and then just disintegrate. Another salvo of fire tore over and between us, one round clearing the back hatches by less than twelve inches and making the 26-tonne Optimist rock violently on its tracks. Still we rushed forward, still the enemy fired. They were now only hundreds of metres away. Directly in front of the Optimist I could see the crew of a T55 tank scrambling out and waving white flags. A rasping whine, a staccato clatter, the chain gun spat and the turret was filled with the acrid smell of cordite. "They are trying to surrender," I shouted at Sergeant Allen. A flick of the traverse handle moved the turret that fraction needed to enabled me to see what he had fired at. A T55 tank, unnoticed and untouched but right on our nose, had its barrel pointing straight at us, the crew inside no doubt frantically trying to reload. The chain gun had hit the tank turret but with just a 7.62mm round we could only hope to distract the crew momentarily. We were now less than 300 metres away and the tank gun was moving from side to side as the gunner fought to bring the Optimist into his sight picture. They would fire at any second and at that range the tank round would annihilate us. In desperation I screamed into the radio for Mike Vickery to *"For Christ's sake, do something"*, to be greeted with a very casual *"Roger."* Seconds later the Emperor fired, the T55 erupted into a ball of fire and spiralling metal and we were through the line and facing open desert.

"Hello Echo One Zero this is Zero Alpha, I think we had better get some armour around you."
Almost immediately I felt shadows across my periscopes as the two Challenger tanks drew alongside, sandwiching the Optimist between their massive bulk. Fearful that the enemy position was even bigger or that we would be counter-attacked, I asked to keep the artillery until we had fully reorganized, and sent down a quick DF (Defensive Fire) list. One by one the Regiments reported that they were out of range. As I sought new targets, David Radcliffe informed me that the artillery was now

The T55 engaged by Sergeant Allen with a chain gun and destroyed by Lieutenant Colonel Mike Vickery, 14th/20th King's Hussars. (AG)

being switched to support 3RRF's attack.

It was now 12.00. The wind was dropping, the sky clearing and the visibility improving by the minute. Our battle for BRASS was over, but the Battlegroup was spread over a vast area. We now had to reorganize and replenish. Control of this vital operation would fall to the Battlegroup 2IC, Major Godfrey Tilney, and his Battlegroup MAIN HQ. Already the order dispatching D Squadron to join 3RRF had been given, as had RVs for the remaining two squadrons and the company. Our small tac group now had to make its way northwards to rejoin the main Battlegroup concentration. We wheeled round and, with the Emperor leading, set off slowly. We were passing through unfamiliar territory. Some areas were open desert which we crossed quickly, others were a criss-cross of sand walls and burning vehicles. Here we proceeded with greater caution, warily approaching any vehicle that looked as if it might still be intact. Many, on closer examination, had been shredded by the artillery and it was soon clear that some of the blackened hulks had been destroyed much earlier during the air campaign.

As we journeyed we came across small groups of Iraqi soldiers. Some held white flags, others waved the leaflets that the air forces had dropped promising good treatment to those who surrendered. Few made any move to approach us and all seemed relieved that the two tanks, enormous by their standards, totally ignored them. As we approached the complex of vehicles that was Battlegroup MAIN, now deployed in its star shaped formation, I heard Dave Marshall, BC with 3RRF, putting the final touches to his Fire Plan. It had taken less than an hour for D Squadron to extract itself, move, receive orders and get onto its new Line of Departure. They made an H hour of 13.00 and I felt the ground again shake as the Divisional artillery opened fire in support of the attack. We parked up close to MAIN and climbed down to stretch our legs. Already there were a number of Iraqi prisoners, sitting cross-legged, in neat lines. Sergeant Major Redhead played Master of Ceremonies by barking at them in the Arabic he had learnt during his service in the Oman. Their numbers grew steadily. Some had come forward from COPPER SOUTH, some had walked back from the Iraqi front line when it was clear to them that their armoured reserve had been destroyed. The bulk, however, were from BRASS. After the initial barrage, the FOOs had lifted the fire early when it was apparent that the enemy infantry was in no state to fight. As we moved through BRASS and the battle situation became clearer they had at times held the artillery fire in order to allow the enemy to surrender. There was room for compassion even amidst the need to protect our own. I know that tank crews did likewise. Those who surrendered were simply driven past, but those who chose to fight were crushed either by the awesome weight of the artillery or the armour moving behind.

It was a chance to relax, eat and, if you were lucky, sleep. The crew of the Optimist did all three, as well as vital maintenance and preparation for the expected REPLEN. As we were parked less than ten yards from the prisoners I spent some time, seated in the turret, watching them. They were a complete mixture. The Regular Army troops from COPPER and BRASS seemed healthy enough and their equipment serviceable. They sat around chatting to each other. Those from the front line were clearly less well provisioned, in a poor state of health and just seemed relieved that for them it was all over. There were both very young and very old amongst them. As the squadron leaders arrived in their tanks for orders and parked up close by, the Iraqis looked in awe at the size, speed and power of the Challengers which stood half as high again as their old, lightweight, T55s. The arrival of the Queen's Company, not one of whom was much under 6' 4", was the final proof, if proof were needed, that further resistance was futile.

At 14.20 we received a Warning Order from Brigade. The Brigade was to seize Objective TUNGSTEN and destroy all enemy within it. The attack would be led by the two infantry battlegroups. We were to despatch our tank squadrons and take under command No 2 Company of the Grenadier Guards. We were to be a 0:2 battlegroup with just the two infantry companies, our engineers, the three FOOs and me. Our task was Brigade reserve and, once TUNGSTEN had been taken, the 14th/20th Battlegroup would pass through, pick up its squadrons and lead the subsequent advance. There was great consternation in the HQ

Iraqi soldiers surrender at Objective BRASS. (AG)

on receipt of the news that they were to be in reserve, with no squadrons under command. I was delighted!

By 15.00 the 3RRF Battlegroup's attack on its portion of BRASS had been successfully completed and they had continued on to clear the next position, STEEL. At the 14th/20th the A1 echelon was distributing fuel, water, ammunition and rations. The weather was now clear, bright, warm and sunny. All around me troops were preparing themselves and their equipment for whatever might come next. Close to the HQ the lines of prisoners grew inexorably. As I worked up in the turret I heard Richard Farndale report that one of the 3RRF Warriors, reorganizing to the east of him, had exploded. He thought that it must have hit a mine. Minutes later his report that a second Warrior had also exploded seemed to confirm Richard's guess that the Fusiliers had indeed run into a minefield. Fearing further casualties, I passed the warning of the possible minefield on up the Battlegroup command net. These reports were the foundation of what was to be a long saga of confusion, which was only fully unravelled after the war. In fact both vehicles had been hit by Maverick missiles fired in error by American A10 aircraft. The missiles had been launched from some 15,000 feet by aircraft completely invisible to those on the ground. Nine soldiers died and a further eleven were wounded. The casualties sustained were the worst the British were to suffer throughout the entire conflict and put an end to any feeling of euphoria amongst the troops of 4 Brigade.

At 16.00 the Colonel and I were summoned to a Brigade Orders Group, a short distance to our rear. As the Emperor still had to be re-armed, we went in the Optimist. It was at Brigade Forward HQ and most of the briefing took place around a map spread over the front of the Brigadier's tank, Nomad. With the fresh news of the Fusiliers' casualties the mood was sombre and businesslike. Brigadier Hammerbeck announced that intelligence indicated that the Iraqis' strategic reserve, the Republican Guard Force Divisions, were moving forward to protect the forces withdrawing from Kuwait towards Basra. This was what General Schwarzkopf had been waiting for. Stripped of their deep protective pits and concentrated anti-aircraft fire, once on the move they would fall easy prey to the Coalition's air power. Also it was reported that the Egyptians were about to attack Kuwait City airfield.

Intelligence indicated that TUNGSTEN was held by the Iraqi 37 Brigade. 4 Brigade's Mission was to clear Objective TUNGSTEN by first light. TUNGSTEN, however, had an obstacle at its rear over which we would have to pass if we were to achieve our mission. The obstacle was an oil pipeline running parallel to a road. In order to protect the pipeline, sand had been piled on top of it to a height of some 15 feet. It was this that would prove a problem and it was assessed that it would take considerable Engineer effort to breach. There was pressure on the

Brigade Commander to move quickly, yet replenishment was not yet complete, orders had to be issued and the re-deployment of troops had still not begun. David Radcliffe briefed the three BCs on the artillery plan. The attack by the two leading battlegroups would be supported by the M109s of 2nd and 26 Regiments and two M110 and two MLRS batteries from the American reinforcing brigade. Being already exhausted, I was heartily glad that, for the moment anyway, the spotlight was off the 14th/20th.

Battlegroup orders were given at 17.00 in a huddle outside MAIN HQ as a large crowd of Iraqi prisoners sat watching, mesmerised, from close by. A Squadron would join the Life Guards Squadron with the RS Battlegroup, B Squadron would join D Squadron with the 3RRF Battlegroup. The Queen's Company would stay with 14th/20th and would be joined by No 2 Company of the Grenadier Guards, from 3RRF Battlegroup. The 14th/20th Battlegroup would move at the rear of the Brigade column. Our Mission was Brigade Reserve. New maps had been issued taking us right to the coast. For this operation, however, we were to move from the southern end of BRASS via a series of satellite way-points. The oil pipeline would be known as CROCUS and the breaching sites were planned to be at Grids PT 552502 (3RRF) and PT 577530 (1RS). H hour for the 14/20H move was 21.30.

As we stood around, intent on absorbing the details of the orders, there was a terrifying explosion less than 10 feet away. The noise was deafening and the sand and the blast threw those closest forwards into the others. The instant conclusion was that we were under artillery attack. Everyone scattered, including the by now 500 or more Iraqi prisoners. For a short time chaos reigned until the realization that the explosion was in the singular. A REME gun fitter had been working on one of the Reconnaissance Troop's Scorpions which was parked immediately behind the Orders Group. He had accidentally fired the 76mm gun and the high explosive round had impacted just feet from the assembled body. We regained our composure relatively quickly. The Iraqis took longer to settle. If this was what the British did to each other, what would we do to them?

Refuelled, fed and rearmed we sat in the darkness waiting to move. The 14/20H Battlegroup, or what remained of it, was now in its march formation - Recce Troop, Tac HQ, the two infantry companies and MAIN. The thankful Iraqi prisoners had departed earlier, crammed on board M548s. These vehicles, originally loaded with jerrycans of fuel, their task complete, had dumped their empty cans and taken on board tired and dejected prisoners. At 21.30 we moved off along a now well-worn track at the rear of the Brigade column. It was very dark and overcast, but dry. I sat high in the turret of the Optimist, following the two Challenger tanks of Tac HQ. Some 20 metres ahead the convoy light, low on the rear of One One

Charlie, bobbed up and down as the tank faithfully followed the wave-like contours that the passage of so many tracked vehicles had generated on the track. It was the only thing visible and I watched it, transfixed, hour after hour, mile after mile. The small white dot would travel upwards, pause, then descend. At the bottom of its trajectory it would go out momentarily as the base of the tank sank down into the dip only to reappear, as if reborn, to start the process all over again.

27 FEBRUARY 1991

It was a long and very dark move to the FUP, some 30 to 40 kms. I sat up in the turret, my eye on the only visible thing, the moving dot of the convoy light. Up, down, vanish. Up, down, vanish. As I watched this seemingly endless ritual the small orb of light made its upward pilgrimage and went out. 'STOP', I screamed into the intercom and the Optimist instantly stood on its nose. Inside, sleeping bodies were sent sprawling and I went slamming against the armoured sight shield, only my body armour saving me from serious injury. I ordered the Optimist forward very slowly. Standing high on his turret seat, Sergeant Allen shone a hooded torch forward and to our left. One One Charlie had driven, nose first, into an enormous crater, its powerful 120mm gun embedded in the sand. The crew seemed shaken but unhurt. I can only guess what Staff Sergeant Geraghty said to his driver. There was nothing we could do to assist, so we hurried on, fearful of losing contact with the Emperor. They were just ahead and the 70-tonne Challenger was negotiating its way up a 15-foot sand rampart, tottering momentarily at the top before descending down the far side. This was CROCUS, the obstacle, the oil pipeline. The Optimist followed cautiously with Sergeant Allen talking Lance Bombardier Covill through the very difficult manoeuvre. Slowly upwards, a slight track to the right, a momentary pause on the pinnacle and we were over.

Ahead of us, in the darkness, the two assaulting battlegroups had crossed the oil pipeline obstacle, without the anticipated problems, and had shaken out into their assault formations - the Royal Scots to the south, the Fusiliers in the north. The 14/20H remained static behind, still in march formation, ready to be called forward when required. The Brigade attack onto TUNGSTEN was heralded by a massive fire plan. As we waited expectantly, the sky was illuminated by the arcing paths of MLRS rockets and the ground shook from the pounding of thousands of shells. Iraqi ammunition bunkers and fuel dumps were amongst the first casualties, lighting the horizon with bright flashes and towering fire-balls. Led by the armoured squadrons, the battlegroups started their assault at about 02.30. TUNGSTEN consisted mainly of artillery and infantry positions. What armour there was tried to escape north and north-east, only to be destroyed by our tanks. We slowly followed up

168

behind, keeping to the centre line. Dawn revealed the results of the night's effort. TUNGSTEN encompassed a large area and everywhere there now lay burnt-out infantry vehicles and devastated gun positions. Inside their pitifully inadequate pits, distorted and blackened ordnance pointed up to the sky like deformed dinosaurs. All around were foxholes and bunkers. Strewn everywhere was paper, abandoned equipment and unexploded ammunition. There were also prisoners, hundreds of prisoners, acres of prisoners. They looked stunned at the speed of the night's assault and the ferocity of the artillery fire. In all, the Brigade took some 2,500 prisoners on TUNGSTEN.

The two assaulting battlegroups reached their limit of exploitation, the 76 Easting, by 07.00. The 14th/20th had gone firm at 06.30, waiting patiently for the squadrons to finish their battle. By 08.00 our squadrons had rejoined us and we were placed at one hour's notice to move. Maintenance of both vehicle and body now went on wherever possible. Tac was parked in what had been the central area of a Divisional Artillery Group. We went exploring. Mindful of the ever-present threat of booby traps and land mines, we investigated the HQ bunker, clearly evacuated in the greatest hurry by the enemy. The position offered a fascinating insight into life in the Iraqi army. Life for them had clearly been austere and perhaps harsh, but we found plenty of fresh food, personal items like radios and, most poignant of all, abandoned pictures of wives, children and sweethearts. Mike Vickery and I explored a series of gun pits in which crouched the menacing shapes of Soviet-built 152mm towed howitzers. Burnt and buckled, they sat surrounded by their remaining stocks of ammunition. I examined each shell carefully, looking for the telltale banding that denotes a chemically filled round. I saw none. What I did see were neat piles of green, wooden ammunition boxes, each distinctly marked, 'JORDANIAN ARMY'.

Jordanian Army artillery ammunition at Objective TUNGSTEN. (AG)

As the squadrons returned exhausted after the night's battle, we again became a 3:1 battlegroup, three squadrons and an infantry company. Resupply was now paramount and the echelon worked frantically to distribute fuel, water and ammunition. I was just stretching out on the Optimist's roof to try and catch some sleep when the order came reducing our notice to move to 30 minutes. It was 11.30. Maintenance was hurriedly completed, meals eaten and kit stowed. At 11.58 the expected Warning Order arrived from Brigade. We were to prepare to exploit eastwards to Objective VARSITY (QT 145715) and then, on orders, advance north along the Wadi Al Batin. The 14th/20th Battlegroup would again lead the Brigade advance. When ordered, we were to move at best possible speed. At 12.58 we received confirmatory orders over the radio net. We were to move at 13.30. With the orders came our first proper SITREP. It was short but encouraging. The Marines had taken the airport outside Kuwait City and airborne forces had destroyed all bridges over the Euphrates. As we moved off in our standard march formation, the wind started to blow and the sky darkened, not from clouds but from the thick black smoke of hundreds of burning oil wells. We made best speed but with caution as Division had confirmed that the area to our front was still occupied by the Iraqi Army. Tac was, as usual, on the centre line of the Battlegroup's advance with A Squadron forward left, B Squadron forward right. At approximately 14.30 call signs 30 and 42, leading the advance of A Squadron, reported heat contacts on their TOGS at a range of about 4,000 metres. Major Peter Garbutt, the Squadron Leader, asked for confirmation that it was safe to fire. After a few moments, Brigade confirmed that there were no friendly forces to our front and curtly ordered the 14th/20th to *"Get on with it."*

We motored forwards, Tac now moving up in line with the lead squadrons in order to see what was happening. At a range of 2,040 metres the two tanks of A Squadron paused at the short halt and engaged the target with five rounds of HESH (High Explosive Squash Head). The splash on their TOGS clearly indicated a hit. Still we moved forwards. With no thermal imaging sight, I had to rely on what I could see with my eyes. For a long time this consisted of nothing more than dark, overcast heat shimmer. However, as we closed, out of the gloom appeared a small red glow, which expanded to a glow and pillar of smoke and then to a burning vehicle. I stared intently at the horizon through my binoculars. From behind the burning vehicle, stretching from left to right, emerged a long line of trucks - a logistic column, a full 3 kilometres long, standing stationary in the desert. To Mike Vickery, desperate to find more lift for the growing number of prisoners, such a large number of trucks was the answer to a prayer. He was convinced that they would surrender at the sight of so many tanks. Unfortunately he omitted to inform me of this 'cunning plan'. I spoke immediately to my Fire Direction Centre,

"*Hello Zero, this is Three Three, Fire Mission three Regiments, over.*"

"*Zero, Fire Mission three Regiments, out.*"

Frantically Sergeant Allen and I worked in the turret, sending down the co-ordinates and instructions that would decimate the column. The loss of so much logistic support, I reasoned, would deal a crippling blow to the Iraqi's ability to prolong the war. The column was divided into three equal parts, and a Regiment assigned to each. '*At my command*' had been ordered. We would fire only when all three Regiments were ready in order to gain maximum shock effect.

"*Regiment One ready, over.*"

"*Regiment One ready, out.*"

Still we closed. In the Optimist we waited impatiently, knowing that the Fire Direction Centre would have to 'crash action' batteries that were on the move and that it would all take time.

"*Regiment Two ready, over.*"

"*Regiment Two ready, out.*"

Our fear was that this mass of vehicles would see the Battlegroup approaching and scatter before the artillery was ready. We motored forward, desperate for the report that would tell us that the third regiment was ready to fire and we could engage,

"*Check Firing, over.*"

"*Check Firing, out.*"

It was the voice of David Radcliffe. From his position in Brigade he was party to the much bigger picture and he was far from certain that these vehicles were Iraqi. His fear was that they were Egyptians, moving up from our right. As we drew within clear visual range the awful truth dawned. Before us were two burning British Army Spartan armoured vehicles and less than a kilometre further on were over 100 trucks of 7 Armoured Brigade's logistic column. Slowly we circled the two burning Spartans. They were locked together by a straight bar, one having been towing the other. The rear vehicle was engulfed in flames, the front vehicle on fire also but the flames had not yet reached the driver's hatch. There was no crew to be seen anywhere. They must have been in the vehicles when the rounds impacted, having no chance to escape. The only hope was for the driver of the front vehicle of which there was no sign. Sergeant Allen was determined to make sure that there was no one in that driver's seat. He ordered Lance Bombardier Covill to stop the Optimist close by and, leaving the turret, ran across to the vehicles only to be driven back by the intense heat. Once back in the safety of the turret he reported that he thought he had seen an arm in the hatch. "We must go back."

With the driver closed down, I guided the Optimist right up against the front of the leading Spartan. As we felt the bump of armour on armour, Sergeant Allen scrambled out of the turret across the front of the Optimist and onto the engine decks of the blazing vehicle. Heat from molten aluminium is fearsome and I could feel its severity even with the protection of my turret. It took him seconds to scramble up, peer through the hatch and confirm that the driver's seat was empty. While this was going on, Robert Fox and the two signallers, armed with first aid box and fire extinguishers, had opened the back doors ready to get him in. As Sergeant Allen leaped off the engine decks the missile warheads in the rear vehicle detonated, engulfing the Optimist in a ball of flame and molten aluminium. Willing hands grabbed him, doors were slammed shut and, still smouldering, we backed away. Minutes later we heard over the net that both vehicles had been unoccupied when struck. The incident happened at approximately 15.00 at Grid PT 827703 in Eastern Iraq.

Relieved, we motored over to Mike Vickery who had parked up close to the logistic column and was deep in conversation. Clearly there were some very angry voices raised over the blue-on-blue. We were saved further trouble by the order for the column to move. I omitted any mention of my aborted fire mission. Had events been allowed to run their course, British casualties from the Gulf War would have been astronomic and my name would have joined the infamous. I still shudder at the thought and it is the only thing vivid enough to drive nerve agent from my nightmares.

The Spartans were a pair from 10 Air Defence Battery, Royal Artillery, and they had been stationed on a flank, protecting the Administration Area of 7 Brigade. When one of the Spartans had broken down, the Bombardier in command of the section had decided that towing was preferable to abandoning the vehicle. They had just put the tow bar on when they noticed a large number of Iraqi soldiers walking towards them. Fearing that the Iraqis might take courage and attack rather than surrender if they saw the British predicament, the Gunners had taken their weapons and gone forward to meet them. They were therefore some hundreds of yards away when the rounds struck. The two crew members who had remained close by the vehicles were casevaced with burns. (This account was given to me long after the war by the Section Commander.) As we watched the column move off, the light finally began to fail. The near-disaster with 7 Brigade had clearly convinced Division that all was not as it should be. We should have been told of the echelon. In fact we were later to learn that the British 1st Armoured Division and the American 1st and 3rd Divisions were also on a collision course. "One of the biggest blue-on-blues in history," to quote General Rupert Smith. We were ordered to stay where we were while the situation was sorted out. We leaguered up and those that could went to sleep. Tac and MAIN were now co-located and as we prepared our evening meal Robert Fox announced that he had been summoned to join Brigadier Hammerbeck at Brigade MAIN. It was with much sadness that the crew of the Optimist said farewell to a journalist who had become an intimate part of our team and our lives.

Shortly after 19.00 I stretched out on the roof of the Optimist. We had been going for nearly 90 hours. My slumber was short-lived. At 23.05 we received orders. 4 Brigade was to move behind 7 Brigade to Objective SODIUM to cut the route north out of Kuwait City. 14th/20th Battlegroup would lead the Brigade advance, moving at 06.30. The route was again given as a series of satellite way-points. On arrival we were to occupy hasty defensive positions, facing east. Enemy positions were now to be bypassed. We were to engage only in self-defence. I wondered if anyone had informed the Iraqis.

28 FEBRUARY 1991

I was woken at 04.20. I was cold, stiff and exhausted. The BBC World Service had just announced that a ceasefire was expected at 08.00. I went back to sleep much heartened. As usual it was short-lived. I was awakened just before 06.00 in preparation for the move. 06.30 saw the start of the Brigade's high-speed dash east. The smoke-filled sky meant that the dawn was late and, as we moved off, visibility was down to less than 1,000 metres. We were to cut the Basra Road in order to prevent the Iraqi Army escaping Northwards. Over on our left and some way forward 7 Brigade was already on the move. We moved as quickly as the ground and visibility allowed. I do not know what I had expected of the Wadi Al Batin. Earlier briefings had left me with a mental picture of a feature somewhat between the Grand Canyon and the Central Pacific Trench. In reality it was barely noticeable - a very shallow but wide indentation in the ground running north to south. The only thing which marked it from the surrounding desert was a sparse greenness at its lowest point, where grass struggled to take root. At 06.45 we crossed and entered Kuwait.

As we left the Wadi Al Batin, the official Iraq/Kuwait border, we had to pick our way around a series of deep quarries. The mounds of sand were the first significant physical features we had seen since our move west to join VII (US) Corps. The workings were extensive and we had no choice but to negotiate our way through them. The Emperor led Tac HQ and I followed behind a now very cautious One One Charlie. There were sand mounds towering hundreds of feet into the air and equally deep pits. Between them wound sand roads, often with a heart-stopping sheer drop on one side. They had been made by tracked Bulldozers so the roadways were wide enough. The Bulldozers were not, however, 60-plus tonnes and I was in constant fear that the road would give way and

An Army Air Corps Lynx helicopter – our eyes as we dashed east. (AG)

we would topple into the abyss. It did not and we emerged to hard, flat 'race track' desert. We pushed on, the light improving.

At 07.05 the lead elements of the Battlegroup were joined by Army Air Corps Lynx helicopters. They would be our eyes as we headed into the unknown. As the visibility improved further we gathered speed. What a sight we made. Some of the tanks now flew Union flags or their squadron or troop standards. To my right and left I could now see columns of racing troops. Tac, led by Mike Vickery, were forward and on the centre line of the 14th/20th dash. Occasionally we would pass an abandoned or destroyed Iraqi vehicle. I remember passing a solitary and forlorn-looking Soviet-built BRDM. What it was doing all alone and so far from its friends could only be guessed at. We charged on. Over on my left, some 200 metres away, and keeping parallel, was Nomad, now flying the flag of the Isle of Man. Why the Isle of Man? I learnt much later that the Brigadier had been asked to do so by the Island's 'Gulf Mums Association'. I would have liked to have had the distinctive blue and yellow Battery Flag with me to fly in the festival. Common sense told me, however, that this was not the time to be conspicuous and with my luck we would have run into the only Iraqi with a grudge against Sweden.

At 08.00 the news of the official ceasefire was broadcast over all nets. We were reminded that we were now only to fire if positively fired upon. There was still confusion as to whether Saddam had accepted all the UN terms. We dashed eastwards, the sky once again becoming blacker and more overcast. We were going at full speed when at 08.30 Mike Vickery came onto the net and announced that Iraq had agreed to all peace proposals and the Battlegroup was to halt where we were to await orders.

The two Challengers and the Warrior stopped, line-abreast and about ten metres apart. We were on top of a barely discernible ridge of soft sand. A feeling of utter jubilation and relief swept over me. We had made it. It was over. We were alive. The 4th Armoured Brigade had covered 350 kilometres in ninety-seven hours of which fifty-four had been in contact with the enemy. We had destroyed some sixty-six tanks, ninety APCs and countless artillery pieces. We had captured three divisional and four brigade commanders, along with all their staff, and taken between 5,000 and 6,000 prisoners.

"Hello Echo One Zero this is Zero Alpha, are there any bumps around you, over?"

174

I scrambled up out of the turret and peered down at the soft sand.

"Echo One Zero, Yes, and they have got two prongs sticking out the top, over."

We were in an enormous minefield, placed to protect Kuwait City. The Iraqi engineers had gone for the easy option and buried the anti-tank mines, row upon row, in the only soft sand for miles - our ridge. Each mound, about the size of half a football, had two small 6-inch antennae pointing skywards in a menacing V shape. The mines that we could see were about 15 feet apart and we had driven about 50 metres into the field. It was a miracle that not one of us had been hit. Looking back down our tracks, the Optimist had crossed two lanes, missing some mines by inches. All further conversation was conducted by shouting from turret to turret. The only thing to do was to try and back out, with someone looking out for the mines. I watched transfixed as first the Emperor and then One One Charlie made their slow, cautious, but finally successful, way back. It was now our turn. A recce from the roof showed that the right-hand track was perilously close, mere inches in fact, to a mine. We would have to track sharply in order to miss it or try to push it out the way. With Gunner Lyons peering carefully over the side and shouting directions to me, I guided Lance Bombardier Covill using the intercom. Slowly we moved, the steering on full lock. The engine screamed against the load and then "STOP." Gunner Lyons looked up despondently: "The track's come off the rear sprocket."

I could not believe this was happening. The war was all but over and we were deep inside a minefield with a track off. Each mine was designed to kill a main battle tank. Their effect on a Warrior would be catastrophic. We were all acutely aware that anti-tank minefields are always liberally scattered with anti-personnel mines - small insidious beasts designed to maim by blowing a single foot off. There would be no telltale mounds for these little beauties. They would be waiting patiently under the sand. None of the 'You are stranded in the desert with....' command exercises the Army was so keen on giving me at Sandhurst came close to this particular problem. I eased myself out of the turret and crossed to the back of the vehicle. The back door was now open and Bombardier Wilkins was peering out. It was our good fortune that the Warrior, unlike the tanks, had its engine forward and was therefore driven by a toothed sprocket at the front of the vehicle. The rear sprocket was a smooth wheel, designed simply to lift and tension the track. It was this top rear sprocket that now had the track hanging precariously half-off.

With Lyons hanging from the roof, crowbar in hand, and Wilkins pushing from the safety of the back door, we set about easing the track back onto its grooved wheel. It took much effort and some skilful tracking of the vehicle but at last it dropped back into place. The relief amongst the crew of the Optimist was tangible. Slowly we made our way backwards to safety and the welcoming cheers of the Emperor and One One Charlie.

We had been told to leaguer up and await further orders. The World Service news reported both President Bush's announcement of the ceasefire and President Saddam Hussein's pronouncement of a great Iraqi victory. The Battlegroup was ordered to go firm where it was and await orders.

We were in an area that was strewn with battlefield debris, burnt-out vehicles, abandoned trench systems and empty gun pits. Our recce troop was parked up close by, a large Union Jack now flying from the radio mast of one of the Scorpions. Like us they were awaiting further orders. The temptation to go exploring was just too great, so the Tac HQ crews dismounted and went walkabout. Logistics clearly was not a problem in this sector of the Iraqi front. The trenches were full of ammunition boxes and all around were the abandoned belongings of a defeated army - clothes, fresh food, books, radios etc. There were also artillery rounds, stacked neatly in sandbag-protected bunkers. Loose shells stood upright in rows ready for immediate use, piles of green wooden boxes, many with the incriminating markings of the Jordanian Army. We picked our way gingerly through the positions. We had to be wary of the many unexploded allied bomblets lying like black sheep-droppings on the hard sand. Easier to see were the bright yellow sub-munitions dispensed by the air forces. Like large shuttlecocks, they lay all around the devastated hulks, the strike onto the sand not being hard enough to cause a detonation. A few hundred yards on from a blackened MTLB we found the cause of its misfortune. About 10 feet long and looking like half a torpedo, lay the green shape of the lower part of a CBU. This was the canister that had broken away from the underside of the aircraft to enable the sub-munitions to rain down on the target. Some wag had written in blue letters on the side 'For no sex in November.' Clearly a reference to his or her enforced stay in Saudi Arabia, thanks to Saddam.

'For no sex in November'. (AG)

Shortly afterwards Mike Vickery stumbled across its sister marked with 'and none in December either.'

By the time we retraced our steps back to the vehicles Battlegroup MAIN had sorted out the deployment and organized the REPLEN. We were to leaguer in box formations. Once we were all mounted, we started to pick our way slowly towards our new location. I was motoring behind the tanks when I noticed a gun barrel sticking skywards from behind a low sand wall. I waved to the Emperor and together we drove over to investigate. There, in the midst of its sand defences was a Soviet-built S60 anti-aircraft gun. Other than a puncture in one of its four wheels, it was in perfect condition. It still had a shiny clip of 60mm shells in the magazine. Clearly the Iraqis had given the serviceability of anti-aircraft guns a high priority in this sector. It was the first fully intact piece of equipment we had come across and, in case it turned out to be the only one, I claimed it as a battle trophy for the Gunners. It was after all a gun. Towing it was not as simple as we at first thought, as the two towing attachments were incompatible. Undaunted, the crew of the Optimist rigged up a coupling using a discarded steel cable and we were in business. Tac HQ and one S60 leaguered up just after midday.

Above all, the ceasefire gave us an opportunity to get out of our NBC suits. With a combat suit, NBC suit, body armour and a helmet, the heat inside the Optimist had been greatly magnified. This plus the occasional bout of utter terror had combined to make us all sweat profusely. The result was that the charcoal lining of the NBC suit had broken free and had impregnated every layer of clothing and a good way into our skin. We looked like minstrels. Fortunately for us, our stocks of canned water, kept primarily for the engine, were high, so we were all able to strip off and have a long-overdue wash.

It's all over. Lieutenant Colonel Mike Vickery and the Emperor. (AG)

When I next saw Mike Vickery he was standing on the front of the Emperor, smart and clean in his sand-coloured pullover, beret on head. He stood there beaming, like a proud father whose sons had all just come home with excellent school reports. On the fume extractor, half way down the tank barrel, his crew had drawn miniature tanks and APCs. Like a Spitfire pilot's trophies, they were the Emperor's score. I must say that at that moment we all felt like 'The Few'.

By 14.00 we had been refuelled and rationed and were at three hours notice to move. The World Service announced that the Iraqis had accepted the ten conditions of the ceasefire document. President Bush also announced that forty of the forty-two Iraqi divisions had either been destroyed or rendered combat ineffective. By mid-afternoon those who were not fast asleep were in the teeth of a sandstorm. Visibility dropped to a few yards and the temperature plummeted. It was in high but shivering spirits that we gathered to listen to the 19.30 SITREP. Four-fifths of Iraq's military equipment had been destroyed and 250,000 prisoners taken. The dreaded Hamarabi and Tawalkana Divisions had been annihilated and the Medina was down to one platoon for each battalion. They were totally beaten, it was all over. With the knowledge that Saddam was still claiming a great victory, Mike Vickery, I and the Tac team celebrated with a decidedly alcoholic drink. The wind howled

Scores! The Colonel and the Adjutant, Mike Vickery and Jonty Palmer. (MV)

outside. Inside the Optimist we were grateful to be where we were and alive. Countless thousands had died because of the ambitions of one man. There but for the grace of God went all of us and we knew it. Thankful and exhausted, I went to bed and slept.

THE LONG ROAD HOME

1 March 1991

I awoke early. Old habits die hard. It was a beautiful sunny day but with a strong wind. I tuned into the World Service. British troops were being dispatched to dig mass graves. Saddam had not been seen or heard from and speculation was rife as to his fate. The Iraqi High Command was still prevaricating and all sorts of threats and ultimatums were being issued. The Battlegroup was in 'wait and see' mode. The tac parties and I would remain with the Battlegroup while there was any chance that fighting would start again. We were, however, a long way ahead of our logistic tail and, until it caught up, drinking water was severely rationed.

I had to attend CO 2nd Field Regiment's orders at 13.00, so set off in the Optimist mid-morning to travel via the Battery who were camped just over a low ridge some 2 kms away. Behind the Warrior we towed the S60. Our arrival at the Battery is one of the high points of my life. The guns were parked in a neat row, cam nets deployed and flags flying - everything from the Union Jack to the White Ensign. We had been spotted at some distance, so that, by the time we drove into the centre of the position, complete with battle trophy, everyone was out cheering and waving. We parked up and were all but mobbed. It was marvellous.

The Optimist returns to the Battery with S60 trophy. (AG)

179

At RHQ 2nd Field the same spirit of euphoria was evident. David Radcliffe beamed at us all as we arrived and we were some time getting down to the business of the day. He had already sent out to each of the Battery Commanders a long list of points from the Artillery Commander, Brigadier Durie. We were to make copious notes on a seemingly endless list of topics while memories were fresh. The information would supposedly go to improving training and equipment. I suspect they got the same answers after the Second World War and Korea. The points from the Orders Group, in order:

1. If we come across any particularly good enemy equipment, mark it '2 Fd Regt RA' and get it recovered. The Regiment would try to get it back as a trophy.
2. All explosives are to be handed in, including those captured.
3. The area is heavily mined. Stay on tracks.
4. The ration would be 10 litres of water per day until further notice.
5. A recce Sergeant had been injured by a booby-trapped mine. It had a trembler device. He has serious injuries to his legs.
6. Get your points for the CRA in ASP.
7. Geoff Ravenhill, fit and well, will rejoin The Rocket Troop today.

The Intelligence update estimated that of the entire Iraqi army only about eighteen battalions remained effective. There were no functioning HQs above brigade level. The forces in the KTO had completely disintegrated. Intelligence staff were interested in a range of equipments and we were to keep a look out for such interesting things as communication systems, missiles and of course anything chemical.

On returning to 14th/20th I was greeted by the news that the recce had discovered an artillery battery quite close by with some intact self-propelled guns. Mindful of Second's desire for a trophy, I dispatched Sergeant Allen and the Optimist to investigate. Before they departed, the Tac P, Tristram Carter, asked if one of his crew could go along as, being inside an armoured vehicle, the young soldier had been able to see very little of events. Sergeant Allen agreed on the strict condition that the soldier, Air Trooper Littler of the Army Air Corps, did not leave the vehicle without permission. I waved them off and then sought out Mike Vickery to pass on the tit-bits from David Radcliffe's Orders.

Mike Vickery and I sat and chatted for a good deal of the afternoon. The word from Brigade was that we would move shortly to a blocking position, north of Kuwait City and on the coast. This would ensure the safety of the City, but, more importantly, would enable us to be re-supplied from the sea. Speculation as to how long we would remain in theatre was rife and ranged from weeks to months, six months being the favourite. What was certain was that 7 Brigade would leave before we did.

180

Sergeant Allen returned. They had found a Soviet-built 2S3 gun in perfect condition and an ACRV command vehicle, also intact. He would return with one of the Armoured Recovery and Repair Vehicles and, with the Warrior, tow both of them back. Before he did, he related the tale of his expedition.

They had found the position easily using the SATNAV. The Iraqi battery had been deployed over a large area, each gun being protected by high sand walls. A 2S3 and an ACRV were the only survivors from the unit, which, to judge from the mass of unexploded bomblets everywhere, had taken a massive pounding from the air. Aware of the dangers, Sergeant Allen had approached both pieces of equipment cautiously, at no time ever getting off the Optimist. However, while he was parked examining the gun, Air Trooper Littler, regardless of the warnings from the crew, had got out through the back and, after a few yards, had trodden on a mine. With shrapnel injuries to his arms and

The liberated 2S3 gun. (AG)

legs, he had lain helpless, unable to move. Bombardier Wicks, in spite of the danger, crawled out and recovered him and, with the help of Gunner Lyons, administered first aid. Between them they managed to stop the bleeding and he was soon with the Battlegroup doctor. His injuries were sufficiently severe for him to be evacuated back to the Military Hospital at Woolwich.

The Optimist and the ARRV duly returned late afternoon towing their trophies. They parked up next to a T55 tank which the 14th/20th had recovered earlier and driven in to great excitement. The ACRV was a real find. It was packed with documents, radios and computing equipment. The intelligence community would think all their birthdays had come at once. The gun, similar in size to our own M109s, was also in perfect working order and was fully bombed up with ammunition. A quick inspection confirmed that there were no chemical munitions on board, only the standard Soviet HE and illuminating rounds. The shells were not a problem. There were piles of shells everywhere and it was just a matter of dumping them at the nearest suitable site. More problematic were the charge bags of propellant. Now stripped of their original packaging they lay in the charge bins ready for use. The only way to make them safe was to burn them, a simple procedure for an expert and normal practice at the end of any artillery firing. Sergeant Radcliffe was an expert and he set about the task with a will. With the help of the crews he made a large pile of propellant some 200 metres downwind of our position. The propellant, in the form of spaghetti-like sticks of cordite held in thin canvas bags, was spread in such a way as to give maximum exposure to the air as each bag burnt. From the main pile a 'fuse' of broken cordite ran for another 50 metres. The propellant was designed to burn in the breach so rapidly that it produces enough pressure to propel the round up the barrel. Free of the constrictions of the gun, the propellant just burns, albeit with considerable intensity. As dusk fell and with most of Battlegroup HQ looking on, Sergeant Radcliffe lit the trail to start the burn of the propellant from some forty Soviet 152mm shells. It was spectacular. A vivid ball of white-hot flame lit the desert for miles. To say that it generated a degree of alarm in 1 (British) Armoured Division, VII

Back to normality – breakfast in 'The Penthouse'. (PN)

(US) Corps, the Egyptian and Syrian divisions and anyone else who saw it would be to understate the reaction. Troops everywhere scrambled for their weapons and the radio nets hummed. We got a tongue-in-cheek bollocking from Mike Vickery.

2 MARCH 1991

A hot day but with a strong wind that whipped up the sand and stung the eyes. The rumour currently doing the rounds was that it would be about six weeks before we returned home. With little happening at the Battlegroup, I decided to spend most of the day at the Battery. The boys were in good heart and were rapidly making themselves comfortable. The GPO and BSM had moved a few of the vehicles to aid admin and refuelling and to provide some collective protection against the wind. Before starting my long round of all the crews, I assembled the Battery and over the noise of the gale spoke to my command. I told them I thought they were wonderful and how proud I was to be their Battery Commander. They had been the pace-setting Battery from the start and throughout had performed magnificently. They had in many ways a much harder war than those in the front line, indeed for much of the war they were the front line. They had started with the artillery raids, had been through the breach before the brigades and were the first Gunner unit to enter Iraq. They had been right behind the 14th/20th Battlegroup on the move out of the breach and had taken the full weight of the Iraqi opening salvo. They had fired in support of both 4 and 7 Brigade attacks and all without the aid of sophisticated night-viewing equipment. The Gulf war had been won not by aircraft, tanks or infantry but by massed artillery fire. I ended with a plea for safety. To have a casualty now would be an unbearable tragedy. During my rounds of the Battery each crew we went through the same routine. War stories. Each exploit magnified in the telling. Everyone had a memory, a moment, a tale to tell. The breach fire plan, the night moves and the moment that Matthew Hubbard came on the air to report 'The BC's in contact.' There were the inevitable 'No, you've got that wrong' and 'You didn't see it....it was much worse than that', and every saga punctuated with black Mancunian humour. That morning I drank countless cups of coffee and listened to countless magical tales. Nothing binds like adversity. We in The Rocket Troop are bound by a fellowship that will hopefully endure all our lives. We went to war together.

Exhausted but elated I returned to the Battlegroup late afternoon. I journeyed back via the Royal Engineer equipment dump. This consisted of a few acres enclosed within hastily erected sand walls. Inside was a slowly growing fleet of Iraqi vehicles, mostly T55 tanks. We parked up close to the entrance and climbed up the berm to survey the catch. It was fascinating. In neat rows tanks that only a few days ago were waiting to kill us now sat harmless and dejected. One wondered where their crews were now or if their commanders had felt towards their commands as I felt about The Rocket Troop. As there appeared to be people walking around examining the vehicles, I decided that this was too good a chance to miss and followed suit. I spent the next half-hour scrambling over equipment that had hitherto been only silhouettes on my Soviet recognition charts. Seeing the Great Bear's technological might in its true colours and now abandoned and dejected, I had to wonder if the Cold War threat had been a reality at all.

On return to the 14th/20th I attended the evening Orders Group. As usual it was dominated by the logistical effort needed to keep us fed, oiled and watered. We were still at three hours' notice to move and six weeks did indeed seem to be the likely forecast for our return, which was a vast improvement on six months. I was relieved that I had ended my talk to the battery with a plea for safety. Mike Vickery's briefing included a similar request for extreme care when examining enemy equipment to avoid injury from unexploded ordnance. Due to the soft sand, some of the small bomblets that had missed the steel hulls had failed to go off. About the size of three golf balls placed in line, and with a small stabilizing streamer of fabric at one end, these unexploded sub-munitions lay scattered all around awaiting an unwary foot-step or a too curious hand.

The good news was mail. Tons and tons of it. I had over twenty letters and a parcel. Letters from Annie, relations, friends and friends of friends. There were even letters from complete strangers who had read Robert Fox's article. Famous for another fifteen minutes. There was the news that my replacement had arrived in Germany, Major Rod Matherson, Royal Canadian Horse Artillery. Strange, I was starting to believe that I would command The Rocket Troop for ever. The parcel from Annie contained, amongst other things, a fruit cake. It was wrapped in about 100 metres of tinfoil. I put it away carefully for a special occasion. Before I went to bed I stood outside in the now calm darkness watching the red flickering glow in the eastern sky which was the oil wells burning around Kuwait City. It was like a sunset that refused to fade.

3 MARCH 1991

We were all up bright and early for the 14th/20th King's Hussars Battlegroup church parade. At 08.30 we formed a hollow square on the desert sand and quietly and movingly said thank you for our deliverance. The Padre, Father Michael Weymes, added his own brand of Irish humour to keep all our feet on the ground. It was a memorable occasion, made more so by the sight of the distant oil fires.

Immediately after the service the management settled down for the daily Orders Group. The intelligence briefing informed us that General

184

Church Parade.
14th/20th King's
Hussars
Battlegroup. (AG)

Schwarzkopf was talking to the Iraqi High Command, but was not making the progress he desired. The problem seemed to be a lack of direction on the Iraqi side. Saddam had not been seen or heard from. There were rumours that he was dead and that Baghdad was in the grip of a power struggle. This prevarication was not acceptable to the allies and plans had been made to deal with the eight remaining armoured brigades in the Basra area which had refused the Coalition's order to withdraw further back into Iraq. This would involve 1st (US) Division (forward left with 2 brigades) and 1st (British) Armoured Division (forward right with 2 brigades) attacking due north. However, the British were the only force currently 'combat capable' as the American division was out of fuel and had not yet been re-supplied. Kuwait City was in a state of chaos and, although the British Embassy had been re-occupied, throughout the city old scores were being settled and tank fire could be heard as the various factions struggled for dominance. Interestingly, the British division was assessed to have been able to move further, faster and more easily than any other division in VII Corps. Apparently the Corps Commander had been severely gripped for holding the British division back. Where these gems of information came from, no one would say. I could believe the first part as the Abrams tank used over twice as much fuel as the Challenger and, like us, most of their resupply was on slow-moving wheels. As for the commander holding us back, I don't believe we could have gone any faster even if we had been ordered to.

We were now at five hours' notice to move and awaiting orders. The rules of engagement remained the same - only fire if fired upon. However, the likelihood of our going back to an active ground war seemed remote and the exchange of POWs was reported to have started. A singularly one-sided flow, I suspected. Resupply was the major priority and plans were well advanced to push a Main Supply Route due north through Haafra Al Batin. Our own divisional engineers had found a bore hole close by which, if it proved uncontaminated, would enable them to start pumping water the next day. More worrying was the report that a specialist monitoring vehicle had found an NBC contaminated area at Grid PL995047. It had positively identified Mustard, Lewisite and Phosgene gases. As for future plans, what was certain was that we would stay where we were for some time. It had been announced that we would withdraw in the order in which we had arrived and that some of the equipment would take a year to be recovered. Once the briefings and plethora of administration had been painstakingly worked through, the Orders Group finally dispersed. I made my way, with most of my crew, to the guns where, it being Sunday, I had arranged for the Regiment's own padre, David Coulter, to hold a church parade. On arrival I was met by the BSM who asked me if I wished to make it compulsory. These things are intensely personal and I told him it was open to all who wished to come, but that there was to be no pressure and no formal parade. At the appointed hour nearly every member of the Battery, Christians, Hindus, agnostics and atheists gathered in the centre of the gun position in a loose half circle. Before the service started I spoke to them all. I cannot remember my exact words but my sentiment was that, whatever we individually thought and believed, today we had something to be thankful for. We had been to war and had survived. That being so, our padre was as good a person as I could think of to lead us in our collective gratitude. As usual David was superb.

I could not spend all day at the Battery for I needed to get my own POR (Post-Operation Report) compiled. I had a long talk with the BK, GPO and BSM about the points they wished to be raised and returned to the Battlegroup. I then spent some time with my own FOOs before sitting down to put my report together. Interestingly, the conclusion I came to was that our training was essentially sound, in particular the Battlegroup training in Canada had stood us in good stead and was a war winner. Our guns were fine, if old, and everything had been made to work by dint of our determination to succeed and the British soldier's ability to shine in adversity. That we started without sufficient radios, logistic vehicles and manpower was something we knew was always going to happen. We were lucky this time. We were given long enough to put it right. The real POR point was that next time we might not have that time.

The evening Orders Group was dominated by PORs and the lessons learnt. The points being raised by both the Infantry and Armoured Corps put my experiences into perspective and confirmed my central comments. We had all made it by the skin of our teeth. Mike Vickery ended the Orders Group with his own personal plea for safety. Today a soldier in the Royal Scots had been reported killed by a mine or grenade. The very interesting Soviet NBC testing boxes, so popular as souvenirs, were to be handed in immediately. They contained real nerve agent.

It was dark when we all finally went outside to stretch our legs. As we

Gathering up Iraqi equipment. (AG)

stood around chatting in the cool of the evening, flares started streaking into the sky and deploying with their familiar 'plop'. Soon there were hundreds of lights floating above the desert on small parachutes. The enquiry as to what was going on was greeted with the news that a peace agreement had just been signed. On the Optimist we opened the side bin and joined in the firework party.

4 MARCH 1991

Up early with the promise of scorching weather. A peace agreement had been signed and the chance of hostilities restarting was fading even further towards the 'no chance' end of the spectrum. I decided that all the artillery crews would move back to the Battery tomorrow. We were all starting to make ourselves comfortable and so, to avoid nugatory work, I gave the order to regroup. I myself had to go to David Radcliffe's Orders Group, so was up bright and early for the short journey. The Orders Group concentrated on the administration to prepare ourselves to live indefinitely in the desert and to ease our return when the word to move eventually came. It would be an ongoing task generated from RHQ. On top of this, David Radcliffe was determined not to sit idly by and waste training opportunities. The Regiment would run a series of courses, aimed primarily at those soldiers who needed up-grading either for promotion or pay. Tasks were discussed and duly allocated to key individuals or to batteries. The Orders Group was denied its usual luxury of an open-ended chat session once the main business was concluded, for a number of us had to be at the Equipment Collection Point in order to meet the Chief of the Defence Staff. I, along with most of the other Majors, took four soldiers and joined the growing throng. Having visited it only two days before, I found the location easily enough. I was, however, staggered by its growth. Extra sand walls had been added and inside these solid corrals was now row upon row of Iraqi armour. Clearly the recovery teams had been working overtime. As a spectacle it illustrated graphically the Coalition's superiority over the Iraqis. As CDS was accompanied by half the world's Press one had to assume that this was exactly the message being put across. I spent a pleasant hour or so in the sunshine talking to friends until at about 12.30 the VIP party arrived. I had been placed in front of some captured guns and stood in line waiting my turn. When it came, Sir David Craig shook my hand, said, 'Well done' and moved on. If I remember rightly he said and did exactly the same thing to me the year before, only we were in Cyprus.

Visit over, I made my way across country to 2nd Regiment's Echelon and scrounged lunch. I needed peace, quiet and a table for I had to write out the citations for honours and awards. If we were running true to form, most would go to Staff Officers close to the great men, and the remainder to the more fashionable regiments. I was determined to turn the unequal tide if I could and armed with some sound advice from Mike Vickery, set about the task. Sergeant Allen was my clear priority and it was over an hour before I was finally happy that I had managed to reflect the magnitude of his action in the few lines allowed. I then turned my attention to Bombardier Wicks and Gunner Lyons and their rescue of Air Trooper Little. A most difficult task, not having been there to witness the action and with the certain knowledge that the system would never give three awards to a single Gunner tac party. By the time I had finished and handed them in to RHQ the sun had vanished and a grey twilight had descended on the desert. The wind had changed and the smoke from the blazing oil wells was now high above us. It was late afternoon when I finally arrived back at the Battlegroup. Just before dusk the wind changed again and started to blow with a vengeance. As

Awaiting the visit of the Chief of the Defence staff. In the centre are Major Dave Marshall RCHA and the author. (AG)

we sat huddled in the 432 penthouse, eating our evening meal, a sand-storm was beginning to rage outside. By the time I had waded through the evening Orders Group, admin conference and final pack prior to tomorrow's move, the rain was beating down on the outside of the tent.

5 MARCH 1991

The morning rose cold, wet and grey. Not the ideal weather to pack up tents and move. By 08.30 the 432 and the Optimist were loaded and ready to go. By 08.45 the three FOO Warriors had arrived from the squadrons and the company and had lined up for our formal farewell to the 14th/20th Kings Hussars Battlegroup. Mike Vickery thanked us all for our efforts, our professionalism, but above all for fitting in so well with his Battlegroup. He then shook hands with every member of the artillery team, personally thanking each individual. With emotions running high and the rain beating down, the Optimist led 'Charlie Charlie Six', the collective call sign for the artillery tac group, back to rejoin The Rocket Troop.

While the crews busied themselves with setting up home yet again, I left to be at RHQ for the 10.00 courses conference. Soaking wet and shivering, I sat through the plan for the immediate future, the programme of courses, cadres and maintenance - all short term activities but aimed squarely at the long-term future of the Regiment. The promotions plot was also made public with my own BQMS, Staff Sergeant Dines, promoted to WO2 and the redoubtable Sergeant Tunley up to Staff Sergeant. David Radcliffe also outlined what he knew of the recovery plan. 7 Brigade would start to fly back on R Day +14, R standing for recovery. All the British would be out by R+42 with 4 Brigade units in the second batch. It was expected that R Day would be announced as soon as there was a formal cease-fire to cement the current peace agreement. It was also announced that the Prime Minister, John Major, would be visiting the next day and so it would be 'places Gentlemen, please' back at the ECP (Equipment Collection Point).

Briefings, discussions and chats over, I returned to the Battery. The crews were now fully deployed, penthouses and tents up, a home from home again. Charlie Charlie Six was in a neat line on the side of the main gun position, close to the two Command Posts and the BK and BSM's 432s. The BSM had been working hard to produce a position close enough to protect and administer, yet with enough space to allow refuelling vehicles and football teams to operate. When you share a metal box with many others, space becomes a valuable commodity. The feeding area (the BQMS's two 8-tonne trucks and our mobile kitchen) was off to one side and down-wind, in an attempt to lessen the flies which were starting to become a nuisance. It was the only area with camouflage nets deployed to provide shade and some fly protection. The final outpost of the position, and furthest down-wind of all, was the rubbish dump. The large hole in the sand, full of black plastic sacks, was daily covered in petrol and incinerated. Makeshift showers had also appeared and toilet facilities (an upturned oil drum over a large hole surrounded by a hessian screen) were strategically placed around the perimeter. Someone getting lost in the dark was still a worry. All across the desert, similar encampments had sprung up. O Battery was the furthest south of the Regiment's sub-units but from the roof of the Optimist most were in view. Some had already had sand walls built around them to contain the people, protect them from the wind and, with luck, deter the flies.

The rain continued to batter down. Some desert! Early afternoon the planned Officers' Mess photograph was formally cancelled. By 14.00 the world had changed from familiar grey overcast to eerie translucent yellow. The wind dropped, the rain stopped and for about two hours it was like being in a science fiction film. I can only surmise that it was strong sunlight filtering through thick smoke, high in the atmosphere. The spectacle was captivating and I remember sitting on the signaller's seat at the rear of the Optimist just staring out at the desert, now bathed in this strange lemon yellow light. By 16.00 the yellow had given way to black. It was so dark that headlamps were needed. This strange unnatural night stayed with us for an hour until the wind changed again and the rain returned.

The Commanding Officer of 39 Regiment, Lieutenant Colonel Peter Williams, enjoys a shower. (PW)

There was a full mail sack today. As well as the familiar blue aerograms there was a parcel for me. It was from Annie and contained, among other goodies, socks. Wonderful. I immediately threw most of my old ones away. Water was becoming more plentiful but was still not plentiful enough. Rather than waste the rain, I hung my dirty combat kit outside and let nature do its best. We ate Annie's fruit cake after dinner.

Well, sixteen of us all had a small bit. One of her best and much appreciated. I went to sleep on my newly deployed cot bed with the rain beating on the canvas next to my head.

6 MARCH 1991

It had stopped raining, though everything was soaked. The sun was now shining but the wind was up and as the sand dried out it was picked up and liberally scattered over damp washing etc. I was starting to hate the desert. O Battery's contribution to the 4 Brigade reception for John Major consisted of myself, BK, GPO, BSM and sixteen Gunners. We travelled down to the Equipment Collection Point mid-morning in a hurriedly emptied 8-tonne truck. On arrival we were shepherded about and placed again in front of the guns. It all took an inordinately long time but it gave me a chance to catch up on the news from the other units, in particular the Battlegroup. Godfrey Tilney, the 14th/20th Second-in-Command, was planning to lead a small party to retrace our route right back to the breach. He asked if I would like to come along, if I could get a Landrover. I readily accepted although I had not heard of my own Landrover since long before the start or the ground war. Had anyone fixed the clutch?

John Major arrived at 10.00 and we gathered around in a great crowd. He again spoke very well and from the heart. He spoke of our achievements and how proud the people at home were. He also mentioned that the Division would be withdrawn as soon as possible. This was greeted by a loud cheer. If he had meant to leave us all with a warm rosy glow, then he succeeded. Brigadier Christopher Hammerbeck then presented the Prime Minister with a beautifully prepared Iraqi AK47 assault rifle. Presentation over, the PM went walkabout and spoke to some of my young Gunners.

The Commander of 4 Armoured Brigade presents the Prime Minister with an AK47 rifle. (AG)

VIP visits to hundreds of troops in the desert are by necessity slow and ponderous affairs. VIP passed did not mean VIP gone, so I was delighted to see Peter Sincock, the Defence Attaché. For him the novelty of playing host on these occasions had clearly worn off, so he was happy to detach himself from the entourage and chat to a friendly face. He could shine little light on the future. Things in Kuwait City were worse than expected and it was taking an inordinate amount of time to get things done. Arab sensibilities had to be considered and, for the sake of Coalition solidarity, they had to move with care. The flight up from Riyadh had been worth it if only to show the PM and Co. the magnitude of the problem. He could give no steer as to when 4 Brigade would start to recover but invited me down to the Embassy as soon as I could scrounge a flight.

Visit over, we made our way back to the Battery. We were now on central feeding so the three-times-a day upheaval required for crew cooking was a thing of the past. We were still on compo, but there was a promise of fresh rations soon. The biggest problem was flies. Having now had time to complete one breeding cycle on all the dead Iraqui soldiers' bodies, they pervaded everywhere in dense dark clouds. Even eating was difficult and it was all but impossible to keep the swarming black bodies off one's food. The sand and rain had conspired to initiate some spring cleaning and the crews were all hard at work. I spent most of the afternoon with those in the Battery who would be running courses, checking programmes and ensuring they had adequate resources for the task ahead. That over, I tackled the plethora of admin required even when the Battery was simply sustaining itself. Early evening the NBC state reduced to LOW. Respirators now no longer had to be carried everywhere. Like Linus and his blanket, it would feel strange without this familiar appendage. After dinner Richard Farndale and Derek Hudson presented me with their proposal to drive back to Germany across country as an Adventurous Training expedition. Enterprising, imaginative but unlikely to be sanctioned from above. The planning would no doubt provide them with hours of constructive fun.

7 MARCH 1991

Last night it rained, not an unusual occurrence in this 'Desert'. During the night a dog was heard howling. As we are miles from any habitation it unnerved a lot of people. Today was bright, sunny and with a strong wind blowing the smoke away from us. Much of the morning was spent at RHQ talking to a team from HQ British Forces Middle East. Their brief was to gather information from those in key positions concerning the training we had received, the tactics we had used and our equipment. The purpose was to learn lessons for the future and hopefully improve matters. The discussions took up most of the morning so it was not until lunch that I was able to tackle Major Steven Young, the Second-in-Command, about a Landrover. The Battery had only the PADS truck, (an overloaded half ton) and a 3/4 ton GS which was the admin work horse. I was reluctant to take either of them. Most of the Battery's Landrovers had been replaced by surplus 432s prior to the start of the ground offensive. These Landrovers had been sent rearwards to be used by the Press, Padres and anyone else who could scrounge one. What Landrovers the Regiment still had were under command of Steven Young and he was reluctant to release any. After much discussion, he finally relented, allocating me a diesel 110 which was currently being worked on by the REME but would be ready that night.

With the promise of the Landrover I went to 14th/20th to mark up my map and get the timings. The expedition would comprise Godfrey Tilney, the three 14th/20th squadron leaders, Majors Peter Garbutt, Richard Shirreff and Alastair Wicks, OC the Queen's Company, Major Grant Baker, the BG IO, Captain Richard Pakenham-Walsh, myself, my BK, Captain Geoff Ravenhill and Mr Robert Fox. We would leave at first light.

For the crew of the Optimist the better weather offered a chance for a much-needed sort-out and Sergeant Allen had them emptying side bins, stowage racks and the back bustle. It was while they were all struggling to get the spare rations and the now sand-filled cam net from out of the large storage bustle on the outside rear of the turret that there was a sharp clang. A piece of metal fell from the net and landed on the back hatches. Investigation revealed it to be a still recognizable Soviet 30mm heavy machine gun round. It must have been this that had produced that sharp clang just behind my head on the night of our first contact. As Gunner Lyons found it, he was awarded the trophy.

I spent the afternoon back at the Battery, sorting admin, touring the guns and making sure all was well prior to my departure. It was late evening before Geoff and I got the Landrover and loaded up – water, sand channels, shovels and a helicopter marker panel. We were going west through what should now be secure Coalition territory. To the north was a strong barrier of American armour and the area we wanted to visit should now be the preserve of American Second Echelon units. Knowing our ally's propensity to shoot first and ask questions later, we flew a large Union Jack from a post at the rear of the vehicle. I went to bed early.

8 MARCH 1991

The small convoy of British vehicles headed west as the sun was rising and promising a clear, bright and dry day. We made good progress across the firm, flat desert, travelling as the crow flies, guided by our GPS. We must have approached the Wadi very close to our eastward advance

The Battlefield Tour.
Left to right: **Grant Baker, Geoff Ravenhill, Godfrey Tilney, Richard Pakenham-Walsh, Alastair Wicks, Peter Garbutt, Andrew Gillespie, Richard Shirreff.** (AG)

Desert Orchids. (PW)

route because we had to transit the quarry workings. Now on wheels, we had difficulty negotiating the steep tracks and soft sand and we stopped to examine the area and have a group photograph. What machinery there was lying about indicated that it had been some time since the quarry was a going concern. What they were extracting remains a mystery. Sand?

The sun was well up when we reached the lowest point of the Wadi Al Batin and stopped to look around. The rain had started to transform this low, narrow, but very long depression. Deep channels, like miniature Grand Canyons, had been cut in the sand by running water. Everywhere green shoots were appearing. Pushing their way skywards and already starting to bloom, were desert orchids. Up to this point 'Desert Orchid' meant a famous race horse. They were beautiful. A single lupin-like spike of yellow flowers rising 6 or 7 inches above the desert sand. No leaves could be seen, but the plants littered the valley bottom, each proudly erect in its own space.

We turned south and then east just before 'NEW JERSEY' and followed the mass of tracks that we had made that first night. It had been dark, cold and wet when we had exited the breach and I had assumed that the desert here was hard, flat and featureless. Certainly what I had managed to glean through the far from clear green world of my II sight had done nothing to dispel this view. In fact the ground gently undulated, not enough to restrict the view to the horizon, but sufficient to provide depressions and hollows into which men and vehicles could hide. The sand, too, was softer, providing clear track marks that the rain had not yet managed to erase. As we approached the area of the first contact I picked up the distinctive track patterns I had been looking for – two wide and one not so wide, moving as a single group between the main formations. This was the Emperor, One One Charlie and the Optimist.

As the others went their separate ways to walk their own individual battles, we stopped the Landrover at the point I had first made contact and got out to explore. On the ground in front of us the whole battle was choreographed in the sand. Slightly deeper track-marks showed where we had waited expectantly in the dark and where the two tanks had first opened fire. On that night, by the light first of burning vehicles and then of artillery illuminating rounds, events had seemed to take place on a very narrow and confined stage. Here, standing in bright sunlight, I was staggered at the scale of the position. This was an area our Intelligence had stated was clear of enemy, yet we believed we had bumped a signals detachment protected by tanks and armoured infantry. Now on view in front of us was the reality – a well planned and constructed defensive location, clearly part of a large prepared position. In the dark and the rain we had clipped one small corner of a formidable enemy force. A few hundred metres further on another part of the battle was inscribed in the sand. The footprints were where Robert Fox had got out of the back of the Optimist and the curving additional tracks were where Nomad had drawn along-side. Close to the sand wall, which marked the rear of the position but was the closest to us, the story was lost in a mass of criss-crossing tracks and footprints. Here the Queen's Company had driven forward with their headlamps on and taken the surrender, herding hundreds of Iraqi soldiers into tight groups and columns.

Standing on top of the low sand ridge we got a better perspective of the position. We were surprised to see that the enemy tanks and APCs were orientated facing our line of advance and not, as we had expected, south towards the Saudi border. The vehicles seemed to be mostly MTLBs, both signals and infantry variants, and T55 tanks. All were in various stages of destruction. One signals MTLB was completely burnt out, whilst others were simply riddled with holes. On the roof of one badly damaged MTLB was an intact aerial. It was for GPS and was identical to the one on the roof of the Optimist. It was not just the Coalition who had access to high-tech navigation.

A T55, stationed strategically on our axis, had been hit just below the mantlet, where the gun enters the turret. This had been the victim of the Emperor's gunner, Corporal Redgrave's opening shot. As we examined the wrecked vehicles more closely, all around us lay the physical evidence that the Iraqi regular troops both intended to and did fight determinedly. Around the MTLBs were thousands of spent machine-gun cases and beside the tanks large brass-coloured 100mm cartridge cases lay discarded. The T55 directly in front of the Tac group had managed to fire five rounds before being hit. Thank God they did not have the advantage of TOGS.

As we gathered together again, the conversation centred upon our amazement as to the size of the position and how much ammunition the enemy had fired. Those who had ventured to the right spoke of clear

MTLB with SATNAV at Objective BRONZE. (AG)

evidence of enemy vehicles vacating their prepared positions and driving away to the south and east. Had the enemy been as surprised and confused as we had been? There was everywhere destruction but no bodies. Either the crews had abandoned their vehicles when the unequal nature of the struggle became apparent or the burial parties had already been through the area. Time was not on our side and it was already close to midday. We remounted and, using the Tac group's tracks as an axis, headed towards COPPER SOUTH.

The battle to clear COPPER SOUTH had been unexpectedly fierce as again the Intelligence assessment was that the position was unoccupied. It had been fought in the dark and in the early dawn. It had largely been a tank battle, the Challengers firing at the short halt using their TOGS or the artillery light. Again the size of the position staggered us all. As we approached we were greeted first by the remains of the ammunition truck and then the fuel tanker. All around, like grim, macabre, contorted statues were the remains of the Iraqi force. Vehicles had been dug into protective sand pits facing south, the presumed direction of the Coalition attack. Most had been unable to traverse their guns and had been destroyed in situ. The rain had left its mark and many of the pits were now full of water and the hulks were turning a rusty brown. Slowly we picked our way across the position, keeping close together, moving between what appeared to be the most interesting locations and equipment. I found it very difficult to equate my memories of the battle to the ground now spread out before me. I remembered the intensity of the enemy fire forcing me back towards the relative safety of the main

The Ammunition truck at Objective COPPER SOUTH. (AG)

Flooded T55 at Objective COPPER SOUTH. (AG)

body. I remembered the hours spent bent double in the Optimist's turret as I followed and fought my battle on the airwaves and my tac map. Most of all, I remembered the fear and horror of being lost and alone on the battlefield in the early dawn. Here, in the sunshine of the afternoon, the now silent hulks seemed both harmless and sad. The large 30mm Soviet cannons, a distinctive feature of the T55s, were particularly poignant. Mounted on top of the turret they pointed skywards like crouched skeletons. Again there were many dead vehicles but no dead bodies. There were, however, the tell-tale signs of large, fresh diggings. Mass unmarked graves? Perhaps the burial parties had passed this way also.

The desert around COPPER SOUTH was different again. The position seemed to straddle a slight dome, the highest feature for miles around. The sand was a mixture of soft powder and hard grit. Most strange of all, there was quite a lot of wispy coarse grass and scrub vegetation. The plants were too well established to be the result of the recent rain, although they were now taking on a rejuvenated green hue. Across the main dome feature, the contours gently undulated and many of the hollows now held quite substantial amounts of water. Flooding was a new and unexpected phenomenon in this desert.

I was determined to return with a souvenir, but what? Already the word had been spread that we would not be allowed back home with machine guns, bayonets, radios etc. Some of our party had acquired weapon sights or name plates. I looked around for inspiration. The position had a full array of equipment, T55 tanks, MTLBs, logistic truck

198

and infantry weapons. As I stood next to the devastated remains of a T55 tank my eye caught something shining brightly in the sand. I carefully scraped the covering away to reveal a ball bearing. It was from the turret ring of the tank and was a full 2 inches in diameter. It was quite beautiful and would be a perfect reminder of events. I put it in my pocket. Mission accomplished.

COPPER SOUTH was the home of a massive HQ complex and the troops and armour seemed to be positioned to protect it. It was situated so that it straddled the highest point of the dome and consisted of both command vehicles dug into shell scrapes with protective sand walls and deep underground bunkers. The entrances to these underground hideaways were either simple but well-cut rectangular holes, almost unnoticeable until you were all but upon them, or sandbagged doorways going down at a steep angle. Invariably, the more sophisticated the entrance, the more important the bunker. I resisted going down. I was well aware that, during the reorganization immediately after the battle, many of these bunkers had been investigated. Some had contained carpets, soft furnishings, shower blocks and all the comforts of home. I was equally aware that allied soldiers had been injured or killed by booby traps. I could live without seeing the odd Persian carpet.

The cries of enthusiasm slowly drew us all to one spot. Upright in front of its trench was a Soviet built grenade launcher. It was mounted on its tripod with a full drum magazine fitted. It was ready to fire, the cylindrical grenades neatly lined up and clearly visible in the circular container. Peter Garbutt and Grant Baker set about it with enthusiasm. It had both a trigger and, so that it could be fired from under cover, a

Majors Peter Garbutt and Grant Baker with the Soviet grenade launcher. (AG)

long cable firing mechanism. We all gathered round expectantly, like excited school boys. All looked well. The trigger was pulled. Nothing! The cable was pulled. Again nothing happened. The disappointment was audible and each one of us chipped in with a solution to the problem. Checks, curses, firm kicks, all failed to produce the desired result. The weapon was well and truly jammed solid and would remain that way. This was probably the reason the Iraqis had abandoned it. All further attempts to sort out the grenade launcher or to explore further were curtailed by the sudden menacing sound of a helicopter. Hovering low, about 20 feet off the ground, some 200 metres away was a solitary American Apache helicopter. The Union Jacks flying on our vehicles were plain for all to see. We were clearly military and Europeans. We waved at the pilot, the age-old sign of greeting. In return we got a movement from the helicopter which means the same in any language. Move! Get off my patch! Discretion being the better part of valour we made our way back to the vehicles and set off for our RV. For over thirty minutes the helicopter stalked us like an ominous shadow.

Our RV was a way-point on the GPS. Here we would, modern technology permitting, meet up with supper. Early evening we drew up next to an 8-tonne truck of the 14th/20th King's Hussars. We were warmly greeted by tables, chairs and a hot meal. The truck had come for two reasons. Firstly it brought our food, water, fuel and comfort. Secondly and more important, it liberated a pristine and very modern generator that had been spotted, and courtesy of GPS, plotted, on the Battlegroup's first visit to the area. We ate extremely well, then whiled away the evening swapping war stories under a magnificent sky. The only minus point was that Geoff Ravenhill discovered that he had lost his wallet. He was certain that it was in the area of the grenade launcher. Next morning, at first light, we would have to drive back to look for it. In the middle of the Iraqi desert our intrepid band slept under the stars.

9 MARCH 1991

Dawn rose bright and clear, promising another magnificent day. I crawled stiffly from my dew-covered sleeping bag, washed, dressed and had breakfast. Leaving the others to move at a more leisurely pace, Geoff and I headed back to look for his wallet. Navigation was easy, our tyre tracks clearly visible from the day before. Getting lost was less of a hazard than running into a 'gung ho' Apache pilot. We reached our objective quickly and without incident and spent about an hour searching by retracing our footprints. Nothing! Despondently we rejoined the main group. BRASS was our next port of call and the 14th/20th King's Hussars Battlegroup's major battle.

We drove slowly up to our Line of Departure, the oil/sand road.

Memories flooded back. Again I was amazed by the size of the position. We had attacked in fog, dust and smoke. Here now, on a sunny spring morning, objective BRASS spread from horizon to horizon. The 4th Armoured Brigade had attacked thousands of troops and hundreds of armoured vehicles and guns deployed over an area some 20 kilometres wide and 16 kilometres deep. Before us now was the armoured heart of the position. There were broken and rusting vehicles everywhere. We made our way southwards, stopping to examine and explore. This was the first time I had seen at first hand the real effects of artillery fire. The new British L15 shell was devastating and trucks and APCs had been ripped apart by the combined downward force of HE and jagged steel shrapnel. Tanks had fared little better. Although the steel shards had failed to penetrate the thick armour of the turret, they had been effective on all the other parts of the vehicle - tracks, engine decks, road wheels, gun barrels. Nothing withstood the power of these airburst shells. Most horrific of all was their effect on trenches. If they were open and exposed then they rapidly filled with sand and the remains of their hapless occupants. Those dug in with extensive overhead cover fared no better. Blast and shock could get into the confines of bunkers and trenches, but could not get out. The resulting over-pressure of tons of high explosive ruptured lungs, burst eyeballs and spared no one.

Occasionally there were groups of neat, single, deep, vee-shaped holes in the sand, testament to the arrival of the enormous 203mm shells of the American National Guard's M110 guns, the most powerful and accurate in the ground force inventory. The impact of these shells must

Robert Fox of The Daily Telegraph. (AG)

201

have severely tested the Iraqi's nerve. The bomblet had been equally devastating. Delivered by the M109 guns and the MLRS rockets, they had cascaded down over the target area bringing destruction to everything in their path. Some burst, sending lethal chunks of jagged shrapnel across the battlefield. Others struck solid metal and punched a deep, white-hot hole.

I clambered onto a T55 tank, now rusting slowly. The armoured engine decks were a mass of jagged steel, bent upwards like brown rusty fingers. The large roof-mounted machine-gun still had belted ammunition hanging from the feeder tray. More ammunition lay close by on top of the track guards, flanked by a solitary eating plate. There was a distinctive yellow panel, about 12 by 6 inches, painted on the side of the turret, with black Arabic numerals similar to a reversed 77. Above this number, wedged in the hand rail, was the light aluminium half-collar from a discarding sabot round. This must have broken away as the round was fired, spinning backwards to find a final resting place on the turret. In the bottom left-hand corner of the yellow-painted panel was a small neat hole, about the size of a tennis ball. At first we thought that this was where a solid armour-piercing round from a Challenger's 120 mm gun had struck. Closer examination showed that the hole did not go all the way into the turret. A bomblet round, carried forwards by the inertia imparted by its carrier, had hit the turret. On impact its copper cone had inverted and, driven by its own integral shaped explosive charge, changed into a jet of liquid metal. It had not managed fully to defeat the armour. Nonetheless this small sub-munition had done all that its makers had promised. The crew had been spared the white-hot molten slug entering the turret, they had not been spared the shock wave that followed. The American burial teams had visited some days before but they had left behind the now blackening and putrefying remains that coated the inside of the tank turret. Millions of flies now worked to complete their gruesome task.

From the evidence of the sabot, the crew had fired at least one round from their main armament and were probably in action when the artillery struck. From the evidence of other vehicles, many crews had fled when they saw the artillery hit their comrades. About halfway down BRASS, about the point where we had wheeled on the dogleg, we came across a Landrover and two people. We went across to investigate. They were civilian 'Boffins', from where I know not but the purpose of their presence was to ascertain the failure rate of the bomblet. The battlefield did have unexploded bomblets, indeed it also had a fair sprinkling of unexploded aerial munitions lying conspicuous and sinister in their yellow markings on the desert sand. The two scientists spoke disparagingly about the bomblet. Feigning ignorance, I enquired of the problem only to be told that the bomblet had, in their estimate, a high failure rate. I enquired on what data they based this calculation. They had counted the few blinds lying about and made an educated guess. I introduced myself and explained that I was responsible for the bomblets being fired. I then tried to get over to two incredulous civilians the reality of modern artillery warfare. There are eighty-eight in each 155mm shell and 644 in each MLRS rocket pod. The bomblets fired at this position numbered in the hundreds of thousands. I don't think I convinced them. I believe they revised their calculations by a factor of ten. A hundred would have been more accurate. The size and scale of Gulf operations is still the most difficult element of the whole campaign to put across to those who were not there.

Making our way slowly across BRASS, it was difficult to determine accurately who had done what. As a major Iraqi strong-point, it had taken its fair share of the air war and perhaps the artillery raids. Clearly some of the vehicles had been destroyed some considerable time ago. Bright yellow air-delivered sub-munitions were a constant hazard as they lay strewn across the battlefield. Some looked very fresh and I can only surmise that they were from the air sorties I had ordered prior to the Battlegroup's attack. Many tanks had been destroyed by artillery and in some areas the Challengers had fired on dead hulks. Equally the position had been so large that the artillery could not hope to cover everything and the Challengers and Warriors had engaged troops fighting hard for their very survival. There was, however, no disputing who had fired the last shot. Those vehicles that had fallen to artillery alone were still largely intact unless the magazine had detonated, in which case the turret lay like a discarded frying pan close by. Those that had suffered at the hands of the Challengers 120mm gun were in various states of total disintegration. Some tanks lay crumpled, their turret lying twenty or so metres away. Some had been all but vaporized and little remained other than a hole in the desert and a few mangled and scattered pieces of steel. It was the shock and force of the artillery and the speed and accuracy of the tanks that had stunned the enemy and led, thankfully, to our achieving our goal without a single Battlegroup casualty.

We moved westward to the part of BRASS attacked by the 3RRF Battlegroup and the neighbouring position, STEEL. The desert was very similar, but the enemy consisted primarily of artillery batteries and their supporting logistics and communications. The Iraqi positions had all been facing due south when the Battlegroup had attacked from the north-west behind a massive Fire Plan from the artillery. The Iraqi guns were all large calibre and towed. Their tractor vehicles had long been withdrawn and so their crews' only options were to flee, fight or give up. Having heard or seen the fate of their comrades, most either fled in advance or chose to surrender. The logistics units, in their soft-skinned trucks and devoid of armoured protection, faced a similar choice. Most, like their artillery comrades, chose to surrender. With the Squadron Leaders keen to follow their own battle routes, Geoff, Robert and I concentrated on the gun positions. Lacking the ability to manoeuvre, the soldiers here had prepared to fight in situ. The gun batteries were deployed in the Soviet style, linked by telephone wires to a central command post. The guns on this part of the position were large, South African-manufactured, G5s. Designed by Dr Gerard Bull of 'Super Gun' fame, they could throw a shell well over twenty miles. Each gun was surrounded by high sand walls. Inside the protective ring and to the rear were the crew dugouts and the ammunition stores. I could have been visiting my own battery. Here, evidently abandoned in great haste, was all that remained of a crew who were probably little different from my own crews. In the crew shelters were the personal effects that all soldiers gather around them. A home-made table, bedding, pinups cut from western magazines, photographs of wives, families and sweethearts, a transistor radio, numerous Yugoslav respirators and decontamination kits and food – surprisingly fresh potatoes, onions and dates. They had clearly been in this location for a long time and to someone it was home from home. Looking at these personal effects I almost felt that I was intruding.

The battery command post was equally familiar, although it clearly served the function of both firing the guns and administering the unit. It consisted of a deep dugout cut into the desert, the superstructure constructed largely of corrugated iron sheeting and steel ammunition boxes filled with sand. Over the structure sand had been piled, but most of the work of the command post seemed to have taken place outside in the open. Inside the underground 'office' we found, neatly hand-written in Arabic script, the personal records of each soldier. In the top right-hand corner was a small black and white photograph and there were numerous entries, presumably recording such things as next-of-kin,

Battery Command Post, Objective STEEL. (AG)

courses, promotion, leave or misdemeanours. These carefully kept pieces of paper, charting the lives of individual people, now blew aimlessly across the desert. It was difficult not to wonder what had become of these unfortunate souls.

The communication cables from the guns came into a modern and sophisticated French telephone exchange. The Command Post had British-made Racal frequency hopping radios, the type the British Army could only dream of, and British NBC kit, both the suit and the S10 respirator – the perks of command? The data needed to fire the guns was calculated manually using a Soviet plotting board and South African firing tables. Neatly pinned to a board were arcs of fire and likely targets – not the action of a unit that had no intention of fighting. As we left the Command Post and started to move across the position I spotted a small, toadstool-shaped anti personnel mine half-exposed in the sand. It was on the side of the bunker just at the point where the roof line started to rise. From it came a thin black trip wire, now partially buried in the drifting sand. Clearly those fleeing had enough time to lay a few booby-traps. We backed away cautiously. The Gypsy had given us her warning.

As a soldier I was puzzled at what the fleeing Iraqi soldiers had chosen to leave behind. If I was on my feet, in a war zone, preparing to face all the hazards of the unknown, I would have taken food, my respirator and certainly my boots. Yet here before us, discarded, were respirators, food and numerous pairs of boots. Such precious equipment was strewn everywhere. I picked up a black beret and removed the badge. It was old and had clearly seen many years service, I presume with the same owner. Pictures of wives and families now blew unwanted across the desert. As a British soldier, to abandon things that were so dear to me would have been difficult, to leave the things that would perhaps save my life seemed madness. Robert Fox told me that he had witnessed similar actions in the Falklands. Argentinean soldiers had taken their boots off before fleeing in sub-freezing temperatures. They also had abandoned treasured photographs and potentially life-saving equipment.

With time pressing we remounted and headed for TUNGSTEN. This was a position that I had seen but briefly, having been in reserve for the whole of the battle. Now we journeyed along the route that Tac and the two infantry companies had taken as we had moved in the dark between and behind the two assaulting battlegroups. Again in the light of day it was all very different. The track we had driven along that night crossed hard, featureless, coarse sand desert. The pipeline which had been thought such an obstacle stood about 4 feet proud of the desert surface and could be seen for miles. Running parallel with the pipeline, but on our side, was an oil/sand service road. As we approached we could see that the crossing was at the sight of a small, disused pumping station.

There was an old, derelict, single-storey building and an idle 'nodding donkey' pump. The remains of old power and telephone cables were also evident. About 50 metres short of the road, to the left of our track, was a deep tank scrape. This had been the unwelcome but fortunately temporary home of One One Charlie. On the road itself we stopped briefly for lunch. The crossing point that had seemed so hazardous consisted of sand piled over the pipeline. It had been some 15 feet high with a knife edge when the Emperor had crossed. Now, having been transited by the two Warrior companies and numerous logistic convoys, it was all but flat and the Landrovers crossed with ease.

TUNGSTEN had taken the full force of the Divisional Artillery. I remember watching the MLRS flashes in the darkness and feeling the impact of the shells vibrating up through the floor of the Optimist. By the battle for TUNGSTEN the Iraqi Army knew that it was beaten and many had abandoned their positions and fled to the relative safety of the open desert. It seemed that on this position it was the artillery units at the rear and therefore closest to our advancing troops that had suffered most. An Iraqi artillery commander, taken prisoner on the night of the attack, reported that he had a battery of over 260 men. After the MLRS strike only eight had survived. 4 Brigade had also captured a Brigadier. He was reported to have been a lawyer by trade, American trained and educated, and with a very good command of the English language. He said that he had started the war with over 100 guns and after prolonged attack from the air his command was still 80% effective. The Air War had come as a terrifying surprise, but they quickly realized that the aircraft targeted their equipment not the men and if they stayed in the protection of their trenches some distance away, then they were safe. What is more they usually

Iraqi heavy artillery at Objective TUNGSTEN. (AG)

Geoff Ravenhill in
B52 bomb crater. (AG)

received some warning of an air strike and often the aircraft would repeatedly re-attack the burnt-out hulks as they were easier to see. With the artillery there was no warning and nowhere to shelter. It covered everyone and everything. "After the artillery barrage, I had only seven guns left."

Although the air war had not been as effective as had been hoped, it nonetheless played its part. In particular the mighty B52 bombers had left their own distinctive calling cards. Unsighted at thousands of feet, the sudden and unexpected arrival of their 1,000 lb bombs must have spilt a few cups of coffee down below. We came across a tank which had fallen prey to one of these aerial giants. It had been lifted off its tracks, separated from its turret and thrown like a toy across the desert. In its place was a crater some 50 feet across and 10 feet deep, excavated not out of the sand but solid rock. Beside it lay the twisted remains of the bomb case. I was so overawed with the effect that I asked Geoff Ravenhill to stand at the bottom of the crater so that I could record the sight on film. He disappeared and I had to content myself with a shot of him standing just below the rim.

Towards the centre of TUNGSTEN we came across a massive logistic

Robert Fox and the Chinese-made bike. (AG)

Guns destroyed by allied Engineers. (AG)

dump - hundreds of tons of artillery and T55 tank ammunition. It was stored in open topped-pits sunk into the desert floor and with some 100 metres spacing between each. The lack of overhead cover allowed easy access and, should one be hit, ensured that the blast went upwards, thus minimizing collateral damage. There were boxes of every shape and size, wooden and steel. They came from America, France, China, Yugoslavia, but, most prominent of all, Jordan. In one pit we found literally hundreds of brand new Kalashnikov AK47 assault rifles. Some had been exposed to the elements and had started to rust, others were in pristine condition, still with the manufacturer's thin film of grease on them. There was ammunition too, in great abundance. It is testament to Mr Kalashnikov's design that even the most rusty fired with ease the very first time. We spent a brief interlude shooting at whatever targets we could find in the desert.

We made our way slowly eastwards through the position and stopped by a bunker which was right next to the sand track along which we were driving. In the dugout was a Chinese-made, sit-up-and-beg bicycle. Robert Fox mounted and, to accompanying cheers, rode across the sand. There was not another moving object from horizon to horizon.

At the far end of TUNGSTEN we rejoined the Pipe Line road. Here were more artillery batteries and we stopped briefly to investigate. The allied engineers had been before us and had neatly blown apart the long barrels of any gun still capable of firing. These guns now looked faintly

ridiculous with their snub and blackened noses. Amongst the guns we found both carefully made mock-up guns and metal reflectors nailed to wooden posts. These simple devices had no doubt played havoc with the American spy satellites and confused the radars of the attacking aircraft. The decoy guns were particularly impressive. These simple tubes with a sheet steel plate to simulate the crew shield had clearly been professionally manufactured and then brought out into the desert in great numbers. They sat inside sand-walled bays just like the real thing, held up on thin legs so that they cast a realistic shadow for the benefit of the aerial cameras.

The road, firm, flat and straight, headed south-east back across the Wadi al Batin and we made good time. Our first indication of Al Abrak was a red and white banded radio mast rising up from the desert floor like a miniature Eiffel tower. As we approached, through the heat shimmer, there emerged, first, lower masts shining silver in the sunshine and then a scattering of single and double-storey buildings. This was the Kuwaiti police post, built to monitor the sensitive tip of the triangle where the borders of Saudi Arabia, Kuwait and Iraq meet. The whole complex of sheds, accommodation blocks, offices, hangers, pylons, masts, garages, trucks, jeeps and armoured vehicles was enclosed behind a high chain-link fence. Al Abrak had been held by the Kuwaiti army, taken by the Iraqis, bombed by the Americans and liberated by the Egyptians.

A decoy gun at Objective TUNGSTEN.
(AG)

The Kuwaiti Police Post at Al-Abrak. Captured by Iraq, bombed by America, liberated by Egypt.
(AG)

As we skirted the perimeter of the camp, looking for a way in, there was no movement or sign of life. The gates at the entrance had gone and we drove cautiously down what had been the central thoroughfare. There was destruction everywhere. Al Abrak had sustained a massive air and artillery bombardment and the buildings lay shattered, masts and cables lying across the roads where they had fallen. The sky was not the only place destruction had come from. The Iraqis had seemed relieved, even keen, to surrender to Europeans, perhaps accepting that our technology was superior, perhaps confident that they would be well treated. They clearly had no such thoughts about the Egyptians. Arab pride or fear of the consequences of capture had caused the fighting to be fierce and bloody. The Egyptians had been forced to fight for every building and the evidence of the ferocity and slaughter was everywhere. Pervading everything was the smell of death which caught in the back of the throat and made you want to retch.

Slowly our convoy picked its way between the fallen masts, burnt-out vehicles and rubble. Suddenly we found ourselves surrounded by small anti-personnel mines, scattered across the road and now around the Landrover's wheels. We had no choice but to weave a delicate path through them, each of us watching one of the wheels and shouting instructions to the driver. It took an agonisingly long time. On the far side of the post, on firm and clear concrete, we stopped and dismounted. It was like being in a horror movie. There was not a building that had not been sprayed with bullets and nowhere was there a pane of glass left unbroken. Every vehicle had either been riddled with holes or gratuitously set on fire. This was Arab settling score with Arab. There had been none of the niceties of the Geneva Convention here. No first

Evidence of the struggle for Al-Abrak.
(AG)

aid given, no prisoners taken. Bodies still lay in their vehicles or where they had fallen. The clouds of flies were thick.

The area we were now in was the small farm complex used to provide the Post with meat, eggs etc. Dividing the small open areas of dry dirt were low, single-storey brick buildings. Long, thin and shed-like, their asbestos roofs had been smashed and not a window or a door remained intact. Here the flies gathered in even darker and more menacing clouds. In an open pen we found twelve camels. They lay in a mass of black, sticky, putrefying blood and feasting insects, their stomachs ceremonially slit open. One had died in the act of giving birth. This was the ultimate insult from Arab to brother Arab. In the still air and roasting heat the noise from the flies droned in our ears and the appalling stench made our stomachs heave. I had come to believe that I was beyond shock. I was not. As we walked slowly back to the Landrovers one in our midst said quietly, "I have smelled the smell of evil."

It was last light when we arrived back at the Battery. We had covered over 400 kilometres and re-lived a war. I was met by the BSM who presented me with two cans of beer – real beer. The Regiment had sent a truck to Bahrain. (Alcohol may have been taboo in Saudi Arabia but this was liberated Kuwait and we had done the liberating.) He updated me on events. We could send three members of the Battery home tomorrow on the first trooping flight to Germany. Anticipating my reaction, he had already warned off the three soldiers whose wives were due to have babies. A good BSM knows how his BC thinks. There was still no word of a return date for the rest of us, but that the system was repatriating anyone was encouraging news. The BK was to go immediately to RHQ to be briefed on the return options. Two soldiers from 7 Brigade had been killed yesterday. They had been out trophy hunting and jumped out of their Landrover onto bomblets. My mind went back to my own recent trip. Otherwise the troops were in good heart, all was well, no change. It had been announced that we were all to get five weeks' leave on return. We spent about an hour over beer and admin until, with images of flies and camels passing before my eyes, I went to bed and tried to sleep.

10 MARCH 1991

A bright sunny day but with a strong wind. Geoff Ravenhill came across as I was wading through breakfast to brief me on the options for the return. Neither were very encouraging. The best forecast was that we would wait until 7 Brigade departed, a scenario that would keep us in theatre for five or six weeks. If, however, there were problems with the Iraqis, and that scenario covered the full Middle East spectrum from non-compliance by Saddam Hussein to the complete collapse of the current Middle East order, then we could be here for five to six months or more. Having sorted out the day's business with Geoff, I left for RHQ. The

CO's 09.00 conference was to confirm courses, orbats etc. Afterwards we chatted about the return options. David Radcliffe was sympathetic towards my plight. As a BC I had now been in command for over three years and, although I could think of no better job, it was too long in career terms. I already had a posting as an instructor to Warminster and my successor, Rod Matherson, had arrived in Germany. He told me that he would post me at the earliest opportunity and if necessary my successor would fly out to relieve me in the desert. Half-heartened by this news and half-saddened that I should perhaps leave the Battery before the task was properly completed, I returned to the guns in time for David Coulter's 11.00 church parade.

Immediately after lunch I visited the Guns Course. Lieutenant Hewlan Morgan was lecturing and I sat at the back of the makeshift desert classroom of sand walls and a cam net, and listened to him instruct. He was striving manfully with a home-made blackboard against a strengthening wind. Content that all was well I took my Landrover and headed for the Brigade RV and the Mobile Bath Unit. I needed to get cleaned up before the 16.00 Officers' Mess photograph. The Brigade RV was much as I had remembered it, only it had moved a few hundred kilometres - an RMP tent, a NAAFI container selling the necessities of life and a Bath Unit. Bath Units are the traditional butt of barrack-room jokes and Goon Show scripts. If you have not had a proper wash for weeks, they are heaven-sent. It consisted of a large black Royal Engineer static water tank which fed shower nozzles inside a brown canvas marquee. On one side of the tent were the changing facilities consisting of a few trestle benches; the remainder was given over to the washing area. The whole thing was powered by a generator-cum-pump. We arrived, parked up, entered and stripped off. We then went through and

The Mobile Bath Unit. (PW)

stood under the shower heads which were strategically placed about 5 feet above the duck-board floor. A head protruded through the tent flap. "Sorry lads, the heater's bust." We had a cold shower. It was wonderful. Not superbly wonderful, just wonderful.

We gathered at RHQ for the photograph. It was a rare meeting of the Regiment's officers and we all made the most of the occasion to catch up with the news. I bade a fond farewell to Mark Vye, who was flying home the following day. The Regiment had liberated much Iraqi equipment and it was parked close by. Two large towed guns had been positioned, barrel to barrel, to provide a fitting backdrop to the photograph. Chairs were moved, tall swapped for short, but finally the great deed was accomplished. Sadly the historic photograph did not turn out well. After my evening admin/orders meeting, the three FOOs and I whiled away the time playing Malefiz. I can't remember who won.

11 MARCH 1991

Another bright sunny morning, clear blue sky but with an annoyingly strong wind that whipped up the sand and stung the eyes. David Radcliffe held his morning Orders Group at 09.30. He opened by announcing the new Battery Sergeant Major's plot and then, after the plethora of administrative points needed to keep a regiment functioning, he updated us on the wider events but confessed few firm decisions could yet be taken. There was now a possibility that 4 Brigade could be home by 15 April. A decision would be taken on 17 March. He could not shed any light on the significance of either of these two dates. The CO also announced that we were all to get a medal. The ribbon would be sand-coloured for the desert with stripes in the colours of the three Services. Afterwards he told me that he had signalled the Royal Artillery postings branch to insist that Mark Vye and I should be given the full five weeks' Gulf entitlement of leave and a further three weeks to get our families moved and resettled. He had also insisted that, if necessary, my successor should replace me in the field.

I emerged from the conference to find the sun losing a battle to the smoke clouds that were now gathering above our heads. I had to remain at RHQ to be interviewed by a reporter from, I was told, *The Times*. He came and we chatted briefly. He was supposedly a professional Defence Correspondent but had little idea about the Army or how it operated. Indeed he was not even clear on the rank structure. As I was preparing to leave I was grabbed by the QM who told me that the three weapons damaged when the M548 had exploded were now repaired and ready for collection at 49 EOD. I laughed. He could not be serious. Surely those weapons were not within hundreds of miles of here. They were, and what was more the boards of enquiry and the paperwork that would be generated if I went back to Germany without them would keep me busy for the rest of my career. I capitulated and agreed to have them collected. Where and what was 49 EOD? It was by the airfield in Kuwait City! What luck! I would collect them personally, tomorrow. Elated, I made it back to the Battery in time for lunch.

As a rule I always briefed the management of the Battery on the salient points of all the meetings I attended at RHQ. I held my Orders Group at 13.00 and gave them the news about the return home. Rumour had been running rife and, as 'six months in the desert' was still the hot favourite, it was starting to affect morale. Although I could not confirm a move date, my information was at least an officially sanctioned rumour. On top of this good news, BFBS, the British Forces Broadcasting Service, were visiting the Battery. Excitement abounded. They arrived just after 14.00, an announcer and a sound man. It was a chance for as many as possible to send a message home to loved ones. As the BC, I was asked to open with a few words. I greeted everyone back in Münster and on behalf of the Battery sent our good wishes. I told them where we were, said a little about our daily life and living conditions and promised that we would all be home soon. I ended by saying hello to Annie and the children. Behind me the BSM was herding all the would-be Terry Wogans into line to wait their turn. The effect on morale of these seemingly trivial events should never be underestimated. By the time BFBS had departed the sky was black and the transition from day to night was marked only by the appearance of a red glow in the east - the oil fires. I spent the evening assembling and briefing a crew and preparing for our journey to Kuwait City.

12 MARCH 1991

Visiting Kuwait City, without good reason, was officially forbidden and the tales of the scores being settled as the various Arab factions struggled for dominance filled the news. I had always determined that I would not return home without seeing the city that we had come so far and fought so hard to liberate. I would go regardless of official decrees. Now that there was a legitimate reason to visit I would make the most of it. The previous night I had elicited the best directions I could from those in the Regiment who had already been part of the way. The Main Supply Route currently stopped short of the city before turning south towards the Saudi border. The guidance was "Due south to the sand road, left to the tarmac road, turn right at 'Shorty', then head for the oil wells until you pick up the military signs for the city." Simple enough!

We left early, two of us in a single Landrover, a large Union flag flying prominently and an escorting 8-tonner. This was not a part of the world to visit on your own or in which to break down. Geoff Ravenhill drove the Landrover. It was a bright clear morning, the wind having cleared away yesterday's smoke clouds. We journeyed due south, keeping the rising sun square to our left. We quickly found the sand road and turned east. Although made entirely of sand, this was an established route, clearly in use in pre-war days for it was hard, flat and straight. We had covered no more than 2 kilometres when we were forced to leave the road to skirt around a column of decimated vehicles. Now brown and rusting, the battery of 2S1 self-propelled guns had been fleeing back towards Kuwait city when the aircraft had found them. Still in line they had attempted to scatter, none of them making it more than a few yards from the road. Led by a Soviet-built BMP, the column of guns and MTLB command posts had stood no chance. The American A10s had used their tank-busting cannon to murderous effect. These vehicles looked armoured but covered in a metal skin would have been a more accurate description. A Renault 5 would have fared just as well. The cannon shells had literally shredded the convoy, bursting the steel boxes open at the seams. The fires that inevitably followed, fortified by fuel and ammunition, did the rest. We stopped to look. Seeing a complete artillery battery destroyed in this way was somehow worse than the hundreds of individual casualties we had already seen. For us to witness the fate of fellow Gunners seemed particularly moving and shocking.

Chastened, we travelled on. The road started to undulate and turn. After about 15 kilometres we found ourselves driving between two enormous tented camps, set some 100 metres back from the sand road. The tents were mostly white and in immaculate straight lines. Behind the tents, as I looked south, I could see row upon row of artillery pieces, their barrels elevated to point skywards. Beside them were Soviet-built T62 and American-built M60 tanks. This was the Arab Corps. On the side of the road, where one camp's entry road joined our route, was a neatly inscribed sign surrounded by white-painted stones. Next to the sign stood a tall and imposing figure, ramrod strait, a British pace-stick under his arm. The sign announced the Egyptian Army. They looked impressive and in very good order. The man wore white British-pattern chevrons on his arm and old British-pattern webbed belt and gaiters. He could have come from the Army of the British Raj.

The 2S1 Artillery Battery destroyed by US A10 aircraft as they fled towards Kuwait City. (AG)

Heading towards Kuwait City, just past 'Shorty'. (AG)

As we journeyed on, ahead of us was a road running from right to left across our path. From a distance most of the vehicles on the road looked to be stationary, only a few showing signs of movement. As we drew nearer it became clear that the stationary vehicles were abandoned wrecks dotting the curbside. This was the tarmac road we were looking for. Turn right at 'Shorty' was the instruction. I had enquired about 'Shorty' only to be met with silent nods and knowing grins. At the T junction, where the sand road met the highway, an MTLB lay on its side, wrecked and abandoned. In front of it was a sand-covered grave. From the grave came a blackened arm reaching skywards, its wrist bent, its hand pointing towards Kuwait City. This was 'Shorty'. Soldier humour at its blackest.

The highway was clear, destroyed vehicles having been bulldozed to the side. The sky was now starting to become grey and there was an acrid smell of smoke in the air that caught in the throat. Shortly afterwards it became so dark that we had to drive on full headlamps. It was 12.00, midday. The sight, sound and smell of the oil wells blazing will live with me for ever. Estimates put the number of wells on fire at ninety-six. The effect was to totally black out the sky. The noise from the roar of the flames was deafening, like a rocket motor, and you had to shout to be heard. Most of the blazing wells seemed to be to the south-west of the city and our route took us through the most dense area. At one point we stopped to examine a Soviet-built ZSU 23/4 anti-aircraft gun. This was the 'bogeyman' of my vehicle recognition classes, one of the Warsaw Pact's great terror weapon. Now it lay useless and abandoned. In photographs it had looked impressive, close up it was much less imposing, completely un-armoured and poorly made. The belts of ammunition which fed the four, radar-directed machine guns still lay in their feeder trays. Around it was nothing but destruction, testament to its failure as an anti-aircraft weapons system.

216

The sides of the road leading towards the city were littered with abandoned and destroyed vehicles. As we approached the built-up area, the road climbed up onto a flyover. From this vantage point we could look down into the city suburbs. It was like a scene from H.G. Wells' *War of the Worlds*, destruction everywhere and virtually no sign of life. The reports that the city had been systematically plundered appeared true. Doors, windows, curbstones, traffic lights, in fact anything that could be moved, had gone. Ahead of us was a military 'Road Closed' barrier with the writing in English. We were forced to leave the flyover and descend down a slip road. As we reached ground level we saw the reason for our diversion. About 500 metres further on a gap, over 100 metres wide, had been blown in the elevated road. We headed south on the only route available to us. As we rounded a bend we saw first the sandbagged sangar, then the road block. This was, however, no Military Police checkpoint. The five or six men controlling the road had shamaags around their heads, concealing everything but their eyes. They waved Kalashnikov assault rifles menacingly. This was the Mujahadeen. Not all were well disposed to the infidel. We approached the road block slowly and cautiously. To turn and flee would have been to invite a hail of bullets into the back of the vehicles. I fitted the long curved magazine to my sub-machine gun, cocked it and lay the short weapon across my lap, the barrel pointing at the centre of the door. If necessary I would fire through the soft aluminium panel. We stopped. A masked gunman looked through my window at me, a second looked in the back of the Rover, while yet more examined the truck. I smiled and held up two fingers in the sign of victory. I prayed that I had got it the right way round. 'English,' I beamed and pointed backwards at the Union Jack which I hoped was still there. It was! It was greeted by cries of 'English, English,' and much good-natured thumping on the canvas and bonnet. Waving, and just a little relieved, we drove on following the signs for the Airport.

Just short of the Airport we ran into another Mujahadeen road block in the form of a sand-bagged chicane. More confident now, we did not stop; rather as we approached, we slowed to a walking pace and we all waved and shouted and held up the victory salute. Taken aback, there was little the gunmen could do but wave and return our greetings. The next barrier was manned by US Marines guarding the airfield. They waved us through without question. The airfield had taken a battering during both the air and the ground offensives and everywhere buildings lay in various states of destruction. The engineers had been hard at work and already runways had been cleared and repaired and some of the offices and hangars were back in use.

Close to the main terminal building lay a British Airways Boeing 747. The distinctive grey, red and blue tail was still recognisable as were parts

Iraqi vandalism in Kuwait City Marina.
(PS)

of the wings and the four engines lying on the concrete. Otherwise all that remained was a blackened mass of twisted metal. It reminded me of a magnificent dead bird, its flesh devoured by maggots. As we walked around the wreckage we were amazed just how big the aircraft had been. Its destruction appeared total. (In 1995 a television documentary programme exposed the fact that parts of this aircraft had been sold for spare parts on the world aviation market.)

Our destination, 49 EOD (Explosive Ordnance Disposal) was located immediately to the east of the airfield in an industrial complex. It was close to where the forward HQs of ARCENT and British Forces Middle East had established themselves, so getting directions was easy. We found the unit without difficulty, situated in an old factory building. We were greeted warmly with the age-old British ritual of tea. The major in charge then took us on a guided tour of their 'collection'. There were mines of every shape size and nationality. Small arms, anti-tank rockets and missiles. It was an Aladdin's cave. The star of the show was kept

218

until last. In a shed, on a trailer, in its distinctive naval grey paint, was a Chinese-made Stix anti-shipping missile. Some 20 feet long, this beauty was built to sink the largest warships. Over more tea we related our experience at the road blocks. The consensus of opinion amongst those at 49 EOD was that we had been extremely lucky. There was effectively a civil war raging between the various factions within the city and most were inclined to shoot at anyone not demonstrably one of their own, the niceties of Coalition solidarity or gratitude for the liberation of Kuwait having been conveniently put to one side. We were given a map, recently printed, which showed the latest factional boundaries. The black and white overprinted map had, marked in red, groups such as Fater, Jabriyah, Hawalli, Kaifan, Ba'ath and Shi'ite. Each controlled a sector of the city and was struggling to control more. North of the airfield a red line ran across the map from left to right. It was marked 'No travel north of this line without prior permission from HQ BFME.' We collected our three missing weapons and prepared to depart. We were told that before we left Kuwait City there was one other place we must visit, the Mutla Ridge. The map would enable us to get there avoiding the danger areas.

We headed south, then west and finally north, skirting the city in a wide, sweeping crescent until we rejoined the tarmac road, Route 80, well clear of the city. We drove past 'Shorty' and continued north. This was the main route from Kuwait City to Basra, the Basra Road. About 20 kilometres north of the city, the six-lane highway rose steeply onto an escarpment. This was the Mutla Ridge. We had heard of the battle along the road, indeed we were ourselves dashing to cut this highway when the ceasefire was called. We had not, however, seen any newspaper or television pictures and so we were expecting the now familiar scene of destroyed tanks etc. As we drove up the road we could see vehicles ahead - a Landrover and a couple of American HMMW Vs. We pulled up behind them.

Had we seen the most graphic newsreels it still would not have lessened the shock. The six-lane road and the roadside for as far north as we could see was littered with broken, burnt and abandoned vehicles. There were not tens, nor hundreds but thousands of vehicles. They lay contorted in every conceivable position. Pervading everything was the sweet, sickly smell of fried chicken. The burial teams had done their best but such was the slaughter that it was impossible to remove all the burnt and dismembered flesh. Sand had been spread to cover the most horrific sights, each spot now marked by a treacly crawling mass of teeming black flies. A bulldozer had pushed its way through the chaos in an attempt to reopen the route, serving only to compound the confusion on the roadside. There were tanks, APCs, military trucks, transporters with vehicles on their backs. There were civilian cars, trucks, buses, in fact

On the Basra Road.
(AG)

anything that could move had been used by the retreating Iraqi Army. There was a clear preference for Mercedes, BMW, Range Rover and Porsche. They had abandoned Kuwait City in a hurry but not without taking everything they could.

We walked slowly and very carefully off the road and onto the verge. Strewn everywhere was discarded ammunition, grenades, rifles, rocket launchers, uniforms, mines. There was also a heavy sprinkling of air-delivered sub-munitions that had failed to find something solid enough to detonate them. There were a few people moving amongst the vehicles - two British soldiers from the other Landrover and a small crowd of American servicemen and women. Occasionally an Arab could be seen picking his way amongst the wreckage. I saw three road tankers crushed together, a multiple rocket launcher, burnt-out buses presumably once packed with people. On the back of one truck were metal railings, neatly stacked. On another curb stones had been piled. A car boot which had escaped the inferno now lay open revealing children's clothes, kitchen ware, cosmetics, shoes. Anything of value, and much which had none,

220

had been taken. It was ghoulish and we were the ghouls. We could not help ourselves.

This vast exodus of vehicles must have been moving in a frantic but orderly column using both sides and all the lanes of the highway – in the dead of night the defeated Iraqi Army running for home in whatever means of transport it could find. We were later told that Abrams tanks, the 'Hounds of Hell,' had knocked out the head of the column in a classic ambush, stopping it dead. Helicopter gunships and F16s, blessed with modern night vision, then fell on the hapless mass of military refugees. Devoid of any form of air cover, anti-aircraft fire or command structure, the result was inevitable. Those vehicles that had not collided tried to scatter as the first cluster bombs rained down. None got further than a few yards. Stuck in the soft, roadside sand, they fell victim to weapons systems designed to destroy heavy armour, and the fire storm that followed. If you can imagine the M4 Motorway leading out of London being carpet-bombed at the height of the rush hour, then you are some small way towards picturing the Mutla Ridge - the 'Highway of Death'. It was a text-book operation, superbly executed. The American troops taking part, isolated in their turrets and cockpits, their vision restricted to a single sight or radar screen, probably had little idea of the scale of the butchery. There had been a third of a million Iraqi troops in Kuwait. The Mutla Ridge accounted for many of them. No doubt historians will debate the justification for this action ad nauseam. For me it was the most deeply disturbing sight I have ever witnessed and I am glad that I had no part in it.

The journey home was sombre and uneventful and I was back in time for the CO's evening Orders Group. The latest officially sanctioned rumour concerning our return home was that we would move to Al Jubayl on 28 March and fly 2 April. There was high hope that an

More debris on the Basra Road. (AG)

advance party would fly earlier. Orders over, I went with the other BCs to Brigade HQ for supper with the Tactical Debriefing Team. After the experiences of the day, food was the last thing I wanted.

13 MARCH 1991

I was up early. The weather promised to be sunny and hot, but with a strong wind. We now knew that a strong wind from the west kept the smoke away and so it was to be welcomed. Yesterday's experience had convinced me of two things. With common sense and a map it was safe to visit the airfield and the Basra road, and it was important that as many of the Battery as possible should have the chance to see what I had seen. I briefed Graham Ambrose carefully on routes and hazards. He then took an 8-tonne truck and as many of the soldiers as could be spared and headed off for Kuwait City. My second task of the morning concerned HMS *Manchester*. Recruiting as it did from the Manchester area, 2nd Field Regiment had an affiliation with the ship which bore the city's name. The Rocket Troop in particular had worked hard to foster this affiliation. During our tour on the United Nations Green Line in Cyprus some of the crew had visited the Battery as the ship passed by on its way home from the Armilla Patrol. Anchored off Cyprus, they had in return hosted some of us on board ship and a print of The Rocket Troop's action at Leipzig now hangs in the Wardroom. I knew they were in the Gulf. It was time to let them know where we were. I drafted a signal inviting them to visit, giving our position in the desert, not in the usual grid form, but in degrees and minutes. I then gave it to one of the Battery to take to the Brigade communications centre for onward transmission. Nothing ventured, nothing gained.

I spent the remainder of the morning on the difficult task of drafting Brigade Commander's Commendations. The afternoon I spent in searing heat watching the Regiment's leadership course grappling with the problems of digging in. The wind had dropped at midday and temperatures were well into the 90s. There was a static charge in the air as if a thunderstorm was imminent. Sadly it was not. At the CO's Orders we were informed that tomorrow a team of twelve reporters from the newspapers and television of the Manchester area would be visiting. They wanted to speak to as many local boys as possible and to hear at first hand what they thought of the war and the desert. I shuddered at the very prospect.

It was a bumper day for mail. As well as two or three 'bluies' from Annie, there was a large bundle of Easter cards from Lisieux Infants School, Liverpool. They had been sent to the all encompassing BFPO 3000 address and the Posties had sent them on up to us, Manchester being, in their eyes, close to Liverpool. As usual I had them distributed amongst the Battery with the strict proviso that anyone who received a card from a child was honour bound to reply. To set a good example I took one myself. It was in a bright green envelope, a home-made card, and a simple letter. The card had a rainbow-striped Easter Egg pasted on the front. The letter read:

> *Dear Soldier*
> *My name is Rosina I have one siser and a littl bady bruther and*
> *I hope you dot get hurt I have brown hair and brown eyes I live*
> *in Norns green I live with my nan.*

It was beautifully and carefully printed in pencil. Looking at the writing I guessed Rosina was about five as it reminded me very much of the letters from my own daughter, Katie. We were all very touched by the thought and the effort of the small children and the insides of Command Posts and guns were soon graced with brightly coloured cards.

That evening I spent a very pleasant few hours touring the guns, sitting and chatting to the crews. Each gun crew had managed to get at least one member away with Graham Ambrose and their experience was the topic of the hour. The trip had been without incident and very worthwhile. I ordered another truck to go tomorrow.

14 MARCH 1991

Another sweltering day, this time with little or no wind. The CO's 09.00 Orders Group confirmed the return dates, with of course the proviso that they could slip. It at least gave us something on which to focus our planning. I did a quick tour of the courses before settling down at the back of the Optimist to start compiling the many Confidential Reports on all my soldiers that I would have to have completed before I could leave the desert. At 12.00 David Radcliffe visited the Battery and stayed for lunch. He had two pieces of news. With luck the Regimental Advance Party would fly out of the desert on the 20th. I would be with them. With him he also had a signal from HMS *Manchester* announcing that their Lynx helicopter would fly in the next day at 10.00. We were asked to mark the landing site in some suitable way.

At 16.00, right on cue, the North-West's press and television arrived. They were a good-natured but very mixed bag. They had been out in the Gulf for a few days and had visited numerous units with local area connections. They had amassed a lot of material already. My mission therefore, as BC, was to ensure that it was my Battery's pictures and stories that they used. Knowing that they fit stories to good pictures and not the other way around, I loaded them into two M548 and took them the few kilometres across the desert to the destroyed 2S1 Battery. The drive was hot, dusty, but for them thrilling and they thought the wrecked battery was marvellous. They used it for the backdrop for most of their local boy photographs. Back in camp and with the light failing, they did their 'in depth' interviews. The television crew interviewed me, asking about my reaction to the war and the problems we now faced in the desert readjusting to the peace. I felt that I spoke quite well and with conviction. As a final question the interviewer asked me "Apart from the obvious, what are you most looking forward to when you get home?" I was not prepared for this question and replied that "I was looking forward to eating food that was green and crunchy not brown and sloppy." It was the only piece of the interview they used and was apparently syndicated worldwide. Famous for another 15 minutes.

That evening we hosted the visitors to dinner and they had a chance to really get to know the crews. When I discovered that one of the reporters was from Liverpool, I told her of the Easter cards and showed her the one I had from Rosina. She was as touched as I was. She knew the school and told me that it looked after one of the most deprived areas of the city. The next time I was at the Regimental Pay Office I took advantage of a mail order service they were running to send Rosina a Gulf Teddy Bear.

15 MARCH 1991

Hotter still. One of the guns had a large White Ensign which we ran up a radio mast next to the position. There could not be many Royal Navy flags in this part of the desert so we hoped this would provide a suitable beacon. At 10.00, bang on time, the Lynx from HMS *Manchester* landed. On board were the Captain, Commander Andrew Forsyth, two pilots and a Sub Lieutenant. They also brought with them beer, about enough for a can per man. They could be with us for only four hours so we had to make the most of our time. With one of the OPV Warriors and an M109 gun, we loaded up and headed out into the desert, the Naval personnel either driving or perched high in the turrets. Commander Forsyth proved to be a dab hand at high-speed motoring with the Warrior. We went via the 2S1 battery spending about thirty minutes examining the Iraqi vehicles. The pilot had sunk an Iraqi ship using the Lynx's Sea Skua missiles so there were lots of war stories to be swapped.

At midday the Captain and I had to go for lunch at RHQ. Major General James Gordon, the Director of Military Operations, was visiting the Regiment. When we arrived he was watching one of the courses being put through its paces. A fellow Gunner, the last time we had met he had taken Annie and I for a tour of the bright lights of Kowloon. Over lunch he was able to confirm that the return plan was, at present, still on schedule. Lunch over we returned to the Battery and a guided tour for the Navy. On departure the Battery presented the ship's company with a pristine Kalashnikov rifle in real gratitude for the beer. As they departed the Lynx gave a short but spectacular flying display before heading east and out to sea.

By early evening the heat and humidity were becoming unbearable. There was an absolute stillness that reminded me of Hong Kong at its very worst. At about 23.00 the storm broke with heavy rain and lightning. It was a merciful relief, but the rain was totally unexpected and caught many asleep in the open or with kit exposed to the elements. I lay on my camp bed listening to the drumming of the rain and watching it find its way inexorably through the hundreds of tiny holes in the canvas. I was too hot to care.

16 MARCH 1991

Steaming hot, with all evidence of the night's downpour gone by mid-morning. This was the day of the 4 Brigade photograph. RSMs and BSMs had been briefed. Brigade had laid down exactly how many vehicles were to be in the line-up. It would take most of the Battery so we had to drop cam nets, crew sleeping tents, disconnect tannoy systems etc. We had started on an ambitious programme of checking, cleaning and withdrawing equipment prior to the homeward move and it was going well. This disruption we could well do without. Saddam Hussein himself had not caused us this much pain and grief. All the Warriors would have to go and, as it was the only place I could sit and write my confidential reports, I had to go with them.

The spot chosen for the photograph was a few kilometres forward of

Lining up for the Brigade photograph. (AG)

225

the Brigade position, on an open flat area of sand, clear of trenches, bunkers, wrecked vehicles and, we hoped, mines. As the BSM lined the Battery up, I could see, from the Optimist's turret, Challengers and Warriors making their reluctant way towards the RV. It was all driven by a master plan. Placing vehicles invariably takes longer than the most pessimistic planning estimates and so we spent a goodly part of the morning waiting at the tail of a massive traffic jam.

Line upon line of vehicles were conducted into place - Ferrets, Spartans, Scorpions, Sultans, Samsons, Samaritans, AFV 432s, M548s, Warriors, Centurions, Chieftains, Challengers, Bridge Layers, M109s, M110s, M578s, MLRS, Landrovers, Landcruisers, 4-tonne, 8-tonne, 14-tonne, DROPS, Tank Transporters. The list and the lines grew. I sat working in the cool and relative peace of the back of the Optimist, listening to order and counter-order and the occasional barbed comment from Sergeant Allen up in the turret. At last all was pronounced ready and we took our places at the front of the vehicle, helmets on. A Lynx helicopter appeared and hovered in front of the assembled mass, I presume with the photographer on board. We stared blinking into the full force of the mid-morning sun. I do not know the outcome of the exercise. Was it a success? Did the photograph come out? I have never seen it and to date have not met anyone who has.

Whatever the outcome, the helicopter was only just in time, for within minutes of getting the order to stand down we were in the teeth of a sandstorm. We made our way back to the Battery position. All the clothing sleeping bags etc that had been hung out to dry after the night's soaking were now stiff with sand. I had put out a set of wet combat clothes which were now rock solid. The storm lasted until mid-afternoon when the weather returned to the now familiar roasting. Nets had to be retrieved, lines re-connected, tents resurrected and, where possible, numerous objects reclaimed from wherever the wind had taken them or the sand buried them. War was starting to feel preferable to this.

Once the weather had cleared I took a Landrover and sought solace with the 14th/20th. I needed to speak to Richard Shirreff and Peter Garbutt and I visited the two Squadrons in turn. I wanted to get their input for my FOOs confidential reports and it also gave a very pleasant opportunity to catch up with old friends and new gossip. Whilst I was on my rounds I called into Battlegroup MAIN HQ. Mike Vickery greeted me warmly and we commiserated over the disruption caused by the Brigade photograph. He kindly invited me to the Regiment's Dinner Night and Band Concert to be held on the 18th. When I raised my eyebrows at the word 'Band' he beamed proudly. Yesterday, Mr Hicks, the Band Master had taken a 8-tonne truck and driven some four hours to a makeshift desert runway. There he had met a RAF Hercules aircraft which had flown the band's instruments up from Al Jubayl. I knew better than to ask how the Colonel had arranged it. The trip was, however, not without incident. The party had been held up by a band of marauding Kuwait Freedom Fighters who mistook the 14th/20th Prussian Eagle for the Iraqi cap badge. Situations like that stretch sign language to the limit and ruin underpants.

Back at 2nd Field Regiment, dinner was a lively and entertaining affair. The Bombardiers' Leadership Course, those being prepared for promotion, laid on a Dinner Night to remember as part of their course. For the Commanding Officer, Battery Commanders, RSM and senior management they cooked the food, prepared the tables, served and provided the entertainment. The food was excellent considering the ingredients they had available and the very restricted facilities. Inside the tent 'dining room' imaginations had been used to the full and elaborate silver candelabra had been manufactured using bottles and silver paper. The entertainment was in the form of skits with no one in authority being spared their acid wit. It was a superb evening and recharged my flagging faith in humanity.

17 MARCH 1991

Yet another scorching day. The sorting of equipment was going well and we did not seem to have the number of deficiencies that I had expected. The equipment was either there or it was not. We had been to war and normal peace-time accountancy had to take second place to operational reality. No one deliberately loses kit that they may need but losses are inevitable. This was very much the common-sense attitude the Regiment had adopted, but Staff Sergeant Dines, the Battery's very efficient and conscientious BQMS would not be content until he had accounted for every nut and bolt. He and his team had set themselves a massive task and were plodding on manfully. At 10.00 the Battery paraded for a photograph, our last opportunity before moving home. The BSM spread everyone across a large sand dune and the Regimental photographer did the honours.

Photograph over, I left the BK/BSM team to allocate tasks for the rest of the day. The normal administration, kit sorting and vehicle maintenance had to proceed, as did the courses we were running. However, there was now increasing time for sport and other activities. We dispatched three 8-tonne trucks to Kuwait City, effectively giving every soldier who wished the opportunity of seeing the city they had helped liberate. In addition, the Regiment had organized a small range where Iraqi weapons, after rigorous checks by the experts, could be fired. It was our turn for the range this afternoon.

Leaving the Battery management to carry on, I headed cross-country to look for 3RRF. Here the Queen's Company were billeted and I needed to see Grant Baker concerning Richard Farndale's confidential. I went by Landrover, returning late afternoon to work in the relative peace of the back of the Optimist. With Richard's complete, I had finally finished all my Officers' reports. I also wrote my last letter home to Annie. It simply said,

"Dearest Darling,
hope to fly home on 24 March.
Love you. XXX"

18 MARCH 1991

Today was 'Pass off Day' for the Cadre course. Fortunately, although it was sunny, there was a light breeze. The BSM and I attended the parade. After lunch I went back via 127 Battery and had coffee with their Canadian BC, Dave Marshall. The rest of the day was uneventful. I washed some clothes and handed in as much kit as I could to the BQMS. I again spent most of the day in the relative cool of the Optimist, working on Senior NCO's reports and answering letters. There was the daily Orders Group at RHQ and afterwards I held my daily conference for the Battery management. The fly-out day for the Advanced Party was now 21 March.

In the evening I drove across to the 14th/20th. An area had been cleared close to RHQ. There were rows of seats, strings of light bulbs, flags on poles and, facing it all, a single Iraqi T55 tank. The dinner itself was in a marquee with Brigadier Christopher Hammerbeck as the Senior Visitor. Guests had been invited from across the Division and a superb party atmosphere prevailed.

Dinner over, we assembled for the band concert. It was inky dark. By the light of two dismounted vehicle search-lights and countless coloured cylume chemical lights, we sat in the warm, balmy desert night and listened. It was both moving and magical. The Regimental March of the 14th/20th King's Hussars, 'Sussex by the sea' now holds a particular place in my affection but I will always remember the finale. Lance Corporal Rodda, the Commanding Officer's Trumpeter, played 'The Post Horn Gallop' on the barrel of the T55. It will remain one of the most memorable evenings of my life.

19 MARCH 1991

Today I wanted to finish my reports, spend some time with the BQMS on the kit problems, wash my clothes and do the thousands of things a BC who has just been to war has to do before he hands over his Battery. Unfortunately, the House of Commons Select Committee on Defence were visiting and I, and many like me, were ordered to be there. The chosen site was some distance away, under command of CO 32 Regiment, Royal Artillery. A representative assortment of equipment had been assembled, hurriedly cleaned up for the occasion. Beside each vehicle stood its crew, there to talk to this august body. The Battery had sent a gun and a Warrior. We stood around in the blazing heat and waited. Eventually they arrived complete with Press entourage. The few who had some knowledge of Defence spoke enthusiastically to the soldiers and visited each piece of equipment in turn. The others just wanted to have their picture taken and leave.

On the way back to the Battery I took the opportunity to revisit the 4 Brigade ECP (Equipment Collection Point). It was no longer a point, it now covered acres. The equipment had been parked up roughly by type. This represented the serviceable equipment. That which had been damaged during the war was still in the desert rusting. It still represented hundreds of vehicles. The ECP was like a rogue's gallery of equipment. There were T55, T59, T72 and T80 tanks, BMP, MTLB, BTR60, and every variant of BRDM. There were giant FROG rockets still on their wheeled launchers and a complete array of anti-aircraft missiles. It was the artillery park which was the most chilling and spectacular. Virtually every gun in the world's armouries was represented - Soviet 2S1 and 2S3, South African G5, American M109, Italian pack howitzers, even British 25 pounders. The ammunition supply must have been a logistic nightmare. I spent an enthralled hour clambering and exploring.

I could not dally too long. I had to be back for mid-afternoon to watch the Guns Course going through their live firing exercise. What the Arabs and Americans in earshot thought the British were up to we could only guess. It probably served only to confirm their worst suspicions. I spent the early evening parcelling up personal kit that I wanted to get home but would not have room for in my luggage. Parcel dispatched, I spent the rest of the evening talking to the gun crews, aware that tomorrow night would be my last with the Battery.

20 March 1991

Very windy with a fierce dust storm. All movement was restricted to essential traffic. Most of the Battery were battened down inside their vehicles. I had lunch at RHQ followed by CO's Orders. By late afternoon I had finished all my admin, handed in all my Confidential Reports, was packed and ready to go. I toured the Battery to say my final goodbyes. I would of course see them all back in Germany before I departed for England, but it was still an emotional experience. In all a quiet day. How I love quiet days!

21 MARCH 1991

I was up early to do my last few bits of packing. It was going to be another scorching day. Once ready I walked slowly around the vehicle that had been my home for so long. In spite of our best efforts she now looked a tired old lady. The sand-coloured paint was now flaking and the black chevrons and tac signs were starting to fade. The area around the exhaust housing, where the massive diesel engine belched out its fumes and heat, was now black with oily soot. I had travelled many miles in her and witnessed many things. Disregarding the countless miles spent on the work-up exercises, we had journeyed from the Concentration Area at KEYES, to the Assembly Area at RAY, through the breach and fought our way close to Kuwait City – a distance of some 400 kilometres. In European terms, Brussels to Berlin. In all that time she had never once faltered, a testament to her makers, GKN. As I looked at her for the last time I found myself almost affectionately brushing the loose sand away from the black lettering across the front which proudly proclaimed OPTIMIST in six-inch-high letters. It had been a good choice of name.

Derek Hudson and I were dropped off at RHQ, with all our kit, just before 08.00. Gathered around a small convoy of trucks were the fortunate few who made up the Regiment's advance party. My pockets bulged with letters that I had faithfully promised to deliver or post as soon as I reached Germany. I clambered into the cab of one of the trucks and we set off for the makeshift desert runway. We seemed to travel for some while, but at last the front truck stopped and we piled out. Already the sun was climbing into the sky and the temperature was soaring. It looked no different from any other part of the desert in our area. There was sand upon which a flattened airstrip spread away to the horizon, the mandatory wrecked vehicle and some low outcrops of rock. On top of the largest outcrop was placed a six-foot table. This was the MCCP, the Movement Control Check Point. It was manned by the Joint Services Movement Staff , immaculate in their pristine combat kit and brand new issue desert boots. They were here not to repatriate war heroes but to move 'pax', their term for any living thing that is not demonstrably one of their own. We fell into line and awaited our turn to be checked against the manifest and given a chalk number. Derek and I were in Chalk Two, the second aircraft. It would arrive when it felt like it. We were briefed on 'Hot Landings' by one of the movement staff. The sand was soft and the air was hot. There was a chance that if the aircraft stopped it would not get going again. It would therefore slow to walking pace and we would run and clamber aboard. Simple!

Interminable briefing and documentation completed, we sat around in the sunshine. There was no shade. With us were the advance parties from the other units in the Brigade – lots of friendly faces, so the time passed quite pleasantly. At last Chalk One was told to pick up their kit and make their way, about 100 metres, to the edge of the air strip. There was not a breath of wind. As we stood waiting, the aircraft approached from our left, a C130 'Fat Albert' Hercules of the Royal New Zealand Air Force. It touched down in a storm of flying sand about 600 metres away so that it had slowed to walking pace as it drew level with the two lines of expectant troops. At the thumbs up sign from the Load Master they moved forward, ran up the ramp and the aircraft was away. Chalk One having departed, we moved down to the strip and were placed into two lines for boarding.

It grew hotter and hotter, the heat shimmer now distorting the horizon some few kilometres away. At last the drone of engines had us on our feet, our kit ready in our hands. The RAF Hercules landed and with engines screaming to slow the aircraft down, drew level with us. The large rear loading-ramp was down – on it stood the Load Master. At the thumbs up signal we ran forward. The two lines were soon parallel behind the ramp, each person jumping on board and then running forwards into the body of the aircraft. There were no seats, not even the familiar string hammocks, just bare metal floor. The Load Master was urging people to pack forwards and to sit on the floor, kit between their legs. It was a tight fit. I was about halfway down the aircraft in the centre of the floor. There was nothing to hold onto, but we were packed so tight that no one could move.

The ramp came up, the engine pitch changed from a scream to a roar and we surged forwards. Seated on the steel floor we bounced and bucked over the desert. The engines were at full power but still we bounced along the ground, struggling to gain speed. Slowly, agonisingly slowly, the nose started to rise and I felt the mass of bodies move towards the rear of the aircraft. Still the main wheels thundered across the sand. The noise was ear-shattering and we sat with our hands clasped to our heads. After what seemed an eternity the bumping suddenly stopped and we were airborne. There was visible relief on the floor. The noise was still deafening as the engines struggled for grip in the hot, still, desert air. We must have been climbing for little more than a few minutes when it happened. The pitch of the engines changed back to a scream and the aircraft plummeted earthwards. It was like being on a roller coaster. Had we survived a war only to die at the hands of some RAF Pilot Officer? I do not know how far we fell in the air pocket nor how close we were to the ground when the pilot finally managed to get enough purchase from the propellers to pull away. As we sat in stunned silence the pilot's voice came over the intercom, "Sorry about that... I think we'll put that one down to the co-pilot."

The rest of the flight was uncomfortable but mercifully without further incident. We landed at Al Jubayl and were unceremoniously loaded onto buses and taken to Black Adder Camp. It had changed somewhat since I had last visited. The original brown canvas marquees were still evident but beside them now stood row upon row of smart white huts. "They needed it for Prisoners of War so they had to upgrade the accommodation," chirped one wag from the back of the bus. Blue portable plastic toilets, 'Tardis,' were everywhere. We were met by our

New cabins at Black Adder Lines. (AG)

own rear party, who had moved across from Pearl Beach, and shown to our new, if hopefully temporary, homes in the tents. Lunch was a self-service affair eaten off trestle tables in the sunshine and flies.

I whiled away the afternoon settling in and chatting to old friends. I also made a first use of the facilities. The 'Tardis' toilets were wonderful for two reasons. After months of deprivation it was bliss to be able to sit in private on a seat. What's more, each plastic box came with its own entertainment package. Graffiti! Not just any old graffiti but that honed with the barb of soldier's black humour. 'For Christ's sake don't beam me up Scottie, I'm having a shi....' was just one gem that I remember.

Black Adder, for all its palatial splendour, was short of about everything and there was a shuttle bus service running regularly to the telephones, medics, shops etc at Camp 4. After supper a group from the Regiment purloined the rear party's Landrover and went to Camp 4. I telephoned Annie. All was well. We spent the remainder of the evening looking for a burger bar. We failed!

232

22 MARCH 1991

Today I was determined would be a lazy day. It was the first day for nearly three months that the only responsibility I had was for myself. Wonderful! After a leisurely breakfast, Derek Hudson, Ray Harper (the Unit Training Officer) and I made our way over to Pearl Beach Camp. It too had taken on a new lease of life and was humming. The Regiment still had its Rear Party base within the camp and we spent the morning washing clothes and standing for hours under the shower. Bliss! Lunch consisted of a burger from the beach-side café and then it was sunbathing time. Most of us looked like Pandas, lily white except for our faces and arms. We relaxed on the beach and swam in the stupefyingly cold sea. That the Gulf should be so cold was both a shock and a serious disappointment. At sundown we headed home. A group of us had arranged to have supper in Al Jubayl so at 19.00 we set off by taxi for the Holiday Inn. It was like a scene from a wartime movie in that everyone in the hotel, men and women alike, was in uniform. Across the dining room sat the QARANC Nursing Sister, Penny Moody who, less than a year ago, had delivered my daughter Louise in a hospital in Cyprus. It is a small world.

Stephen Young, Ray Harper and Derek Hudson at the Pearl Beach R and R Centre, Al Jubayl.
(AG)

233

23 MARCH 1991

Sadly for the rest of my suntan, today was overcast and humid. After breakfast the Movement Staff, with the tact and compassion of a hanging judge, informed us that our return flight had been changed from 12.30 tomorrow to 00.30 the day after. Oh how I hate them!

Derek and I scrounged a lift to the telephones in Camp 4, then got dropped off in the centre of Al Jubayl. The old part of the town, the commercial centre, was run down and tired. It comprised mostly two-storey buildings, the ground floor invariably taken up by a shop. They were run by Pakistani or non-Saudi Arab traders. The exodus from Al Jubayl had been short-lived. They were now back and doing a roaring trade in T-shirts and tacky souvenirs. US troops were there in abundance, weighed down by African masks, Moroccan jewellery and Samurai swords. To be fair to our North American cousins, genuine souvenirs were difficult to find. Other than oil, Saudi Arabia's only other product is sand. We made our way slowly down the main street taking in all the sights, sounds and smells. At the main road junction we waited to cross. As the lights changed we started forward only to be brought up short by the sound of a car horn. A large black Mercedes with Kuwaiti plates had ignored the lights. It had stopped in the middle of the road. Its horn blared again. The woman passenger haughtily draped her veil across her face. The male driver, in pristine white robes, waved his hand dismissively to shoo us out of his way. My blood boiled. They may not have been typical of the Kuwaiti people but from that moment forth my sympathies were with the poor bloody Iraqi soldiers.

We took a taxi back to camp, arriving in time for lunch. We killed the afternoon by playing cards. There were a few welfare cars available and we struck lucky. Tonight we would head south along the coastal highway to the port of Dammam and the shopping centre at Al Khubar.

As we prepared to depart I was approached by two young female soldiers. They asked for a lift to the market. They had heard horror stories about the Saudi treatment of women and were too frightened to go shopping unescorted. We all crammed into the small Japanese saloon and headed south. I cannot remember who drove, it might even have been me, but I do remember the endless yellow lights that seemed to accompany every inch of the journey.

Al Khubar was an old-established market town now serving the oil port of Dammam. It was linked to Al Jubayl by a modern motorway. The town itself was a mêlée of sounds, smells, hustle and bustle. The streets were crowded with shoppers and traders and of course troops. Mostly American, they wandered around under the weight of their purchases. There were also a very large number of American women soldiers in their desert fatigues so things in Al Khubar would never quite be the same again. We British, in our desert combats, excited the occasional good-natured greeting. We were clearly something of a novelty. In the centre was the main market. It seemed to sell only one thing, gold. It was everywhere - jewellery, watches, ingots, most with a very distinctive deep yellow colour. Delicate filigree necklaces seemed to be the local speciality but which I did not find particularly attractive. I decided to buy Annie a watch. In a large jewellery shop I pointed to the one I wanted. The shopkeeper beamed,

"American, Yes?"

I was quoted a quite outrageous price.

"No, British"

"British! Ah! Special price for the British."

He came down a fraction.

"I live in Riyadh! Three years! I want a Saudi price."

"You work with Saudi Army, Yes?"

"No, the Police!"

He paled noticeably and the price came tumbling down. I bought the watch, smiled and left. Wonderful what two years of hard bargaining in the Far East can teach you.

24 MARCH 1991

We were all up late, 08.00, so no breakfast. We made our way to Pearl Beach via Camp 4 and had brunch from the beachside café. A sunbathe, a final swim, a shower and back to Black Adder for 15.30. A final pack and a few goodbyes. At 18.30 we boarded buses that would take us to the MCCP back in the port area. Manifests were checked, baggage searched, dire warnings of smuggling grenades, rifles, etc. given, then all aboard for Dhahran Air Base. Again I watched the yellow lights flash by, looking out for the occasional distinctive red. There were still convoys on the road but that sense of drama and expectation had gone. The excitement was over. We arrived at 22.00 and were given a boxed meal clearly prepared for POWs but never eaten. Speculation was rife as to the aircraft. Memories of the newspaper pictures of the British Airways' air hostess's stockinged thigh were still vivid, as was mine of the Caledonian Airway's bust. Rumour control announced that an earlier flight had been a Saudi Airways 747 and, horror of horrors, it had been alcohol free.

25 MARCH 1991

At 01.30, clasping our hand baggage, we walked across the tarmac and boarded a RAF Tri-Star tanker aircraft now fitted with seats. We were greeted by a smiling RAF hostess and as soon as we were airborne, given a free drink. Within an hour most of the aircraft was sound asleep. We landed at RAF Gütersloh, Germany, at 06.20. There was a surprisingly large crowd gathered there to meet us. Not being able to rely on flight times or even airports, I had told Annie to wait in Münster. Our CRA

The 'O' Battery Cannon, Waterloo Barracks, Münster, Germany. (AG)

from Germany, Brigadier John Dean, was the official host but lots of the families were there also. They had thrown caution to the wind, risking being disappointed if our flight was delayed or diverted. After a brief pause for 'hellos', 'well dones' and 'good to have you backs', we gathered up our kit and boarded the transport. As I watched the awakening German countryside pass by, my face pressed against the window of the coach, I remembered the last time I had made this journey. It was less than a year ago and I had been returning with the Battery from UN duty in Cyprus. A lot had happened in those few months.

At 08.30 the coaches swung through the gates of Waterloo Barracks. It was as if we had never been away. As we headed through the camp we passed The Rocket Troop's offices. Opposite, the Napoleonic cannon had been hung with ribbons in the Battery's blue and yellow colours. There was a large crowd waiting to greet us on the Regimental square. Sergeant Murphy and the Battery rear-party, wives, friends, children. Annie and my own three children were waiting also, four welcoming faces in the crowd.

The front of my married quarter was also draped with blue and yellow ribbons and colourful balloons. As we walked up the path I could see a sign hanging on the front door. It had been made by my children and in large letters said 'WELCOME HOME DADDY.'

Afternote:

For his bravery, 24343227 Sergeant S Allen was awarded the Queen's Gallantry Medal.

Under the 1991 Options for Change Defence Review the 14th/20th King's Hussars and the Second Field Regiment, Royal Artillery were struck from the British Army's order of battle. The title of O Battery (The Rocket Troop) passed to the Headquarters Battery of First Regiment, Royal Horse Artillery. The Battery has no guns.

236

APPENDIX 1
O BATTERY (THE ROCKET TROOP)

Maj Gillespie	Capt Ravenhill	Capt Ambrose	Capt Farndale
Capt Hudson	Capt Keleghan	Capt Norton	Lt Greaves
Lt Hubbard	Lt Morgan	WO2 (BSM) Steadman	WO2 Barma
WO2 Bates	WO2 Lee	WO2 Mullin	WO2 Windle
SSgt (BQMS)Dines	SSgt Fender	Sgt Allen	Sgt Bolger J
Sgt Bolger P	Sgt Brown	Sgt Chauhan	Sgt Devenish
Sgt Fullick	Sgt Humphries	Sgt Johnson	Sgt Joyce
Sgt Lewis	Sgt Radcliffe	Sgt Scotford	Sgt Sharp
Sgt Stevenson	Sgt Tunley	Sgt Webber	Bdr Allison
Bdr Babbington	Bdr Bailey	Cpl Barron	Bdr Blay
Bdr Collinson	Bdr Dawson	Bdr Edgar	Bdr Fisher
Bdr Gooding	Cpl Harrison	Bdr Heap	Bdr Keable
Bdr Lacey	Bdr Lal	Bdr Lee	Cpl Macleod
Bdr North	Cpl Parton	Cpl Portsmouth	Bdr Reid
Bdr Smith	Cpl Smith	Bdr Taylor	Bdr Tilson
Bdr Turl	Bdr Whitford	Bdr Wicks	Bdr Wilkins
Cpl Woodhouse	LBdr Astley	LBdr Baldwin	LCpl Ball
LBdr Barker	LBdr Bebb	LBdr Bennett	LBdr Boase
LBdr Bonehill	LBdr Bright	LBdr Campbell	LBdr Cartwright
LBdr Chapman	LBdr Covill	LBdr Davies	LBdr Douglas
LBdr Eccle	LBdr Edwards	LBdr Elliot	LBdr Flint
LBdr Gillespie	LCpl Gowans	LBdr Greenwood	LBdr Hall
LBdr Hickman	LBdr Holt	LBdr Hulse	LBdr Hutchinson
LBdr Jarvis	LBdr Jeffcoate	LBdr Kempin	LBdr Lilley
LBdr Louis	LBdr Musson	LBdr O'Shea	LBdr Parker
LBdr Round	LBdr Rowlands	LBdr Sharples	LBdr Smith
LCpl Souter	LBdr St Louis	LBdr Sumner	LBdr Tomlinson
LBdr Weir-Ansell	LBdr Westhead	LBdr Whitehead	LBdr Williamson
LBdr Witt	LBdr Worsley	Gnr Atkinson	Gnr Ayres
Gnr Backhouse	Gnr Backhouse W	Gnr Ball	Gnr Bancroft
Gnr Banham	Gnr Beardmore	Gnr Bell	Gnr Bleakley
Gnr Booth	Gnr Brooke	Gnr Cooper	Gnr Corcoran
Gnr Cork	Gnr Corris	Gnr Craig	Gnr Crawford
Gnr Curtis	Gnr Daly	Gnr Dixon	Gnr Doherty
Gnr Dry	Cfn Duncan	Gnr Durant	Gnr Endacott

Gnr Evans Gnr Farrell Gnr Finn Gnr Fisher
Gnr Ford Gnr Fordham Gnr Foster Gnr Gibbon
Gnr Gillibrand Gnr Greybanks Gnr Gunn Gnr Hallam
Pte Hawkins Gnr Hayes Gnr Heaton Gnr Helliwell
Gnr Higham Gnr Hiorns Cfn Holmes Gnr Hough
Gnr Joyce Gnr Keegan Gnr Lally Gnr Leyland
Gnr Lyons Gnr Maddocks Gnr McCabe Gnr McCord
Gnr Meecham Gnr Miller Gnr Morrell Gnr Mullany
Gnr Mullen Gnr Murch Gnr Murphy Gnr Mycock
Gnr Newell Gnr Newton Gnr Nock Gnr Owen
Gnr Parker Gnr Peak Gnr Perrin Gnr Phillips
Gnr Phillips 950 Gnr Pickett Gnr Pinnick Gnr Rawlinson
Gnr Rawlinson Gnr Redding Cfn Reilly Gnr Richardson
Gnr Richmond Gnr Roberts Gnr Robertson Gnr Rowe-Cousins
Gnr Saltmarsh Gnr Shepherd Gnr Sides Gnr Simpson
Gnr Smith Gnr Spendlove Gnr Sproat Gnr Steadman
Gnr Tebay Pte Thompson Gnr Tierney Gnr Vickers
Gnr Walmsley Gnr Warburton Gnr Watson Gnr Whitehead C
Gnr Whitehead Gnr Whittaker Gnr Whitworth Gnr Wood
Gnr Worsley

APPENDIX 2
KEY EQUIPMENT

CHALLENGER 1
Crew 4, Combat weight 62 Ton,
Max speed 56 Km/H, Armament 1 x 120 mm,
2 x 7.65 mm MG

M1 ABRAMS
Crew 4, Combat weight 54.5 Ton,
Max speed 72.4 Km/H, Armament 1 x 105 mm,
1 x 12.7 mm MG, 2 x 7.62 mm MG

M60
Crew 4, Combat weight 52.6 Ton,
Max speed 48 Km/H, Armament 1 x 105 mm,
1 x 12.7 mm MG, 2 x 7.62 MG

T55/59
Crew 4, Combat weight 36 Ton,
Max speed 48 Km/H, Armament 1 x 100 mm,
1 x 12.7 mm MG

WARRIOR BCV/OPV
Crew 5, Combat weight 26 Ton,
Max speed 82 Km/H, Armament 1 x 7.62 Hughes
Chain Gun

M2 BRADLEY
Crew 3 + 7, Combat weight 22.6 Ton,
Max speed 66 Km/H, Armament 1 x 25 mm
Cannon, 1 x 7.62 mm MG, 2 x tube TOW
launcher

AFV 432 (Command Post)
Crew 5, Combat weight 15.2 Ton,
Max speed 52 Km/H, Armament 1 x 7.62 MG

M113 (Command Post)
Crew 5, Combat weight 10 Ton,
Max speed 64.3 Km/H, Armament 1 x 12.7 mm
MG

MTLB
Crew 2 +11, Combat weight 11.9 Ton,
Max speed 61.5 Km/H, Armament 1 x 7.62 MG

SCORPION
Crew 3, Combat weight 8 Ton,
Max speed 80.5 Km/H, Armament 1 x 76 mm,
1 x 7.62 mm MG

SPARTAN
Crew 4, Combat weight 8 Ton,
Max speed 80.5 Km/H, Armament 1 x 7.62 mm
MG, Javelin AD Missiles

SULTAN
Crew 5, Combat weight 8 Ton,
Max Speed 80.5 Km/H, Armament 1 x 7.62 mm
MG

M109 A2
Crew 6, Combat weight 24.9 Ton,
Max speed 56.3 Km/H, Armament 1 x 155 mm
Howitzer (Max range 35.4 Km), 1 x 0.5 inch
MG

M110
Crew 6, Combat weight 26.3 Ton,
Max speed 54 Km/H, Armament 1 x 203 mm
Gun (Max range 21.3 Km)

240

M548
Crew 2, Combat weight 25.4 Ton,
Max speed 61 Km/H, Armament 1 x 7.62 MG

AFV 434
Crew 4, Combat weight 17.5 Ton,
Max speed 47 Km/H, 1 x 7.62 MG

BEDFORD TM 14 TON (6 x 6)
Crew 2, Max load 14 Ton,
Max speed 90 Km/H

BEDFORD TM 8 TON (4 x 4)
Crew 2, Max load 8 Ton,
Max speed 93 Km/H

HMMWV
Crew 2, Combat weight 3.8 Ton,
Max speed 105 Km/H

LANDROVER 3/4 TON
Crew 2, Combat weight 2 Ton,
Max speed 90 Km/H

JCB FORK LIFT
Crew 1, Combat weight 6.8 Ton,
Max speed 57 Km/H

MLRS

Crew 3, Combat weight 25.2 Ton,
Max speed 64 Km/h, Armament 12 x 227 mm
Rockets (Max range 48.3 Km)

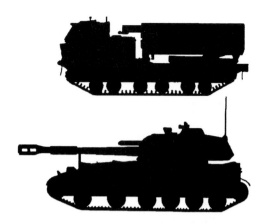

2S3

Crew 6, Combat weight 30 Ton,
Armament 1 x 152 mm Gun (Max range 24 Km),
1 x 7.62 MG

ZSU 23-4

Crew 4, Combat weight 20.5 Ton,
Max speed 44 Km/H, Armament 4 x 23 mm
Cannon (Max range 4.5 Km)

CHIEFTAIN AVLB

Crew 3, Combat weight 53.3 Ton,
Max speed 42 Km/H, Bridge length
24.38 m, Armament 2 x 7.62 MG

CENTURION AVRE

Crew 5, Combat weight 51.8 Ton,
Max speed 34 Km/H, Armament 1 x 165 mm
Demolition Gun, 2 x 0.30 MG

COMBAT ENGINEER TRACTOR

Crew 2, Combat weight 17 Ton,
Max speed 56 Km/H, Armament 1 x 7.62 MG

M578

Crew 3, Combat weight 24.3 Ton,
Max speed 55 Km/H, Armament 1 x 7.62 mm
MG

242

INDEX

Note: Page numbers in bold refer to illustrations

Adie, Kate, 35
Aircraft
    Apache helicopter, 84
    Gazelle helicopter, in FAC role, 37
    Harriers, US Marine Corps, 37
    Lynx helicopters, 174, **174**
    RNZAF Hercules, 230-31
    US, A10 and C130 gunships, 86
Aitken, Vanessa (Jayney), 124
Al Abrak, battle for Kuwaiti police post at, 209-11,
    209, **210**
Al Haniyah feature (Objective COPPER/BRONZE),
    146, 152-53
Al Jubayl, 5-7, **5**, **19**, 76, 221
    Convoy Marshalling Area, 8-9, **9**
    return to, 231, 233, 234
    unloading, 18, **19**
Al Khubar, market, 234-35
Allen, Sgt Steve, ix, 48, 51, 70, 91, **156**, 193, 236
    advance into Iraq, 148-49
    battle trophies, 180
    and burning Spartans, xiii, 172
    navigationals skills, 96
    Objective BRASS, 160, 162, 163, **164**
    Objective TUNGSTEN, 168
    and Robert Fox, 94
Allison, Bdr, 36
Ambrose, Maj Graham, FOO, 16, 21, 52, 152, 222, 223
    Objective BRASS, 162
    'Odyssey', 113
    rescue of Landrover, 31-32
Ambulances, in Battle Group work-up, 60-61
Anker, Lt Col Clint (US), xii
Archiroden Lines, 6, 18, 76
Arndt, Herr Peter, 116
Artillery, xii, 108, 201-03
    ammunition, 27, **28**, 50, 92
    limbers, 36, 40, 42-43
    Hughes Chain Gun, 49, 91, 115
    illuminating rounds, 150-51
    Iraqi decoy guns, 209, **209**
    M109 SP Howitzers, 25, 27-28
    M483 bomblets, 38-39, 176, 202-03
    MLRS, 117
    for Objective BRASS, 157, 159
Ayers, Gnr, 45
Aziz, Tariq, Iraqi foreign minister, 122

Baghdad talks, 44, 48
Baker, Maj Grant, Grenadier Guards, 52, 227
    battlefield tour, 193, **194**, 199-200, **199**
Ball, LCpl, ACC, 27
Basra Road, 173, **220**, **221**, 222
Battle trophies, 177, 179, 180-81, 181
Battlefield tour, 191, 192-211
BBC World Service, 19, 40, 51-52, 119, 124
    news of ceasefire, 178
    news of war, 58, 59, 173
Bedouin camps, 11, 69
Beer, Saudi non-alcoholic, 16
Black Adder Camp, 6, 7, 9-10, **10**, 231-32, **232**
Blackpool, ix
'Blue on blue' incidents
    Air Defence troop Spartans, xiii
    near misses, 149-50, 171-72
    RRF Warriors hit by American A10s, xiii-xiv, 166
    vehicles destroyed by Apache, 121, 128
British Army units
    1 (BR) Armoured division see Coalition forces
    Army Air Corps, 174
    Brigades
        4th Armoured, xi, xxiii, 25, 110, 116-17
            Battle orders, 131-32
            Brigade RV at KEYES, 81-82, 87
            Objective BRASS, **158**
            Objective TUNGSTEN, 166-69
            photograph, 225-26, **225**
        7th Armoured, xi, xxiii, 110, 141, 142-43,
            171, 172
            advance into Iraq, 142-43, 147-48
            return of, 189
    Regiments
        14 Signal, 119
        14th/20th King's Hussars, ix, xxiii, 62, 128-29,
            236
            advance into Iraq, **143**, 145-47
            Battlegroup, 6, 33, 59, 69-70, 183
                at area KEYES, 77, 82-94
                church parade, 184, **185**
                Objective BRASS, 156-57, 159-60, 161,
                    162-64
                Objective TUNGSTEN, 167, 168
                Orders (21 Feb), 132-33
            at Black Adder Camp, 9-10
            eve of battle service dinner, 102, 114
            Regimental Dinner and Band Concert,
                226-27, 228

16th/5th Royal Lancers, 45, 141
Grenadier Guards, Queen's Company, xxiii, 52, 59, 151, 165, 167, 195
Life Guards, xxiii, 52, 167
Queen's Royal Irish Hussars, 143
Royal Regiment of Fusiliers (3rd Bn), xxiii, 33
    Battlegroup, 83, 149, 156, 166, 167, 168, 203
    'blue on blue' incident, xiii-xiv, 166
Royal Scots, xi, xxiii, 186
    Battlegroup, 52, 58, 69, 147-50
        Objective BRASS, 156, 157, 159
REME, 14, 134
Rocket Troop (O Battery), ix, xxiv, 183, 189, 236
    author's address to, 101-02, **101**
    Orbat, 23
    Robert Fox's article on, 113-15
Royal Artillery
    2nd Field Regt, ix, xxiii, 12-13, 157, 167, 236
        and end of war, 180, 227
        Officers' Mess photograph, 212, 213
        in Saudi, ix, xxiii, 12-13, 24, 67-68, 71
        see also Rocket Troop (O Battery) (above)
    10 Air Defence Battery, 172
    26th Field Regt, 50, 157, 167
        16 Battery, 150, 151, 152
    27th Field Regt, xxiii
        23 Battery, xxiv, 15
            in Saudi, 24
    32 Heavy Regt, 122
    39 Heavy Regt, 117
    40th Field Regt, 8, 10-12, 157
        137 (Java) Battery, 12
    49th Field Regt, xxiii
        127 (Dragon) Battery, xxiv
            in Saudi, 24
Royal Corps of Transport, 21
Royal Engineers
    bridge layer, **26**, 27
    obstacle demolition, 55
    sand wall construction, 87-88, **88**
    see also Coalition forces; United States Army units
British Forces Broadcasting Service (BFBS), 214
Buchanan, Maj John, 22, 67-68, 82
Burns, WO2 Patrick, 115
Bush, George, US President, xiv, 125

Carter, Capt Tristram, 105, 180
Casualty procedures, 61
Chauhan, Sgt, 15, **121**
Chemical warfare
    risks of, 132, 142
    see also NBC

Clayton, Lt Col Rory, 12
Coalition forces, 185
    3rd Army Group, mission, xiv, 130
    and air war, 52, 63-64, 86, 87, 107-08, 206-07
    Divisions
        1 (BR) Armoured, 12, 94-95, 109-10, 131
            Divisional RV, 80-81
            orbat, xxiv
            to join VII (US) Corps, 48
            Warning Order, 141-42
        6th (French) Daguet, 108
    force deployment, **106**
    and ground war, 64, 107-10
    Joint Force Command North, 108, 130, 141
    Orders for war (21 Feb), 130-33
    pilots captured, 65
    projected plan for Desert Storm, 63-64
    Rhino Force, 109, 119
    VII (US) Corps, 48, 62, 108-09, 130, 131
    XVIII Corps, 108, 130, 139
Collett, Maj Alan, Battery Commander, 23 Battery, 6, 148, 149, 156, 159
Combined Services Entertainment, 44, 65
Combo pens, 49, 57
Communications, 104, 120-21
    Iraqi, 205
Container City, 75-77
Cookhouse, **17**
Coulter, Rev David, 103, 186, 212
Covill, L/Bdr Alan, 69, **91**, 96, **156**, 168, 175
    and burning Spartans, 171-72
Craig, Sir David, CDS, 187, 188

Daily Telegraph, The, xi-xii
    see also Fox, Robert
De la Billière, General Sir Peter, 48
Dean, Brig John, 236
Deception, role of, 109, 119
Desert conditions, 39-40
    darkness, 30, 41
    Sabka, 25, 40, 43, 47-48, **47**
    sand dunes, **30**, 31, 33, 69
    sandstorms, 104, 226
Dhahran military air base, 4
Dines, SSgt, **121**, 189, 227
Donkey, lone white, 93, **93**
Dosimeters, 49
Doyle, Capt Peter, families officer, 105
Durie, Brig Ian, CRA, 22, 180

Egyptian forces, 108, 130, 166, 215
Equipment
    accounting for, 227

battle trophies, 180-81
desert boots, 20-21
excess of, 75
Iraqi, 207-08, 216, 229
missing rifle, 74-75
in new Warriors, 49
Soviet grenade launcher, 199-200, **199**
TOGS sighting system, 65
US field telephone, 22
Equipment Collection Point, 229
Euphrates, River, 139, 170
Exercises
Cracker Barrel 1, 15
Cracker Log, 50
Dibdibah Charge, 116-17
Dibdibah Drive, 94-100
Jerboa Drive (CPX), 46
Mussanah Storm (CPX), 84-85
Nessum Dorma, 68
Explosive Ordnance Disposal (49 EOD), 218-19

Falklands, x-xi
Farndale, Capt Richard, FOO, 16, 45, 52, 75, 89-90,
192, 227
breakdown, 67, 68
'Orion', 113
and RRF 'blue on blue' incident, 166
Fender, SSgt, REME, 77
Fire Base Manchester, 12, 19
FOOs, 52, 147, 149
letter from, 3-4
named vehicles, 113
Objective BRASS, 162, 165
see also Ambrose, Graham; Farndale, Richard;
Hudson, Derek
Forsyth, Commander Andrew, RN, 224
Forward Air Controlling, 37-38
Fox, Capt Ray, Tech QM, 20, 74
Fox, Robert, Daily Telegraph journalist
with 14th/20th Battle Group, 86, 135, **137**
and advance into Iraq, 143, 144-45
article, 113-15
battlefield tour, 193, **201**, **208**
and burning Spartan, 172
'interviews' with author, 93-94
leaves 14th/20th, 173
with Rocket Troop, ix-xiv, 143
France, 51
Franks, General Fredrick M., VII (US) Corps, 108, 128
Fullick, Sgt, 121

Garbutt, Maj Peter, 170, 226
battlefield tour, 193, 194, 199-200, **199**

Geneva, peace talks, 39, 40, 41
Gerahty, WO2, x, 168
Gerboa (desert rat), 103
Gillespie, Allan (author's brother), 21, 66
Gillespie, Annie (author's wife), 1, 106, 236
letters to, 137-38, 228
parcels from, 48, 190-91
phone calls to, 18, 22, 73
GKN, engineers from, 67, 70-71
Gordon, Major General James, 224
Gossage, Capt Andrew, 121-22
Greaves, Lt Nick, 12, 14-15, 18, 110, 120, 121
Grimwood, Peter and Avril, 94
Gulf War
attempts at peace negotiations, 37, 39, 40, 41, 51
Baghdad talks, 44, 48
Battlegroup Orders (21 Feb), 130-33
ceasefire, 173, 174, 176, 178
G-Day, 110, 122, 125, 139-40
peace agreement, 187
statistics, xii-xiii
Gutersloh, RAF, 235-36

Haafra Al Batin, 185
Hammerbeck, Brig Christopher, xiii, xxiii, 166, 173, 228
at COPPER SOUTH, 150, 154-55
'Meet the Press' day, 26
visit to 2nd Field Regt, 100
and visits of PM, **34**, 35, 191
Harper, Capt Ray, 72, **233**
Harris, Paul, GKN engineer, 70
Haynes, Maj Dick, Battery Commander, 49 Battery, 3
Hewitt, Maj James, Life Guards, 52
Hillman, Lt Col Jim, 128
Honours and awards, 188, 213
Hopkins, Joyce, 123
Hough, Gnr, injured, 45
House of Commons Select Committee on Defence,
visit, 228-29
Hubbard, Lt Matthew, 43, 118, 121, 183
Hudson, Capt Derek, FOO, 16, 52, 75, 149, 150,
192, 230, **233**
432 breakdown, 67, 68
and Objective BRASS, 156, 162
'Odin', 113
sabka incident, 48
Hygiene, 72

Identification chevrons, 106-07
Inge, General Sir Peter, 44
Inoculations
Anthrax, 24, 85
Bubonic plague, 24, 85-86, **86**
see also NBC

Intelligence
    briefings, 18-20
    Kuwait, 73
    reports, 87, 93
Iran-Iraq war, 20
Iraq
    agreement to withdraw from Kuwait, 119, 133-34
    ceasefire, 174
    threat to Israel, 43
    use of Scud missiles, 59, 64, 65, 117
    see also Saddam Hussein
Iraq Border, breaching operation, 128, **129**, 142-46
Iraqi forces, 20, 120, 130
    12 Armoured division, 125, 130
    17 Armoured division, 125
    52 Armoured division, 125, 130, 154
    Hammurabi division, 125, 178
    Medina division, 125, 178
    Objective TUNGSTEN, 169
    Republican Guard divisions, 87, 108, 125, 130, 166
    retreat from Kuwait, 219-21
    Signals (Electronic Warfare) unit, 151
    Tawalkana division, 87, 125
Iraqi prisoners, xiii, 150-52, 164-65, 167
Iraqi troops
    crew shelters, 204-05
    regular, 165
    surrenders, 150-51, 153-54, 162-63, 164, **165**
Israel, 43, 51
    Scud missile attacks on, 59

James, Maj Julian, 102, 157
Johnson, Sgt, 112
Joint Services Movements Staff, 2-3, 230
Jordan, ammunition for Iraqi army, 169, **169**, 176
Joynson, Capt Henry, 150

Keleghan, Capt Paul, 115, 135, 135
KEYES Forward Concentration Area, 62, 71, 77, 81-94
KEYES Tactical Staging Area, 109
Khafji, Iraqi attack on, 85, 86, 120
Kurds, expulsion of, xiv
Kuwait
    advance into, 64
    Iraqi invasion of, xxiii
    Mutla Ridge, 219-21
Kuwait City, 192
    airfield, 166, 217-18
    Arab factions, 214, 217, 219
    Marina, **218**
    visit to 49 EOD in, 214-19
Kuwaiti forces, 108, 130
Kuwaiti Freedom Fighters, 227

Laundry, 66
Lee, WO2 Eddie, 40
Leipzig, ix, 116
Lilley, L/Bdr, injured, 123, 125
Littler, Air Tpr, 180, 181-82, 188
Live-firing exercises, 35-37
    Air/Aviation day, 37-38
    Check Bearing, 44
Live-firing range, Devil Dog Dragoon, 27, 28-29, **30**, **39**, **65**
Lloyd, Maj Simon, Battery Commander, 137 Battery, 12
Lyons, Gnr Sean ('Killer'), xiii, **91**, 96, 175, 182, 188, 193

Main Supply Route DODGE, 77-80, **78**, **79**, **80**, **81**
Major, John, Prime Minister, 27
    first visit, 33-35, **35**
    post-war visit, 189, 191-92, **191**
Manchester, ix
Manchester, HMS, 222, 223, 224
Maps, 30
Marshall, Maj Dave, Battery Commander, 127 Battery, 6, 39, 149, 164, **188**, 228
Matherson, Maj Rod, 184, 212
Media
    British Forces Broadcasting Service, 214
    Meet the Press day (6 Jan), 25-27, **26**
    North-West press visit, 223-24
    relations with military, xi-xii
    Times correspondent, 213
Minefield, outside Kuwait City, 174-76
Mobile Bath Unit, 212-13, **212**
Moody, Maj Penny, QARANC, 233
Moore, Capt Barry, 115
Morgan, Lt Hewlan, 29, 149, 212
Mujahadeen, in Kuwait, 217
Mullin, WO2 Ian, 101
Münster
    families video from, 105-06
    Waterloo Barracks, 1, 236, **236**
Muntz, Capt Sebastian, 149
Murphy, Sgt, 1, 236

NAPS (nerve agent pretreatment), 49-50, 58
Navigation, 43
    APES, 31, 70, 147
    GPS system (on author's Warrior), 63, 67
    maps, 30
    PADS, 29-30
    SATNAV, 127, 136, 142, 147
    sun compasses, 42
NBC
    drill, 54-55

false alarms, 53-54, 56-57
NAIAD detector machines, 55
protection against, 49-50
reports of contaminated sites, 186
Newell, Gnr, 6, 7, 12, 25, 29, **88**

Objectives
BRASS, 146, 155-57, 158, 159-60, 161, 162-64, 165
battlefield tour, 201-03
BRONZE, 146, 196
COPPER, 146, 147, 148, 152-53, 153, 154, 155
COPPER SOUTH, 150, 152, 153, 154-55
battlefield tour, 197-200, **197, 198, 199**
SODIUM, 173
STEEL, 156, 166, 203-05
TUNGSTEN, 165, 166-69
battlefield tour, 205-09, **206, 207, 208, 209**
VARSITY, 170
Oil pipelines, sand bridges over, 29, 166-67, 168
Oil refineries, Al Jubayl, **5**, 6-7
Oil wells, burning, 216
Operation Desert Sabre, 129, 130-33
Operation Desert Shield (defence of Saudi Arabia), 4-52
Operation Desert Storm (to liberate Kuwait), 63-64
Operation Granby, xxiii, xxiv

Pakenham-Walsh, Capt Richard (13th/18th Hussars), 87
battlefield tour, 193, **194**
Pakistani forces, 108
Palmer, Capt Jonty, x, 34, 59, 73, 154, **178**
Palmer, Capt Neil, 83
Passage of Lines, Exercise Dibdibah Drive, 97
Passwords, 50-51, 125-26
Patriot missiles
Al Jubayl, 8
interceptions of Scuds, 59, 117
Pearl Beach, 76, 233, **233**, 235
Pérez de Cuéllar, Javier, UN Secretary General, 44, 45
Preston, ix
Pylon Line Road, 12-13, **13**, 25, 71-72, 76

Radcliffe, Lt Col David, RA, 10, 14, 38, 68
and burning Spartans, 171
and end of war, 180, 187, 212, 213, 223
and navigation problems, 43
and Objective BRASS, 157, 163-64
and Objective TUNGSTEN, 167
and start of war, 136, 137
Radcliffe, Sgt, 21, 46-47, 51, **88**, 90, 92
432 breakdown, 119-20
and 432 engine replacement, 58, 62, 65, 71, 72-73, 89
and advance, 142
and NBC false alarm, 53-54

and propellant, 182
Radio Baghdad, 45
Rain, 18, 46, 47, 48
storm, 126
Ravenhill, Capt Geoff, Battery Second in Command
(BK), 5,   7-9, 45, 78, 180
battlefield tour, 193, **194**, 200
and chances of return, 211, 214
wounded, 110-11, 115
RAY Tactical Assembly Area, 95, 109, **129**
Redgrave, Cpl `Reds', ix, x, 162, 196
Redhead, WO2, 164-65
Repair Point 7 Alpha, 90, **90**
Rodda, L/Cpl, 228
Ross, Capt Alistair, 84
Row-Cousins, Gnr, 77
Royal Air Force, xxiii
Royal Navy, xxiii
see also Manchester, HMS
Russia, 43
peace initiatives, 66, 128, 133-34

Sabka (dry salt lake), 25, 40, 47-48, **47**
Saddam Hussein, xiv, 185
claims victory, 176, 178
invasion of Kuwait, xxiii
'Mother of all Battles' speech, 128
and UN resolution, 44, 52
Saudi Arabia, 5, 7
Saudi forces, 108, 130
Schools, letters from
Lisieux Infants, Liverpool, 222-23, **224**
Walthamstow, 21
Yateley, 123-24
Schwarzkopf, General Norman, 86, 166, 184-85
Security, passwords, 50-51, 125-26
Sharp, Lt Ben, 82
Shirreff, Major Richard, 102, 226
battlefield tour, 193, 194
Showers, makeshift, 43
Sincock, Brig Peter, defence attaché (Riyadh), 35, 192
Sincock, Ginnie, 105
Smith, General Rupert, GOC, x, 22
on Corps Concept of Operations, 109-10
Snakes, 33, **33**
Steadman, WO2 (BSM), 12, 42-43, 121
Sweden, King of, ix
Syrian forces, 130

Tactical Air Control Parties, 105, 157
TAP (Trans Arabian Pipe) Line Road, 11, **11**
Taylor, Dvr, 76
Taylor, Maj David (14th/20th paymaster), 45, 103

Tilney, Maj Godfrey, 47, 55, 127, 142, 164, 191
  battlefield tour, 193, **194**
Training
  Battlegroup work-up, 55-56, 58-62, 58
  CRA's exercise, 67-68
  live battle runs, 64-65
  see also Exercises
Tunley, Sgt, 29, 74-75, 189
Turkey, 43

United Nations
  Baghdad talks, 44, 48
  deadline for Saddam to withdraw, 44, 52
United States
  and media-military relations, xi
  negotiations with Iraq, 37
United States Army
  code word system, 50-51
  MREs (Meals Ready to Eat), 98
United States Army units
  2 Armored Cavalry Regt, 131, 141
  3 Armored Cavalry Regt, 108
  Air Cavalry Regt, 84
  Brigades
    3 (US), 131, 139-40, 142
    142 Field Artillery, 157, 159-60
  Divisions
    1st Infantry (Mechanized), xii, 84, 97, 127,
      136-37, 136, 141
      1/41 Infantry Battalion, 127-28, 134
      out of fuel, 185
    7th (US) Cavalry, 130
    24th Infantry, 108, 130
    82nd Airborne, 108, 130
    101 Air Assault, 108, 130
  Marine Corps, 12, 13, 16-17, 55, 170
    and live-firing range, 27
    M60 tank battalion, 24
  Marine Expeditionary Force, 8, 18
  Military Police, 96, 98
  National Guard nurses, 80
  'Tent City' in Saudi Arabia, 11
  see also Coalition forces

Vehicles
  AFV 432, 21-22, 31
  AFV 432 (engine replacement), 58, 62, 65, 71, 72-
    73, 83-84, 89, **89**
  abandoned by Iraqi forces, **196**
  Abrams tanks, **145**
  ammunition limbers, 36, 40, 42-43, 50
  battle trophies, 177, **179**, 181, 183-84, 187, **187**
  Challenger tanks, 22, 65

Chobham armour fitting, 90, **90**
'Emperor' (Col. Mike Vickery's tank), ix, **95, 177**
Iraqi T55s, **151**, 154, **155**, 163, 196
Landrover (author's), 21, 31-32, 62, 191
M113 APC, 127
M548 explosion, 110-12, 111, 112
M548s, 50
'Optimist' (author's Warrior), ix, xiii, **91**, 112, **140**,
  175-76, 193, 229-30
Spartans (burning), 171-72
Sultan, 46
US air cargo nets, 15-16
Warrior, 22, 31, 48-49
BCV (author's), 46, 63
Vickery, Lt Col Michael (14th/20th King's Hussars), ix,
  73, 114, **156**, 170, 226-27
  Battlegroup Commander, 10, 47, 150, 186, 189
  Battlegroup work-up, 59-60
  COPPER SOUTH, 152, 153
  and end of war, **177**, 178, **178**
  Exercise Dibdibah Drive, 94, 96, 99
  and live battle runs, 64
  and NBC false alarms, 54, 55, 56
  Objective BRASS, 159-60, 162, 163
  and start of war, 122, 134, 135-36
  and visit from PM, 33-34
Vye, Maj Mark, Battery Commander, 46 Battery, 6, 213

Wadi Al Batin, 173, 194
Webber, Sgt, 25, 112
Weymes, Father Michael, 184
Wicks, Bdr, 123, 182, 188
Wicks, Maj Alastair, battlefield tour, 193, **194**
Wilkins, Bdr Brian ('Pip'), xiii, **91**, 96, 175
Williams, Lt Col Peter, RA, 117, **190**
Windle, WO2, 40, 74
Witt, L/Bdr, 72, 77, 82, 83, 85

Young, Maj Steven, 28, 71, 193, **233**